'David Almond's books show a formidable and continuously lively intelligence, and these critics match his range of thought, lucidity and clarity: an admirable, ground-breaking collection.' – **Peter Hunt,** *Cardiff University, UK*

David Almond is one of the most exciting and innovative authors writing for children and young people today. Since the publication of his award-winning first book, *Skellig* (1998), his novels have pushed the boundaries of children's literature and magical realism.

This vibrant collection of original essays, by leading international children's literature scholars and researchers, provides a theoretically informed overview of Almond's novels and fresh analysis of individual texts. Exploring broad themes such as philosophy, theology and cognitive science, the volume also introduces new concepts such as mystical realism, literary Catholicism and radical landscape.

Rosemary Ross Johnston is Director of the International Centre for Youth Futures (previously the Australian Centre for Child and Youth Culture and Wellbeing) at the University of Technology, Sydney, Australia.

New Casebooks
Collections of all new critical essays

CHILDREN'S LITERATURE

MELVIN BURGESS
Edited by Alison Waller

ROBERT CORMIER
Edited by Adrienne E. Gavin

ROALD DAHL
Edited by Ann Alston & Catherine Butler

C. S. LEWIS: *THE CHRONICLES OF NARNIA*
Edited by Michelle Ann Abate & Lance Weldy

PHILIP PULLMAN: *HIS DARK MATERIALS*
Edited by Catherine Butler & Tommy Halsdorf

J. K. ROWLING: *HARRY POTTER*
Edited by Cynthia J. Hallett & Peggy J. Huey

J. R. R. TOLKIEN: *THE HOBBIT & THE LORD OF THE RINGS*
Edited by Peter Hunt

DAVID ALMOND
Edited by Rosemary Ross Johnston

NOVELS AND PROSE

JOHN FOWLES
Edited by James Acheson

FURTHER TITLES ARE IN PREPARATION

For a full list of published titles in the past format of the New Casebooks series, visit the series page at www.palgrave.com

---

New Casebooks Series

Series Standing Order ISBN 978–0–333–71702–8 hardcover
Series Standing Order ISBN 978–0–333–69345–2 paperback
(outside North America only)

You can receive future titles in this series as they are published by placing a standing order. Please contact your bookseller or, in the case of difficulty, write to us at the address below with your name and address, the title of the series and the ISBN quoted above. Customer Services Department, Macmillan Distribution Ltd, Houndmills, Basingstoke, Hampshire, RG21 6XS, UK

New Casebooks

DAVID ALMOND

Edited by

ROSEMARY ROSS JOHNSTON

palgrave
macmillan

First published 2014 by
PALGRAVE MACMILLAN

Palgrave Macmillan in the UK is an imprint of Macmillan Publishers Limited, registered in England, company number 785998, of Houndmills, Basingstoke, Hampshire RG21 6XS.

Palgrave Macmillan in the US is a division of St Martin's Press LLC, 175 Fifth Avenue, New York, NY 10010.

Palgrave Macmillan is the global academic imprint of the above companies and has companies and representatives throughout the world.

Palgrave® and Macmillan® are registered trademarks in the United States, the United Kingdom, Europe and other countries.

ISBN 978–1–137–30116–1   hardback
ISBN 978–1–137–30115–4   paperback

This book is printed on paper suitable for recycling and made from fully managed and sustained forest sources. Logging, pulping and manufacturing processes are expected to conform to the environmental regulations of the country of origin.

A catalogue record for this book is available from the British Library.

Library of Congress Cataloging-in-Publication Data

David Almond / [edited by] Rosemary Ross Johnston.

pages cm. — (New casebooks)

Summary: "David Almond is critically acclaimed as one of the most innovative authors writing for children and young people today. This collection of original essays by international leaders in children's literature criticism provides a theoretically-informed overview of his work as well as a fresh analysis of individual texts"—Provided by publisher.

Includes bibliographical references and index.

ISBN 978–1–137–30115–4 (paperback)
1. Almond, David, 1951—Criticism and interpretation.   2. Young adult literature, English–History and criticism.   I. Johnston, Rosemary Ross, editor.
PR6051.L588Z57 2014
823'.914—dc23

2014021332

Typeset by MPS Limited, Chennai, India.

Printed in China

For our children
Emily-Jane, Annabel, Malcolm, Sarah and Robert
and in loving memory of
Malcolm Charles Ferguson Johnston

Contents

Series Editor's Preface

Welcome to the latest series of New Casebooks.

Each volume now presents brand-new essays specially written for university and other students. Like the original series, the new-look New Casebooks embrace a range of recent critical approaches to the debates and issues that characterize the current discussion of literature.

Each editor has been asked to commission a sequence of original essays which will introduce the reader to the innovative critical approaches to the text or texts being discussed in the collection. The intention is to illuminate the rich interchange between critical theory and critical practice that today underpins so much writing about literature.

Editors have also been asked to supply an introduction to each volume that sets the scene for the essays that follow, together with a list of further reading which will enable readers to follow up issues raised by the essays in the collection.

The purpose of this new-look series, then, is to provide students with fresh thinking about key texts and writers while encouraging them to extend their own ideas and responses to the texts they are studying.

Martin Coyle

Notes on Contributors

Karen Coats's publications include *Handbook of Research on Children's and Young Adult Literature,* co-edited with Shelby A. Wolf, Patricia Enciso and Christine A. Jenkins (Routledge, 2011) and *The Gothic in Children's Literature: Haunting the Borders,* co-edited with Anna Jackson and Roderick McGillis (Routledge, 2007). *Looking Glasses and Neverlands: Lacan, Desire, and Subjectivity in Children's Literature* (University of Iowa Press, 2004) was selected as a Choice Outstanding Academic Title for 2004, won the Children's Literature Association Honor Award for Best Book in Literary Criticism in Children's Literature for 2004 and was translated into Korean in 2008 and Chinese in 2009.

Valerie Coghlan is President of Bookbird, Inc. and a former President of iBbY Ireland, and was recently awarded an honorary doctorate in children's literature by Trinity College, Dublin. She is now an independent researcher and commentator on children's literature. She has a particular interest in visual texts and in religion as a social and cultural signifier in children's literature.

Nolan Dalrymple is Head of English and Drama at Longridge Towers School, Northumberland, England. His doctoral thesis explored representations of north-east England in children's fiction; it was the product of the first MHRA collaborative doctoral award to be hosted jointly by Newcastle University and Seven Stories, the National Centre for Children's Books. He has published a number of chapters and articles on regional identity and children's fiction, particularly in relation to the work of Robert Westall.

Carole Dunbar is a tutor in the English Department of St Patrick's College, Dublin and lectures on their MA course in Children's Literature. Her doctoral thesis examines the portrayal of the poor in the novels of Mrs Molesworth, Mrs Ewing, Silas Hocking and Frances Hodgson Burnett. She is a regular reviewer of books for the young and has contributed essays to various publications dealing with children's fiction, the most recent of these being a study of the influence of her native city on the work of Frances Hodgson Burnett, entitled 'A Manchester Woman' and published in August 2012 in the Children's Books History Society's newsletter.

Hannah Izod is the archivist at Seven Stories, National Centre for Children's Books in Newcastle -upon -Tyne, England. Hannah has worked at Seven Stories since 2006, initially working on two successive HLF-funded projects before becoming a permanent member of staff in 2010. She is responsible for cataloguing the archive material, as well as working with colleagues across the organisation to develop routes of access into the archive material for a wide range of users.

Rosemary Johnston is Professor and Director of the International Centre for Youth Futures at the University of Technology Sydney, Australia. She is the author of the Children's Literature section of *Literacy: Reading, Writing and Children's Literature* (Oxford University Press), which is about to go into its fifth edition, and of many chapters and journal articles in the fields of literature and education. She is an active researcher, has held three large government-funded research grants, is one of three international partners on a Leverhulme Project, 'Children and War 1890–1919', and leads several large literacy projects in remote, regional and urban areas.

Michael Levy is a Professor of English at the University of Wisconsin-Stout, USA. He has published numerous articles on David Almond, and other children's literature-related topics. His next book, *An Introduction to Children's Fantasy*, co-authored with Dr. Farah Mendlesohn, will appear from Cambridge University Press in late 2014 or early 2015. He is co-editor of the peer-reviewed scholarly journal *Extrapolation*.

Perry Nodelman is Professor Emeritus of English at the University of Winnipeg, Canada. He is the author of Words *About Pictures: The Narrative Art of Children's Picture Books, The Pleasures of Children's Literature* (third edition, in collaboration with Mavis Reimer), *The Hidden Adult; Defining Children's Literature,* and about 150 journal articles and book chapters about various aspects of writing for young people. He has also written four novels for children, and seven more in collaboration with Carol Matas.

Roberta Seelinger Trites is the author of *Waking Sleeping Beauty: Feminist Voices in Children's Novels* (1997); *Disturbing the Universe: Power and Repression in Adolescent Literature* (2000); *Twain, Alcott, and the Birth of the Adolescent Reform Novel* (2007); and with Betsy Hearne, has co-edited *A Narrative Compass: Stories That Guide Women's Lives* (2010). She has served as the editor of *Children's Literature Association Quarterly* and as president of the Children's Literature Association. She is a professor of English at Illinois State University, USA, where she teaches children's and adolescent literature.

List of Abbreviations

Note: The abbreviation [*A*] is added where a citation is from the US edition.

BCM	*The Boy who Climbed into the Moon*
BD	*The True Tale of the Monster Billy Dean telt by hisself*
BSP	*The Boy who Swam with Piranhas*
C	*Clay*
CS	*Counting Stars*
FE	*The Fire-Eaters*
HE	*Heaven Eyes*
JS	*Jackdaw Summer* (also published as *Raven Summer*)
KCM	*Kate, the Cat and the Moon*
KW	*Kit's Wilderness*
MBSW	*Mouse Bird Snake Wolf*
MDAB	*My Dad's a Birdman*
MNIM	*My Name is Mina*
S	*Skellig*
SD	*Slog's Dad*
SH	*Secret Heart*
TS	*The Savage*
WGWB	*Wild Girl, Wild Boy*

Acknowledgements

An early version of Chapter 9 appeared in the *New York Review of Science Fiction*.

Every effort has been made to trace the copyright holders, but if any have been inadvertently overlooked, the publisher will be pleased to make the necessary arrangement at the first opportunity.

1

Introduction: David Almond and Mystical Realism

Rosemary Ross Johnston

> *Tyger tyger, burning bright*
> *In the forests of the night …*
> > William Blake, 'The Tyger', from *Songs of Experience*
> > > (1794)

It has been both challenging and exhilarating to work with eminent researchers across the world in preparing this Palgrave Macmillan Casebook on the work of British writer David Almond. David Almond's books have somehow struck that elusive balance of appealing to both critics and readers, including and most especially young readers. In 2010 Almond won the highly prestigious biennial Hans Christian Andersen Award, which recognises the lasting contribution to children's literature of a living author. He has also won the Carnegie Medal (for *Skellig* in 1998), the Whitbread Children's Award (twice), based both on literary merit and popular appeal, and numerous other international awards and prizes. A complete list of books may be found in the Further Reading section.

David Almond is an author whose books may appear deceptively simple – they are not excessively long (some are quite short), the stories are usually told in simple language and indeed spare prose, and there is very little actual description of characters or place. (*My Name is Mina*, 2010, is more descriptive in these areas than the other books.) Yet, as the contributions to this volume attest, Almond's work attracts international discussion of highly complex issues; his prose is lyrical and likened to poetry; his use of landscape is evocative and mostly clearly recognisable, and his characters are unique and unforgettable. Somehow, this is achieved both nimbly and poignantly. For these and many other reasons discussed in this volume, Almond is an intriguing and enigmatic writer whose work defies easy classification, and who requires and deserves robust and innovative scholarly examination.

A brief note about the use of lines from William Blake's 'The Tyger'[1] in this Introduction: Almond is such a richly layered writer and Blake such an acknowledged influence that it just seems fitting to add this beautiful coruscation of images as a sort of *thought provocateur* (*pensée provocateur*).

Brief biography and works

> I live with my family in Northumberland. We live just beyond the Roman Wall, which for centuries marked the place where civilisation ended and the waste lands began. (www.davidalmond.com/author/bio.html)

David Almond was born in Newcastle-upon-Tyne, England, in 1951, and grew up in Felling, which had been a coal-mining town. He was one of six children in a large Catholic extended family, was an altar boy at the local church, and attended primary schools in Felling and Sunderland, and later St Joseph's Roman Catholic Grammar School in Hebburn. When he was 8 his sister Barbara died, and his father died when he was 15. He studied English and American Literature at the University of East Anglia and graduated with Honours.

Almond worked variously as a hotel porter, postman and labourer, then trained to be a teacher and worked for five years in a primary school in Gateshead, across the river from Newcastle. He began to publish short stories for adults, went to live in Norfolk for 18 months, wrote literacy booklets, and took another job teaching children with learning difficulties. He published two collections for adults, *Sleepless Nights* in 1985 and *A Kind Of Heaven* in 1997, edited a fiction magazine, and as well as writing a novel that was not accepted for publication, wrote a collection of stories as a memoir of his childhood, later published as *Counting Stars* in the UK in 2000 and in the USA in 2002. This book provides a fascinating and moving commentary or metafictional meditation (even perhaps a hypertext) to his later works.

His first book for children, *Skellig*, was published in 1998, to immediate public and critical acclaim. It has been translated into over thirty languages and has been made into a radio play, a stage play, an opera and a film. Other books followed: *Kit's Wilderness* (1999), *Heaven Eyes* (2000), *Secret Heart* (2001), *The Fire Eaters* (2003), *Clay* (2005), *Jackdaw Summer* (2009), *My Name is Mina* (a prequel to *Skellig*) (2010) and *The True Tale of the Monster Billy Dean telt by hisself* (2011), which was published for both an adult and young adult readership and was advertised as his first book for adults. He has also collaborated with artists to produce picture books/

illustrated books/graphic stories: *Kate, the Cat and the Moon* (2004), with Stephen Lambert; *My Dad's a Birdman* (2008) and *The Boy who Climbed to the Moon* (2010), with Polly Dunbar; *The Boy who Swam with Piranhas* (2012), illustrated by Oliver Jeffers; and *The Savage* (2008), *Slog's Dad* (2010) and *Mouse Bird Snake Wolf* (2013), all with Dave McKean. As well as stage adaptations of *Skellig (Skellig he Play)* and *Heaven Eyes*, he has written *Wild Girl, Wild Boy*, *My Dad's a Birdman* and *Noah and the Fludd*.

Almond will publish three new books in 2014: *The Tightrope Walkers*, published as an adult novel in the UK and as a novel for Young Adults in the USA; *Half a Creature from the Sea*, a short-story collection; and *A Song for Ella Grey*, a Young Adult novel.

Almond is a Fellow of the Royal Society of Literature, Professor of Creative Writing at Bath Spa University and Distinguished Writing Fellow at the University of Newcastle. He holds honorary doctorates from the universities of Newcastle, Sunderland and Leicester.

Almond as writer

> *And what shoulder, & what art,*
> *Could twist the sinews of thy heart?*

As the following chapters demonstrate, Almond's literary world is unusual. Consider these opening sentences from *Skellig* (1998) and *The Fire-Eaters* (2003):

> I found him in the garage on a Sunday afternoon. It was the day after we moved into Falconer Road. The winter was ending. Mum had said we'd be moving just in time for the spring. Nobody else was there. Just me. The others were inside with Doctor Death, worrying about the baby. (*S*, p. 1)

> It all starts on the day I met McNulty. I was with my Mam. We left Dad at home beside the sea. We took the bus to Newcastle. We got out below the statue of the angel then headed down towards the market by the river. She was all in red. She kept singing 'The Keel Row' and swinging my arm to the rhythm of the song. (*FE*, p. 1)

There are certain characteristics here which provide an interesting context and prelude to the essays that follow. The writing is simple – short sentences, simple words, conversational if not colloquial style, first-person narration (often with northern English idioms and cadences[2]), a family setting, and the ready sense of the beginning of an episode of events that will clearly be significant. Location is specific – immediately and very much so in *The Fire-Eaters* – it is Newcastle, England. The *Skellig* sentences convey an informality that feels loose and contemporary; *The*

Fire-Eaters has a nostalgic feel of slightly past times, and we are to find out quite soon that it is indeed a very particular time, clearly identified as 1962, the weeks of the Cuban missile crisis, and a time when the threat of a global nuclear war came perilously close.

Yet somehow, in the stories that unravel from these beginnings and the way in which they are told, the international researchers represented in this volume – some of the most respected children's literature scholars of our time – have been inspired to consider Almond's work through unusual critical lenses: that of philosophy and cognitive science; of a contro-versial type of theology; of religion, particularly Catholicism; of the idea of class and its relationships to home, place, identity and belonging. They have discussed his work as an ur-story with complex variations; as the expression of a radical landscape yet one that is clearly identified as northern England; and as a reflection on words and truth and the writing process. In diverse ways, these perspectives may reflect not only Almond's singular contribution to the field of children's literature, but also, as the writers note, may expand critical possibilities for that field itself.

These are big ideas, but Almond is a big writer. As the contribu-tors all comment in various ways, his work is different – sometimes strangely different (yet, as they also note, strangely the same). How then can we – indeed, can we? – define the work of this complex and highly individual author?

Almond and the fantasy tradition

> *And when thy heart began to beat,*
> *What dread hand? & what dread feet?*

The rich stories at the roots of modern literature – the myths of Greece and Rome, legends, folk tales, the *Iliad* and the *Odyssey*, *Beowulf*, Yggdrasil (that giant tree in Norse mythology which connects to nine worlds), Gilgamesh, the South American jaguar (the Master of Fire), and so on and so on – all bear various and varied historical relation-ships to fantasy. Considering fantasy in the children's literary domain, in the *Norton Anthology of Children's Literature* (2005) Zipes *et al.* write:

> Fantasy literature for children encompasses many kinds of works – legends, ballads, romances, myths, literary fairy tales, magic realism, animal fanta-sies, time-slip fantasies and science fiction.[3]

There is a long and lovely tradition of fantasy in children's liter-ature, especially perhaps British children's literature, which is trans-lated and celebrated across the world. Almond's work may be seen as part of this rich, even sumptuous, body of work, which includes Carroll's Alice and the magic of Wonderland, Kingsley's Water Babies, George MacDonald's Princess, Barrie's Peter Pan and Neverland, Lewis's Narnia, Tolkien's Ring trilogy, Susan Price's ghostly Drum, Sewell's talking Black Beauty, Grahame's Willows, Milne's Pooh and Christopher Robin, Potter's parade of little animals and Mr McGregor, Nesbit's 'It', Pearce's Garden, Garner's Weirdstone, Wynne Jones's Christomanci, and more latterly Rowling's Hogwarts and Pullman's Golden Compass. The very diversity of this list poses a critical challenge: what in this context are the defining characteristics of fantasy and how far do they relate to the work of David Almond?

The *Oxford Companion to Children's Literature* notes that fantasy describes 'works of fiction, written by a specific author (i.e. not traditional) and usually novel-length, which involve the supernatural or some other unreal element'.[4] J.R.R. Tolkien's well-known study *On Fairy Stories* (1938) refuses to define but places these stories in 'Faërie, the realm or state in which fairies have their being'.[5] Tolkien understood fairies as a manifestation of the supernatural — that is, of a *Secondary World* (imaginative world), rather than of a *Primary* ('real') *World*. In this same essay he also notes the importance of the 'good ending' — what he called the *eucatastrophe*:

> It is the mark of a good fairy story, of the higher and more complete kind, that however wild its events, however fantastic or terrible the adventures, it can give to child or man that hears it, when the 'turn' comes, a catch of the breath, a beat and lifting of the heart, near to (or indeed accompanied by) tears, as keen as that given by any form of literature, and having a peculiar quality.[6]

Brian Attebury rephrased Tolkien's 'turn', 'catch of breath' and 'beat and lifting of the heart' as *wonder*, 'not merely a meaning but an awareness of and a pattern for meaningfulness'.[7] Tzvetan Todorov, writing about eighteenth- and nineteenth-century literature (not children's literature), identified three categories: the fantastic, the marvellous and the uncanny. In brief, his 'fantastic' is any seemingly supernatural event that breaks the natural laws of the world, and the reader has to make the decision whether this event was illusion or 'real'. The 'uncanny' refers to supernatural events that turn out to be explained rationally; the 'marvellous' is when the supernatural element is seen as 'real'. The fantastic is that moment of hesitation where the reader has to decide.

Whilst Todorov's work is controversial, it does have some pertinence here, particularly in relation to the idea of the reader's hesitation. Maria Nikolajeva proposes that Todorov would place children's fantasy in the category of the marvellous:

> since the young reader is supposed to believe what he is told, while the essence of fantasy for Todorov lies in the hesitation of the protagonist (and the reader) [when] confronted with the supernatural, which is anything that goes beyond natural laws.[8]

It is interesting indeed that these critics describe fantasy basically in terms of the effect it has on (or provokes in) the reader – that is, of the reader response. So does Farah Mendlesohn who, tracking the way in which the fantastic enters the narrated world, identifies four categories within the fantastic: the portal-quest, the immersive, the intrusive and the liminal,[9] and picks up this idea of 'the reader's relationship to the framework', stressing the importance of the assumptions that readers bring to the text:

> I believe that the fantastic is an area of literature that is heavily dependent on the dialectic between author and reader for the construction of a sense of wonder, that it is a fiction of consensual construction of belief.[10]

So, is Almond a fantasy writer? Some publishers in particular classify him as such and clearly there are strong grounds for this. In varying ways there is in his writing that sense of the supernatural, of wonder, the fantastic, the uncanny and the marvellous. There are, with some provisos, 'good' if not always 'happy' endings (and debating that difference is a book in itself). There is that 'intrusion' of the apparently unreal. However, there is also a strong sense of the real, and I think a reader relationship that in most cases sets up expectations not of the fantastic but of the ordinary – but of a sort of 'poetic ordinary'. Almond's novels – like Pullman's, I would argue – carry another, deeper element that does not fit easily into the idea of children's fantasy, or 'epic' or 'high' Rings-type fantasy, or the allegorical fantasy of Narnia, or the romantic fantasy of a boy who never grows up and a family whose nanny is a dog. Almond's 'secondary world' (if that is what it is) is not accessed through any magic wardrobes or doors or windows or rabbit holes, but pertains more to ordinary worlds and to ordinary people (if there are such things, which may be Almond's point, or at least one of them). His fantasy world exists alongside or within or as part of the world of the everyday.

There are numerous examples in the books, and the plays, where this everyday is infused with a sense of Tolkien's supernatural 'Faërie': in the magic of the allotment in *Wild Girl, Wild Boy*; in *Skellig the Book* but even more dramatically in *Skellig the Play*, when Michael, Mina and Skellig join hands in the unity of their ghostly winged dance. Fantasy often has a sense of temporal distance, and part of the impact of Almond's fantasy is an unusual sense of *pastness*, of a lost past but a past that is remembered, that has been experienced, and that is now being viewed and re-created from the knowingness of subsequent events. It is past shadowed by its future. Consider again the opening lines from *The Fire-Eaters* (quoted above) for example, and the opening lines of *Clay*:

> He arrived in Felling on a bright and icy February morning. Not so long ago, but it was a different age, I was with Geordie Craggs, like I always was back then. We were swaggering along like always, laughing and joking like always. (*C*, p. 1)

Several of the contributors to this volume refer to the little book, *Counting Stars*, which is a memoir rather than a novel, but in a way it illuminates these elements of Almond's literary vision, of his construction of the fantastic, his own brand of Faërie, his sense of the marvellous, and his sense of wonder at the everyday.

Indeed, it is the delicacy of Almond's ability to discern and depict the extraordinary in the ordinary that has inspired scholars to seek more precise ways of describing his writing. Zipes *et al.*, in the definition quoted at the beginning of this section, include 'magic realism' as one of their categories or sub-types of fantasy. This possibly confuses mode with genre, but it does open provocative ways of thinking about and describing Almond's work.

Magic realism

> *In what distant deeps or skies*
> *Burnt the fire of thine eyes?*

What is real? What *is*, and what is *not*? Perhaps this is the dilemma at the very heart of being human; at the very heart of intellectual endeavour. Northrop Frye writes:

> Both literature and mathematics ... drive a wedge between the antithesis of being and non-being that is so important for discursive thought. The symbol neither is nor is not the reality which it manifests. The child beginning geometry is presented with a dot and is told, first, that that is a point, and second, that it is not a point. He cannot advance until he accepts both statements at once. It is absurd that that which is no number

can also be a number, but the result of accepting the absurdity was the discovery of zero. The same kind of hypothesis exists in literature, where Hamlet and Falstaff neither exist nor do not exist.[11]

Much has been written about Almond and magic realism, and this is the generic description commonly applied to his work. This follows on from the impressive contribution made to Almond scholarship through the work of Don Latham, in his book *David Almond: Memory and Magic* (2006)[12] and many other articles. Latham considered *Skellig* in relation to a short story by Gabriel García Márquez (1927–2014), 'A Very Old Man with Enormous Wings', not only comparing but demonstrating the influence of this story on Almond's book. His consideration went beyond narrative. As part of his study, Latham identified the Almond text as an illustration of magic realism,[13] making the point that magic realism can play an important role in children's literature and noting that part of the liminal territory explored by the book is the transition of Michael, the narrator, and his friend Mina into adulthood.[14] These are significant ideas, although I am not sure that I agree with the last; in this particular book the transition to adulthood is not as clear-cut as Latham suggests. It is far more subtle.

The term 'magic realism' has an interesting history which, for what it reveals about its characteristics, it behoves us to explore. The concept was originally created by the German historian, art critic and photographer, Franz Roh (1890–1965), who applied it to describe the type of art, emerging after Expressionism, which portrayed scenes of imaginative fantasy through realistic documentary-style painterly techniques.[15] For Roh, magic realism related to but was different to *surrealism*, because magic realism focused on the things of this world, rather than on the 'surreal' things of imaginative or psychological worlds. The 'magic' was in the capacity of the artist to make apparent 'the wonder of matter that could crystallise into objects' so that they could 'be seen anew' (1925). In other words, Roh emphasised that the magic was in perceiving and visually representing the everyday (the 'normal') in different and special ways. It is fascinating to follow the traceries and spillovers and overlaps of international critical thought that both had preceded and then followed this idea as it grew and flourished into philosophy and literature. For example, from a literary/philosophical point of view, it could in some ways, in these early stages at least, be considered in relation to both the philosophical theory of *haecceitas* – *thisness* – proposed centuries before by the Scottish Franciscan monk Johannes Duns Scotus (*c.*1266–1308), and the idea of *inscape* as described by English poet Gerard Manley Hopkins

(1844–1889). Both relate to the concept of individualising difference, a sort of glimpse or subjective experience of final perfection or
essence (of 'deep down things'[16]) as part of a unique and almost 'out-
of-this-world' observation of everyday life. It also could relate in this
way to Irish novelist James Joyce's (1882–1941) idea of the revelation
of the *epiphany* (*quidditas*, 'whatness'): '[W]hen the parts are adjusted
to a special point, we recognise that it is *that* thing which it is... .The
soul of the commonest object, the structure of which is so adjusted,
seems to us radiant.'[17]

After the 1927 translation of Roh's paper into Spanish by Fernando
Vela,[18] a disciple of the Spanish phenomenologist José Ortega y Gasset,
Roh's concept of magic realism was adopted, albeit with differing
meanings, within the artistic expression of literature. It was a ripe
moment. Phenomenology – the science of perceptions, the 'study
of consciousness and its immediate objects'[19] – was a twentieth-
century school of thought that emerged from the work of the German
philosophers Edmund Husserl (1859–1938) and Martin Heidegger
(1889–1976). Husserl believed that experience was the source of all
knowledge and that a sense of fundamental essence could be perceived
through phenomenological reduction; Heidegger argued that Being
must be unhampered by preconceptions and knowledge of the world,
but can be 'unfolded'[20] through language.

I mention all these briefly as part of an international context that
was ready to accept, nurture and evolve the ideas of magic realism.
Its ethos and generative impulse gathered momentum with the publication of *Historia universal de la infamia* (1935) by Argentinian writer,
essayist, poet and translator, Jorge Luis Borges (1899–1986), whose
short stories were characterised by themes relating to dreams, animals,
mirrors, God, philosophy and religion.[21] Another contributing idea to
the burgeoning genre came from the Cuban writer Alejo Carpentier
(1904–1980), who in a famous prologue to his novel *The Kingdom of
this World* (1949), wrote: 'What is the entire history of [Latin] America
if not a chronicle of the marvellous real [*lo real maravilloso*]?'[22] For
Carpentier this marvellous real was inherently Latin America and
Latin American, and represented its multicultural and heady mix of
the European (rational) and non-European (magical, such as voodoo).
Venezuelan intellectual and writer and contemporary of Carpentier,
Arturo Uslar Pietri (1906–2001), described the movement as the 'mystery of human living amongst the reality of life'.[23] Carpentier's idea of
the marvellous real – a sort of marvellous realism – was to hybridise
with or perhaps blend into magic realism, but it is a lovely description
and one that offers an *other* and richly tilted way of thinking about

Almond's writing. Critic Angel Flores, in his essay 'Magical Realism in Spanish American Fiction'(1955),[24] which was to be pivotal in the international development of the genre, traced some of its characteristics – blends of history, myth and fantasy – back to the sense of 'wonderment and exoticism experienced by the Europeans who first colonised Latin America'. (Carpentier, however, has been criticised for perpetuating 'exotic' stereotypes of Latin American culture.) This offers an interesting sense of different worlds – of two worlds coming together – which also I think provides a rich critical focus for considering Almond's work.

The term magic realism (sometimes magical realism) is now more commonly applied to literature than to art and is diversely and often vaguely defined. It is sometimes referred to as a genre, but as David Macey points out, the discussion of genres is 'one of the oldest discourses in the arts, and can be narrowly prescriptive or purely descriptive or classificatory'.[25] And any such label is an imposed mapping or label; as Mendlesohn notes:

> Genre markers (whether tropes or patterns) are useful analytical tools but they are constructions imposed on a literary landscape. The same landscape may be susceptible to quite a different cartography.[26]

The argument can go both ways, but for our purposes here it is enough to consider magic realism as a literary mode; it is a way of telling, a way of writing, rather than, for example, 'a form of social codes governing individual texts'.[27] Basically, it is that literary mode in which magical and fantastic elements (relating to character or plot or location) are introduced into an otherwise everyday or mundane setting, usually without being remarked upon or attracting any explanation or comment, either from author or characters. These elements clearly break the ordinary rules of the real world but are simply accepted. In his famous essay Flores describes Magical Realism as a transformation of the unreal into part of reality and identified Cervantes's *Don Quixote* and Franz Kafka's *Metamorphosis* as examples. As well as obvious fantastic elements, hybrid and multiple planes of reality, inconstancies of time and unexplained time shifts, and blurring of distinctions between everyday life and dreams, Carpentier noted an 'extraordinary plenitude' of unsettling detail, which the author does not explain or necessarily even comment upon. The idea of plenitude will be discussed below.

Magic realism was promoted in Italy by Massimo Bontempelli (1878–1960), poet, playwright, novelist and composer. Well-known international writers subsequently identified with this literary mode include Gabriel García Márquez, Carlos Fuentes, Salman Rushdie, Toni Morrison, Isabel Allende and Angela Carter. The character Saleem in Rushdie's *Midnight's Children* (1981) describes it as 'Matter of fact descriptions of the outré and bizarre, and their reverse, namely heightened, stylized versions of the everyday'.[28] Wendy B. Faris and Lois Parkinson Zamora have made contemporary contributions to understanding through their book *Magical Realism: Theory, History, Community* (1995) and in other papers. Faris identifies as characteristics (and Latham also quotes these): an irreducible element of magic; a grounding in the phenomenal (natural, realistic) world; the production of unsettling doubts in the reader because of this mixture of the real and the fantastic; the near-merging of two realms or worlds; and disruptions of traditional ideas about time, space, and identity.[29]

This, then, is a brief synopsis of the narrative mode of magic realism, and highlights its international and complex heritage. How far does this describe the work of David Almond, or is there a more nuanced way of understanding and discussing this highly original author?

Mystical realism

> *What immortal hand or eye*
> *Could frame thy fearful symmetry?*

As Almond's corpus has grown, I think perhaps there is a more enlightened and enlightening way to consider his writings. At the least it is *another* way, which may offer different insights and a complementary schema of reference. All the contributors to this volume have noted a *something more* in Almond's work, and these *something mores* make surprising and certainly interesting connections to each other. Nodelman's analyses of the centrality of wildness across almost the whole of the corpus, and of incarnation, relate to Dalrymple's descriptions of radical landscapes and of what we could call a sort of deep and sacred history; they both reflect on what Levy describes as difference and transcendent wildness, and Dunbar's discussion of the celebration of distinctiveness – another version of 'wildness' – in the social landscapes of class and community. While Seelinger Trites's discussion of embodiment and embodied cognition pushes towards a *more* in the spaces of cognitive science and philosophy, Coats takes her discussion of embodiment into theology and the idea of the numinous; both writers offer another perspective on and are themselves enlarged by Coghlan's *something more* which is the pervasiveness throughout Almond's work of the rituals and beliefs of Catholicism. The discussion of *The True Tale of the Monster Billy Dean telt by hisself* argues that *something more* as a reflection on the personal act of writing – not only the writer's art but the writer's tools, responsibilities and struggles; indeed, on what it is to be a writer, and what it is to write life.

This sense of the *more* goes to the complexity and profundity of the construction of Almond's literary world. The cultural geographer Edward Soja refers to an idea of 'Thirdspace', that place where

> everything comes together … subjectivity and objectivity, the abstract and the concrete, the real and the imagined, the knowable and the unimaginable, the repetitive and the differential, structure and agency, mind and body, consciousness and the unconscious, the disciplined and the transdisciplinary, everyday life and unending history.[30]

This is a fascinating description and one that offers another way of thinking about magic realism,[31] but its focus is on the accumulation of identity and cultural hybridity and Almond's *something more* is more metaphysical. And while the development of the magic realism as sketched above shows various elements that we surely may recognise in Almond's work, this does not seem quite to give the whole picture. Irrespective of a literary context, the idea of 'magic' carries semantic associations of illusion and conjuring, of not being real, of being deliberately distracted and not seeing the sleight of hand. In the discussion of magic realism, descriptive fantasy – with all its associated ideas – plays an important role: consider the scene describing the 'light rain of tiny yellow flowers falling' from the book frequently cited as a paradigmatic example of magic realism, *One Hundred Years of Solitude* by Gabriel García Márquez:

> They fell on the town all through the night in a silent storm, and they covered the roofs and blocked the doors and smothered the animals who slept outdoors. So many flowers fell from the sky that in the morning the streets were carpeted with a compact cushion and they had to clear them away with shovels and rakes so that the funeral procession could pass by.[32]

This wonderful image carries that sense of the marvellous real, of the inexplicable; of the power of seeing something more, something other; of an extravagance of vision that defies ordinary convention; of alternative possibilities and phenomenology of perception, of a *thisness* or inscape of moment, of epiphany. Almond's writing also describes happenings that are mysterious, miraculous and inexplicable, but there is a difference. First, his characters do not leave these happenings unnoticed; they remark on and question what they don't understand. Indeed, they are perplexed, confronted, in awe of it:

> [Skellig] didn't move. She [Mina] slid the sleeves down over his arms, took the jacket right off him. We saw what both of us had dreamed we might see. Beneath his jacket were wings that grew out through rips in his shirt … .

> I felt the feathers, and beneath them the bones and sinews and muscles that supported them. I felt the crackle of Skellig's breathing. (*S*, pp. 89–90)

Michael then goes to the window and looks out through the shutters; when Mina asks him what he is doing, he replies: 'Making sure the world's still really there' (*S*, pp. 89–90). Similarly, when they see that Skellig eats live animals and passes pellets like those passed by owls, Michael cries, 'What does it mean?', and Mina replies, 'We can't know. Sometimes we just have to accept there are things we can't know' (*S*, p. 131). In other words, both children are fully aware that these are strange and inexplicable occurrences, somehow set apart. Amaryll Beatric Chanady argues that magical realism can be distinguished from the fantastic by differences in narrative stance: the narrator of/in magical realism accepts occurrences of the supernatural without question; the narrator of a fantastic text questions but the questioning is left unresolved.[33] *Skellig* does not quite fit either category – the children question, and the questioning is not so much unresolved as perceived as being part of something mysterious, supernatural, mystical: 'We'll remember forever,' Mina says after their farewell dance with Skellig, 'hearts and breath together', turning higher and higher, with 'ghostly wings' rising from their backs (*S*, p. 158).

The second major difference is in the authorial symbology – the authorial backdrop, if you like, even the symbolical *mise-en-scène*. This does not necessarily refer to the author's personal life nor to his personal beliefs (Almond has spoken about these at length in various places and they do not concern us here), but rather to the conscious and unconscious imaginary that can be detected through his works as feeding and inspiring that writing life, the reservoir or repertoire or creative archive of ideas into which he delves and out of which he writes. This imagery and these creative ideas, as Coghlan points out in her chapter, and indeed as each contributor has noted in ways pertinent to their focus, resonate with a sense of the religious, and particularly of Catholicism. As Almond has said:

> When you stop being a Catholic you have no religion to fall back on, but you do have a sense of possible transcendence. And it seems to me that this is the transcendence. *Heaven is here.* The more I live, the more gorgeous and wonderful the world is, but it is also terrifying and constantly endangered.[34]

There is an echo of these comments in *Skellig*, when Mina tells Michael that William Blake used occasionally to faint, because of 'great fear, or enormous pain, or too much joy'; she says, 'It was possible to be overwhelmed by the presence of so much beauty in the world' (*S*, pp. 142–3). Such comments invoke ideas of the *sublime*, described by the Greek Longinus writing in the first century AD as transport and rapture (*ekstasis*), and 'the echo of a noble mind'.[35] Longinus claimed that the greatest of works 'leave more food for reflection than the mere words convey', and that they make us feel 'as though we had ourselves produced what we had heard'.[36] Edmund Burke's *Philosophical Inquiry into the Origin of our Ideas on the Sublime and the Beautiful* (1757) concludes that while beauty is characterised by smoothness, delicacy and subtle variation, the sublime 'is inspired by ruggedness, irregularity, vastness, power and obscurity'.[37]

As has been widely noted, and as Almond himself acknowledges, the English poet, painter and printmaker William Blake has been a profound influence on his work. W.B. Yeats, in his Preface to the 1873 three-volume edition of Blake's works, wrote: 'He had learned from Jacob Boehme and from old alchemist writers that imagination was the first emanation of divinity, "the body of God".'[38] William Blake is seen as a nonconformist Christian mystic, mostly unknown and unpopular in his own time, but growing to exert a profound influence over many subsequent writers; he did not like organised religion but believed that imagination – and the work of artists and poets – was a God-given and God-inspired work. He revered the Bible and, like Almond's Billy Dean, was taught to read through Bible stories. He believed in invisible worlds that are accessible through love. On the day of his death Blake, as noted by biographer Peter Ackroyd, sang hymns and verses[39] – a young painter who was present wrote:

He said He was going to that Country he had all His life wished to see & expressed Himself Happy, hoping for Salvation through Jesus Christ – Just before he died His Countenance became fair. His eyes Brighten'd and he burst out Singing of the things he saw in Heaven.[40]

The events of *Skellig* continuously unfold against a rich and evocative Blakean intertext. As the children draw and discuss Skellig and the sick baby, Mina's mother tells them that she sees them as 'two angels at my table'; she says they are 'The kind of thing William Blake saw. He said we were surrounded by angels and spirits. We must just open our eyes a little wider, look a little harder' (*S*, p. 122). She then sings the words of the poem from Blake's *Songs of Experience*, 'The Angel' (*S*, p. 124):

> Guarded by an Angel mild
> Witless woe was n'er beguiled ...
> So he took his wings, and fled;
> Then the moon blushed rosy red ...

Almond's imagery emerges from a specific creative impulse that is more ontological than phenomenological (but includes both), that is eschatological, and that is symbolically inspired by Christian, and specifically Catholic, ideas, beliefs and practices. Christianity and Catholicism are his inspirational intertexts, his wellspring of words and symbols. And it is here that he can be seen as either exhibiting a very individual form of magic realism, or writing within a different but related mode that is more accurately and specifically described as *mystical realism*. The terms magic realism or magical realism bring opposites together (each in a slightly different way); so too the idea of mystical realism draws together conceptual opposites – the alterity and otherness of the imprint of the fantastic and the inexplicable on the conventional everyday. But here they emerge not randomly or as random events, but coherently, as part of a connected togetherness of figurative, other-worldly thinking. This coherence is a sense of a spiritual supernatural that becomes almost a semiotics of Christian symbology: angels, Heaven, love, joy, praying ('"You still say your prayers for her?" asked Mum', *S*, p. 148). Magic realism is mysterious and inexplicable but does not always have that edge of the spiritual (Isabel Allende is an exception that comes to mind; perhaps mystical realism would also be a better descriptor of her work). There is also a sort of internal palimpsest, the old writing can be glimpsed in bits through the new, and the old beliefs – although mostly rubbed out – still show through in spots. There is a sense that this alterity and otherness are somehow profoundly 'real', and somehow related to a Divine being and a place called Heaven. This sense of a religious supernatural is not commonly seen as part of magic realism; Roh himself in a sort of late postscript to his work wrote that his use of the idea of magic was 'of course *not* in the religious–psychological sense of ethnology'.[41] Almond is not conducting an ethnological study of human culture per se, but a study of human beings living at once on the edges of a cosmological abyss, on the rim of the cosmological sublime. For Almond, as the chapters in this volume indicate, there is a sense of a fullness, a living and lived reality that is infused with the hyper-real, super-real, meta-real, that informs the phenomenology of perception and even at times transcends it.

I want to pick up this notion of fullness. Philosopher Arthur Lovejoy identified a theory of plenitude, or a plenitude principle,[42] which he believed could be traced back to Aristotle, who said that no possibilities that remain eternally possible will go unrealised.[43] This may be seen as relating to the parallel worlds (Universal Wave Function) of quantum mechanics, but the idea that every possible explanation is also true if not in the current world then somewhere else in a universe that is infinite and eternal has tantalised many thinkers through the ages, and can be traced back as far as the ancient Greek philosopher Epicurus (341–270 BC). Almond writes of a world that is rich in the way it overlaps with other worlds; in *The True Tale of the Monster Billy Dean telt by hisself*, as I point out in Chapter 10, this is symbolised in the island of Lindisfarne, which is sometimes one world and sometimes another; in Billy's words, 'a little bit of Heven … a plase that sumtyms floted on water & sumtymes rested on the land' (*BD*, p. 8).

All of this points to something that is not just fantastic but that at some deep level is, actually, real. Skellig is not a magical figure but he is a mystical one, portrayed as healing through love – not fantasy, not magic, but some sort of mysterious, mystical truth-inspired tenderness and compassion. He, like Jesus, was not an expected sort of saviour. Michael's mother describes how a man with 'a great hunch on his back' in 'filthy' clothes and 'matted' hair but with 'such tenderness in his eyes' suddenly appeared at the hospital, and lifted the sick baby out of her crib:

> 'They stared and stared into each other's eyes. He started slowly to turn around …' 'Like they were dancing,' I said … .
> '… And then the strangest thing of all was, there were wings on the baby's back. Not solid wings. Transparent, ghostly, hardly visible, but there they were. Little feathery things …'. (*S*, p. 150)

This is a depiction that can best be described as meta-real – it is a meta-reality – an above-and-beyond reality, a second order reality-about-reality. I don't think Skellig is a Christ figure, but he is an unlikely, superficially unlovely figure who brings about healing and love. In an appearance-obsessed secular world, he is something beyond appearance. Almond invites us to contemplate the overlap and tumble of possible worlds, not as science fiction, not as fantasy, not as magic, but as another form of realness, another real, a sort of 'Heaven is here' as another manifestation of reality.

The distinguishing feature of mystical realism is a coherent and pervasive sense of the spiritual.

Finding space for the spiritual

> *What the anvil? what dread grasp,*
> *Dare its deadly terrors clasp!*

The idea of truth has been treated as a master narrative of suspicious intent in a postmodern world. And any idea of religion as a universal experience is even more suspicious. Of course there are reasons – some very good – for this, and a global world in touch with itself needs to rethink, embrace and pluralise its philosophical syntagms (traditional conceptions of linear strings of relationships) and paradigms (vertical mindsets of possibilities). But as I wrote years ago, that rush to the head of twentieth-century postmodernism itself was itself a master narrative – a very pervasive and consuming one.[44] There has of more recent years been a subtle but growing review of the significance of religion in Western culture. This is a timely context when we consider that two of the most powerful children's writers in England today (they are of course Almond and Philip Pullman), in very different, unorthodox, superficially at least quite opposite ways, are bringing religion back to the artistic table. Several of the contributors to this volume comment on this. Is Almond's work – emerging as it does from the strong Western roots of religion – unconsciously (or consciously?) prefiguring what Stanley Fish predicted after the attacks on the World Trade Center and the Pentagon on 11 September 2001? This respected and controversial American literary theorist, famous among other things for his work in reader-response theory and interpretive communities, and frequent contributor to the *New York Times*, wrote in 2005 that there is

> a growing awareness of the difficulty, if not impossibility, of keeping the old boundaries in place and of quarantining the religious impulse in the safe houses of the church, the synagogue, and the mosque … .

When Jacques Derrida died I was called by a reporter who wanted to know what would succeed high theory and the triumvirate of race, gender, and class as the center of intellectual energy in the academy. I answered like a shot: religion.[45]

Terry Eagleton, in *After Theory*, writes that global political pressures and religious confrontations force the West 'more and more to reflect on the foundations of its own civilisation'.[46] But, as he goes on to say:

The West, then, may need to come up with some persuasive-sounding legitimations of its form of life, at exactly the point when laid-back cultural thinkers are assuring it that such legitimations are neither possible nor necessary. It may be forced to reflect on the truth and reality of its existence, at a time when postmodern thought has grave doubts about both truth and reality. It will need, in short, to sound deep in a progressively more shallow age.[47]

Jean Baudrillard warns that the West and indeed Western education have lost the unifying reason for values such as truth, justice, goodness and beauty, and that the contemporary culture of knowledge is '*le cadavre en spirale*' – the spiralling cadaver.[48] Jean-François Lyotard claims that in this dehumanising and dehumanised postmodern world, humans 'are like Gullivers ... : sometimes too big, sometimes too small, but never the right size'.[49] He goes on to say that in the 'expressions of thought' that include 'visual and plastic arts', literature, philosophy and politics, the idea of 'a kind of work, a long, obstinate and highly responsible work', which was part of the true process of modernity and the *avant-garde* (and, by the way, remember that Cuban writer Arturo Uslar-Pietri believed that magic realism was an extension of the avant-garde – *the vanguardia*) must be restored as part of human 'responsibility'. Without this, Lyotard continues, 'we will surely be condemned to repeat ... the West's "modern neurosis" – its schizophrenia, paranoia, and so on'.[50]

Jens Zimmerman cites all these to argue that 'The identity crisis of the West, and the exhaustion of secular reason, has a number of philosophers and politicians calling for a return of religion into the heart of the academy and public policy.'[51] As Richard Lane notes in his introduction to the piece: 'Zimmerman turns to Nietzsche, Heidegger, Lévinas and Derrida to show how these exemplary critics of logocentric thought also reignite debate about "the Divine Logos and the humanistic tradition".'[52]

Margaret Wertheim, in a book devoted to the exploration of cyberspace within a more expansive cultural history of space, also writes of the confusions, difficulties and losses facing a secular post-modern Western society:

> Like the late Romans, we too live in a time marked by inequity, corruption and fragmentation. Ours seems to be a society past its peak, one no longer sustained by a firm belief in itself and no longer sure of its purpose.[53]

Wertheim's thesis is that 'conceptions of space and conceptions of ourselves are inextricably intertwined', and that 'it is the language we use – the concepts that we articulate and hence the questions that we ask – that determines the kind of space we are able to see'.[54] It is interesting to consider her ideas not only in relation to Almond's literary world but also to the discussions of embodiment in the chapters by Coats and Seelinger Trites. Wertheim writes:

> [W]hile we have been mapping and mastering physical space, we have lost sight of any kind of religious or psychological space … .
>
> How did such a monumental shift occur? How did we go from seeing ourselves at the centre of an angel-filled space suffused with divine presence and purpose to the modern scientific picture of a pointless physical void? What was at stake here was not simply the position of the earth in the planetary system but the role of humanity in the cosmological whole. How did we go from seeing ourselves embedded in spaces of both body and soul, to seeing ourselves embedded in physical space alone? And, critically, how has this shift in our vision of space affected our understanding of who and what we are as human beings?[55]

Perhaps part of the growing receptivity to such a critical restoration has grown out of increasing knowledge, acceptance and respect for Indigenous spirituality and Indigenous religions. Indigenous peoples across the world have taught the sceptical and secular West that there is a place for the spiritual in everyday life, and they bring it to life in imageries of landscapes and mindscapes, spaces of being and belonging, cultures of immanence and transcendence. The Australian Aboriginal artist of the Arrawar region known as Kame expressed her life and being in a series of paintings of sweet potatoes: as tubers and deep tangled roots entwined underground; as shoots beginning to form and break through the dry, cracked earth; as a golden explosion of blossom. Kame was a Sweet Potato woman.[56] These are totems, spiritual connections to self, landscape, community and Dreaming – an ongoing spiritual community of past, present and future, perhaps another way of thinking about Ricoeur's idea of time as a public space,[57] another way of thinking about the work of a writer such as Almond.

Science and the spiritual

> *When the stars threw down their spears*
> *And water'd heaven with their tears:*
> *Did he smile his work to see?*
> *Did he who made the Lamb make thee?*

Wertheim's deracinated world is a literary and cultural conception of physical space; a *scientific* conception of the physical reveals physical unity and connection rather than the postmodern disconnection Wertheim describes. The scientist Brian Greene, one of the world's leading string theorists, writes in his award-winning book *The Elegant Universe: Superstrings, Hidden Dimensions, and the Quest for the Ultimate Theory*:

> [A]ccording to string theory, the observed properties of each elementary particle arise because its internal string undergoes a particular vibrational pattern, This perspective differs sharply from that espoused by physicists before the discovery of string theory; in the earlier perspective the differences among the fundamental particles were explained by saying that, in effect, each particle species was 'cut from a different fabric.' ... String theory alters this picture radically by declaring that the 'stuff' of all matter and all forces is the *same*. Each elementary particle is composed of a single string – that is, each particle *is* a single string – and all strings are absolutely identical. Differences between the strings arise because their respective strings undergo different resonant vibrational patterns. What appears to be different elementary particles are actually different 'notes' on a fundamental string. The universe – being composed of an enormous number of vibrating strings – is akin to a cosmic symphony.[58]

It is fascinating to compare a scientific explanation of the physical universe such as the above with the Australian Aboriginal idea of the Dreaming: ancestor beings made a noise, the noise became singing, and the singing created land, landforms, and themselves as beings. 'You dream, You sing, It is.'[59] This becomes even more significant when Greene goes on to discuss 'the music of string theory'.[60]

Like magic realism, like mystical realism, I have no conclusion to draw from this. It is all part of the mystery – the deep and real interconnectedness of the siloes of thinking we tend to separate as 'science' and 'arts' and 'literature' and 'spirituality'. It just *is* – but awareness of it enlarges the way we think about the here and now, and the way that a writer such as Almond helps to make us think. Literary thinking needs to be expansive, interdisciplinary, transdisciplinary – as literature is. Here are other descriptions of other possibilities and other worlds. Here are other ways of seeing. Apart from the obvious literary considerations, and as the number of respected theorists have declared in their different ways, there are certainly important implications here for Western culture. As Lyotard says, it is in artistic 'expressions of thought' that 'a kind of work, a long, obstinate and highly responsible work' must be restored as part of human 'responsibility' for human progress.[61]

The chapters in this volume

> *On what wings dare he aspire?*
> *What the hand, dare seize the fire?*

So, it should be no surprise that we have sought innovative thinkers as contributors to this volume. In remarkably diverse ways, and from very diverse perspectives, they have arrived at some similar critical places: in summary, that Almond's books are not startlingly different to each other, that there are clearly discernible similarities across the whole corpus, yet that there is something elusively unique in each one.

Any study of Almond should not be limited to a single text, so there has been a deliberate effort to be wide-ranging and to consider those books which each author felt most appropriate for their critical purposes. There remains a fair distribution of commentary on *Skellig* as a pivotal text, but some contributors, especially Nodelman and Coats, carry their discussions across the oeuvre. The chapter on *Heaven Eyes* is important not only because it is a complex variation, but because of its female protagonist. *The True Tale of the Monster Billy Dean telt by hisself* is the first Almond book to be directed towards an adult as well as young adult readership; it is also a sort of extension of some of the themes in *Clay*, and in a deep way appears to be a culmination of Almond's ideas – to this point anyhow – on writing. This selection of texts encourages creative and interesting applications that will enhance the reading not only of those particular texts but also of others in the Almond corpus.

In a wide-ranging discussion that includes almost all of Almond's texts, in Chapter 2 of this volume, 'Living Just Beyond the Wall: Versions of the Savage in David Almond's Novels', Perry Nodelman identifies an *ur-story* involving the author's plots and characters: 'Almond's novels tend to read as versions or variations of the same story, a story intriguingly and obsessively engaged with the border between civilisation and savagery in the lives of young people – especially boys.' An ur-story (the German prefix '*ur-*' denotes original, ancient, primitive) is one that in literary terms can usefully be seen as archetypal; in Almond's case, this may be seen to pertain to personal archetypes, but as Nodelman strongly argues, they are also the archetypes of children's literature. His description of the social and physical geography of the Almond ur-story complements Nolan Dalrymple's descriptions of landscapes in Chapter 6 and Carole Dunbar's description of class in Chapter 7. He also notes as part of that story the philosophical and religious resonances that are subsequently considered in different ways by Roberta Seelinger Trites in Chapter 3, Karen Coats in Chapter 4 and Valerie Coghlan in Chapter 5. The idea of the 'person, animal, or creature identified as being somehow savage, an exotic and often magical "other" who comes from or is otherwise connected with a wilderness beyond the borders', and the subsequent 'consideration of the wilderness within' also relate to Michael Levy's chapter on *Wild Girl, Wild Boy* (Chapter 9), and to my own chapter, which focuses on the idea of truth and the writing process in *The True Tale of the Monster Billy Dean telt by hisself* (Chapter 10). Noting that despite common situations, concerns and character types, Almond's books represent a variety of different kinds of fiction, and that 'each one offers a quite different experience from the rest', Nodelman writes: 'The Almond ur-plot is essentially a story of incarnation – becoming one with the wild natural world.'

In 'Ontology, Epistemology and Values: Philosophy and Cognitive Science in David Almond's *Skellig* and *My Name is Mina*' (Chapter 3), Roberta Seelinger Trites offers creative new insights into the field of children's literature by exploring these two books through the lens of cognitive science, particularly examining the intersection of cognitive science with philosophy and how this plays out in Almond's works. She begins with an acknowledgement of the importance of children's literature as one of the significant ways that children learn philosophical and ethical values about what it means to *be* – ontology – and what it means to *know* – epistemology. She relates this particularly to the work of, first, F. Elizabeth Hart, who notes the significant influences of bodily, social and cultural contexts on the mind and on the development of imaginative process, and secondly, George Lakoff and Mark Johnson, who, in rejecting the Cartesian split, argue that in an embodied mind philosophical questions emerge from three things: 'a reason shaped by the body, a cognitive unconscious to which we have no direct access, and metaphorical thought of which we are largely unaware'. As well as discussing Almond's multiple metaphorical imageries, Trites notes the contribution that 'deeply philosophical books' such as these make not only to children, but to their literature.

Chapter 4, 'The Possibilities of Becoming: Process-Relational Theology in the Works of David Almond', Karen Coats also notes the idea of embodiment and goes on to break innovative ground both in the study of Almond and, notably, in the study of children's literature. Again there is that complex sense of Almond's almost contradictory similarity and originality – she notes: 'Almond was doing something with his characters that I had not seen before.' Coats goes on to identify this as a sense of the power of 'numinous possibility', and begins her study with a discussion of the 2013 book by Almond and Dave McKean, *Mouse Bird Snake Wolf*, a fable she sees as not only lending itself to multiple interpretations, but also as the author's most overt expression of 'an ideological thread' that can be traced throughout his oeuvre. She introduces the controversial idea of process theology, built upon the world-view of process philosophy, and applies this as a critical lens to Almond's work, identifying its basic tenets as creativity, interrelatedness, free will, responsiveness to the past and the lure of the divine. She notes that Almond's characters – 'Kit, John, Allie, Erin, January, Heaven Eyes, Blue, Harry, Sue, little Ben, Slog, Michael, Mina, and Skellig – all find the source of grace by following the lure of God into a darkness out of which they emerge remade.'

The complexity of religion in Almond's work is explored in a different way by Valerie Coghlan in '"A sense sublime": Religious Resonances in the Work of David Almond' (Chapter 5). Coghlan begins her chapter with a quotation from William Wordsworth, 'a sense sublime of something far more deeply interfused', as one way of describing and seeking to understand the metaphysical qualities and 'lurking sense of the mysterious' in Almond's writing. She describes and places in context the rich imagery of what she calls Almond's 'literary Catholicism', the intersection of plots with Catholic ritual and belief, and the influence of Blake, particularly of his *Songs of Innocence and of Experience*. She argues, however, that Almond's works express the idea that experience does not necessarily have to shatter innocence – that indeed the characters are not entirely innocent, and that experience is ongoing. She discusses Almond's belief in the power of story to offer hope: '[t]here are moments of great joy and magic.

The most astounding things can lie waiting as each day dawns, as each page turns' (*HE*, p. 215).

Critical focus shifts in the next chapter to the significance of landscape in Almond's writing. Nolan Dalrymple's 'Birdmen from the Depths of the Earth: Radical Landscape in the Fiction of David Almond' (Chapter 6) describes and discusses the significance of Almond's radical vision and depiction of the landscapes of north-east England. Dalrymple sets in that different critical context some of the themes discussed by other contributors to this volume – its modern and ancient influences, the edges and what he calls the 'marriage' of rural wildness and urban civilisation, the wastelands and wildernesses, the undercutting of natural spaces by mines, and the environmental and social legacies of industrial decline. He notes that Almond's landscape imagery is essentially Romantic, and that the Romantics associate creativity with natural landscapes and wild places, including gardens and birds. Dalrymple describes a sense of 'radical knowledge' that evokes the sacred within the profane, and makes a particular point about the significance of the relationship between what lies above and what is below the ground, down in 'the history of the landscape'. Almond's is a North-East in which the landscape is at one with its traditions, derelict though they may be.

In '"They thought we had disappeared, and they were wrong": The Depiction of the Working Class in Almond's Novels' (Chapter 7), Carole Dunbar draws critical attention to Almond's social landscapes and his continuing identification with the working-class life he portrays. Dunbar argues that this gives his writing a vibrancy, depth and individuality which are indivisible from his own social roots. She draws attention to important parallels with the work of Alan Garner and Peter Dickinson, and particularly stresses the class emphasis on the value of education: in *The Fire-Eaters*, Bobby's dad tells his son, the first member of the family to attend grammar school, 'you can do anything … you're privileged and free' (*FE*, p. 60). As most of the other writers represented here also do, Dunbar refers to the autobiographical memoir *Counting Stars* as an intertext both to Almond's writing and his life. She notes the ambivalent attitude of teachers to the working-class poor, and comments on the use of folk songs and ballads to suggest the poor through theme and dialect.

Nodelman's second chapter in this volume, 'Almond's *Heaven Eyes* as a Complex Variation' (Chapter 8), follows on from the earlier one but draws attention both to the significance of the female protagonist (Almond's first, and the only one, excepting of course the play *Wild*

Girl, Wild Boy, until *My Name is Mina* in 2010), and to this novel's similarities yet dissimilarities within a pattern that is intensely familiar in literature for children – the home/away/home story of escapes to dangerous freedoms and returns to restrictive safety. Nodelman points out the ambivalences that help to make this novel – on the surface a 'surprisingly Utopian fairy tale' – so mysterious and even problematical. He discusses themes relating to the idea of Tyneside landscape and history, the importance of story to identity, the use of pictures to recover the past, and the symbolism of the 'Black Middens'. He draws attention to the imaginative territory explored by Almond in *Heaven Eyes* but also notes its unsettling dissimilarities from Almond's other works.

Michael Levy, in Chapter 9, 'The Transcendent in David Almond's Play *Wild Girl, Wild Boy*', focuses on an Almond play, and explores Almond's idea of the supernatural as well as developing further extrapolations on the idea of wildness. He notes that for Almond, transcendence is finding 'that great sense of joy and the miraculous' in such simple things as the taste of a raspberry, and notes the parallels between Elaine's difficulties in writing and Wild Boy's difficulties in speaking.

This sense of unsettling dissimilarities amid similarities is amplified in the book examined in Chapter 10, *The True Tale of the Monster Billy Dean telt by hisself*. Here I describe how Almond's tale is told, and what this reveals about words and truth, writing and language, and more importantly what Almond thinks about words and truth, writing and language. This chapter notes the continuing imageries of stars and dancing and birds singing and the power they contribute to the story, and the way they thread as leitmotifs through the narrative. It discusses the construction of tale, teller and readers; the idea of an ethics of hope that permeates Almond's work; and how and what this book – his first for a dual readership – contributes to the Almond oeuvre.

The Appendix by Hannah Izod outlines the invaluable resource to researchers that is available for Almond scholars at Seven Stories, the National Centre for Children's Books in Newcastle, England. It is an archive of original artwork and manuscripts, holds exhibitions, and runs events and learning programmes. As Izod points out, Almond has donated rough draft material for two of his books – *Heaven Eyes* and *My Dad's a Birdman* – to the collection. The latter book also has correspondence and notes in relation to preparing this book for publication in the USA. She outlines the fascinating way that this material – although not huge in quantity – can reveal so much about Almond and the writing process. Indeed, it contains worthwhile tips that researchers could also apply in other contexts.

Hopefully these chapters will assist critical understandings and provoke further discussion about the work of this complex and highly individual author. Perhaps they will help explain why imageries that are used over and over again avoid becoming repetitive and instead become somehow enriched and enlarged with every appearance – colours deeper, meanings more profound. Stars, dancing, larks, the 'ancient', mice, beasts, the dark, angels – they crop up again and again, with intense familiarity, and become part of a sort of collective conscious, if not unconscious. As Mina's mother tells her daughter, 'Your head holds all those stars, all that darkness, all these noises. It holds the universe' (*MNIM*, p. 282)

Perhaps Almond's skill is that he does not actually, as in popular literary parlance, *engage* with issues. Rather, he tells his stories and in the telling – out of the characters and events and their chronotopical relationship to time and place – issues and their associated philosophical and religious and theoretical and literary implications emerge, sometimes inconclusively, sometimes ambiguously, but always elegantly. There is a within-ness and a without-ness, reality upon reality – meta-reality: 'I close my eyes,' writes Mina in her journal, 'and stare into the universe inside myself' (*MNIM*, p. 287).

So, read if you can each chapter in this volume as part of the story of a children's literature giant of our time. The authors have worked independently but there are surprising echoes in their critical examinations, and surprising, uncontrived, links between the contributions.

This collection thus offers contemporary discussions of Almond's work and provides critical material in order both to provide a sense of the whole of his literary oeuvre and to bring new ideas to the examination of individual texts. It also contributes new ideas into the scope and endless possibilities of children's literature criticism.

> *What immortal hand or eye,*
> *Dare frame thy fearful symmetry?*

Notes

1. William Blake, *Songs of Innocence and Songs of Experience* (London: R. Brimley Johnson, 1901 [1794]).
2. To really appreciate the accents and idioms represented in Almond's narration and dialogue, listen to some of the author's readings on

YouTube. There is a particularly interesting one of him reading the early pages of *The True Tale of Billy Dean telt by hisself*, http://www.youtube. com/watch?v=YhqzewH_UFo.

3. Jack Zipes, Lissa Paul, Lynne Vallone, Peter Hunt and Gillian Avery, *Norton Anthology of Children's Literature: The Traditions in English* (New York and London: W.W. Norton, 2005), pp. 551–8.

4. Humphrey Carpenter and Mari Prichard, *Oxford Companion to Children's Literature* (Oxford and New York: Oxford University Press, 1995), p. 181.

5. J.R.R. Tolkien, 'On Fairy Stories', in *The Tolkien Reader* (New York: Del Rey, 1986 [1966]), p. 9.

6. Tolkien, 'On Fairy Stories', p. 14.

7. Brian Attebery, *Strategies of Fantasy* (Bloomington: Indiana University Press, 1992).

8. Maria Nikolajeva, *The Magic Code: The Use of Magical Patterns in Fantasy for Children* (Stockholm: Almqvist & Wiksell, 1988), p. 10.

9. Farah Mendlesohn, 'Rhetorics of Fantasy', http://www.farahsf.com/ extract.htm (accessed 24 January 2014).

10. Mendlesohn, 'Rhetorics of Fantasy'.

11. Northrop Frye, 'The Anatomy of Criticism', http://northropfrye-the-anatomyofcriticism.blogspot.com.au/2009/02/tentative-conclusion. html (accessed 13 January 2014).

12. Don Latham, *David Almond: Memory and Magic* (Lanham, MD, Toronto and Oxford: Scarecrow Press, 2006).

13. Latham quotes the following as examples, and notes that in interviews Almond has variously embraced and rejected the characterisation of his work as magical realism: Ilene Cooper, 'The Booklist Interview' (1 January 2000) and Mark Mordue, 'The Gentle Dreamer', *Sunday Age* (Melbourne), 1 June 2003. In a personal interview with Latham (21 April 2005), Almond acknowledged both his debt to magical realism and the tendency of writers to resist all labels.

14. Gabriel García Márquez, 'A Very Old Man with Enormous Wings', in *Collected Stories*, trans. Gregory Rabassa and J.S. Bernstein (New York: HarperCollins, 1999), pp. 217–25. Don Latham, 'Magical Realism and the Child Reader: The case of David Almond's *Skellig*', *The Looking Glass: New Perspectives on Children and Literature*, 10(1) (2006).

15. Franz Roh, 'Magical Realism: Post-Expressionism' [1925], in Lois Parkinson Zamora and Wendy B. Faris, *Magical Realism: Theory, History, Community* (Durham, NC: Duke University Press, 1995), p. 426.

16. Gerard Manley Hopkins, 'There lives the dearest freshness deep down things', 'God's Grandeur' [1877], in *Poems and Prose of Gerard Manley Hopkins* (Harmondsworth: Penguin), p. 27.

17. James Joyce, *A Portrait of the Artist as a Young Man* (Melbourne: Penguin, 1960 [1916]), p. 213.

18. Franz Roh, 'Realismo mágico: Problemas de la pintura europea más reciente', trans. Fernando Vela, *Revista de Occidente* 16(47) (abril–junio 1927): 274–301.

19. *Oxford English Reference Dictionary* (2nd ed., 20 vols, Oxford: Oxford University Press, 1996).

20. Martin Heidegger, 'Letter on "Humanism"' [1949], http://archive. org/stream/HeideggerLetterOnhumanism1949/Heidegger-LetterOn (accesed 10 January 2014).

21. Jorge Luis Borges, *Historia universal de la infamia* [1935]. Published in English as *A Universal History of Infamy*, trans. Norman Thomas di Giovanni (New York:, Dutton, 1972). English edition: *A Universal History of Iniquity*, trans. Andrew Hurley (London: Penguin Classics, 2004).

22. Alejo Carpentier, 'The Baroque and the Marvelous Real', in Lois Parkinson Zamora and Wendy B. Faris, *Magical Realism: Theory, History, Community* (Durham, NC: Duke University Press, 1995), p. 107.

23. Arturo Uslar Pietri, *Letras y Hombres de Venezuela* (Mexico City: Fondo de Cultura Económica, 1949), p. 161.

24. Angel Flores, 'Magical Realism in Spanish American Fiction', *Hispania* 38(2) (1955): 187–92.

25. See, among others, David Macey, *The Penguin Dictionary of Critical Theory* (London: Penguin, 2000).

26. Mendlesohn, *Rhetorics of Fantasy*.

27. Richard Harland, *Literary Theory from Plato to Barthes* (Basingstoke: Macmillan, 1999), p. 232.

28. Salman Rushdie, *Midnight's Children* (London: Jonathan Cape, 1980), p. 303.

29. Lois Parkinson Zamora and Wendy B. Faris, *Magical Realism: Theory, History, Community* (Durham, NC: Duke University Press Books, 1995), pp. 1–11.

30. Edward W. Soja, *Thirdspace* (Malden, MA: Blackwell, 1996), p. 57.

31. It is interesting to note that Soja's idea builds on the concept of spatial infinity developed by Borges.

32. Gabriel García Márquez, *One Hundred Years of Solitude* (London: Penguin, 1972 [1967]), p. 144.

33. Amaryll Beatrice Chanady, *Magical Realism and the Fantastic: Resolved vs. Unresolved Antinomy* (New York: Garland, 1985), pp. 30–1.

34. Nicolette Jones, 'David Almond: Story is a Kind of Redemption', *Daily Telegraph* (25 October 2008), http://www.telegraph.co.uk/culture/books/3562549/David-AlmondStory-is-a-kind-of-redemption.html (accessed 31 March 2014; emphasis added).

35. T.S. Dorsch, *Classical Literary Criticism* (Harmondsworth: Penguin, 1965), p. 109.

36. Longinus, 'On the Sublime', http://evans-experientialism.freewebspace. com/longinus01.htm (accessed 17 January 2014).

37. Edmund Burke, *Philosophical Inquiry into the Origin of our Ideas on the Sublime and the Beautiful* (London: Routledge & Kegan Paul, 1958 [1757].]

38. William Butler Yeats, Preface to *The Works of William Blake: Poetic, Symbolic, and Critical*, ed. Edwin J. Ellis and W.B. Yeats, 3 vols (1893).

39. Peter Ackroyd, *Blake* (London: Sinclair-Stevenson, 1995; Minerva, 1996), p. 389.

40. George Richmond was a follower of Blake and part of a group of young painters who called themselves 'The Ancients'. In later life he painted portraits of Cardinal Newman, Henry Hallam, Charlotte Brontë, Elizabeth Gaskell and many others. Geoffrey Grigson, *Samuel Palmer: the Visionary Years* (London: Kegan Paul, 1947), p. 38.

41. Parkinson and Faris, *Magical Realism* contains a translation of Roh's original essay.

42. Arthur Lovejoy, *The Great Chain of Being* (Cambridge, MA: Harvard University Press, 1936).

43. Aristotle, *Physics*, III, 4, 203b 25–30, in *Aristotle's Physics Books III and IV*, trans. Edward Hussey (Oxford: Oxford University Press, 1993).

44. 'Postmodernism asked questions about perspectives (whose truth?) and sought new, inclusive ways of thinking, and new equities. Ironically, its pervasiveness has created its own grand narrative, and it has influenced and continues to influence not only literature but all the creative arts, engineering, architecture, religion, business.' Rosemary Ross Johnston, 'Literacy', in Gordon Winch, Rosemary Ross Johnston, Paul March, Lesley Ljungdahl and Marcelle Holliday, *Literacy: Reading, Writing and Children's Literature* (4th ed., Melbourne: Oxford University Press, 2010), p. 492.

45. Stanley Fish, 'One University Under God', *Chronicle of Higher Education* (7 January 2005), http://chronicle.com/article/One-University-Under-God-/45077 (accessed 10 January 2014).

46. Terry Eagleton, *After Theory* (London: Allen Lane, 2003), pp. 72–3.

47. Eagleton, *After Theory*, p. 73.

48. Jean Baudrillard, *Simulacra and Simulations* – XVL, 'The Spiraling Cadaver', trans. Sheila Faria Glaser (Ann Arbor: University of Michigan Press, 2004 [1994]).

49. Jean-François Lyotard, *The Postmodern Explained: Correspondence 1982–1985*, afterword by Wlad Godzich (Minneapolis and London: University of Minnesota Press, 1992), p. 29.

50. Lyotard, *Postmodern Explained*, pp. 79–80.

51. Jens Zimmerman, 'Western Identity, The Exhaustion of Secular Reason, and the Return to Religion', in Richard Lane (ed.), *Global Literary Theory* (London: Routledge , 2013), p. 798.

52. Lane, *Global Literary Theory*, p. 798.

53. Margaret Wertheim, *The Pearly Gates of Cyberspace: A History of Space from Dante to the Internet* (Milson's Point, NSW: Doubleday, Transworld, 1999), p. 23.

54. Wertheim, *Pearly Gates of Cyberspace*, p. 306.

55. Wertheim, *Pearly Gates of Cyberspace*, pp. 38–9.

56. I wish to express my appreciation to Dr Pam Johnston for telling me about the work of the Aboriginal artist, Kame.

57. Paul Ricoeur, *Time and Narrative,* trans. Kathleen McLaughlin and David
    Pellauer (Chicago: University of Chicago Press, 1984).
58. Brian Greene, *The Elegant Universe: Superstrings, Hidden Dimensions, and
    the Quest for the Ultimate Theory* (London: Vintage, 1999), pp. 145–6.
59. As reported to me by community elders, 2002.
60. Greene, *Elegant Universe*, p. 146.
61. Lyotard, *Postmodern Explained*, pp. 79–80.

2

Living Just Beyond the Wall: Versions of the Savage in David Almond's Novels

Perry Nodelman

In a note 'About the Author' in his novel *Secret Heart*, David Almond tells readers that he and his family live 'just beyond the ancient Roman Wall, which once marked the place where civilisation ended and the wastelands begin'. As Almond suggests himself in an online interview, that geographical location can stand as a metaphor for the fictional space created by his novels: saying that 'beyond the wall was where the kind of wild things happened'. He adds, 'Good books have kind of been into the wilderness and have come back again and they're kind of controlled, they're kind of civilised, but if they're any good they've still got that kind of hint of wildness about them.'[1] As a result of their shared (and sizeable) 'hint of wildness', Almond's novels tend to read as versions or variations of the same story, a story intriguingly and obsessively engaged with the border between civilisation and savagery in the lives of young people – especially boys. The commonalties in Almond's descriptions of life on both sides of the wall where civilisation ends not only mark his work as distinctively his but also, at the same time, reveal its allegiance to some key characteristics typical of writing for young people, itself a literature about life on both sides of the wall where adulthood begins.

The ur-story lurking behind the apparently wide variety of characters and experiences described in Almond's novels centres around a boy in early adolescence who lives at the edge of a town in northern England, near but apart from both a wilder space and a more urban or interconnected or global culture. The story involves the boy's dealings with a person, animal or creature identified as being somehow savage, an exotic and often magical 'other' who comes from or is otherwise connected with a wilderness beyond the borders of the boy's normal life (and is often, also, connected to the past), and whose presence engages the boy in a consideration of the wildness within himself. At a key point in the story, the boy joins the savage being in a wild, dark place, most often a cave, and finds a way of acknowledging his own connection with it that both releases him from it and it from what troubles it and has connected it to him.

Some of Almond's books express this story more obviously than others do – especially the novels that feature boys as protagonists. In what follows I describe the relationships between the ur-story and these novels: *Skellig, Kit's Wilderness, Secret Heart, The Fire-Eaters, Clay, The Savage* and *Raven Summer*. Then, after discussing how Almond's other books relate to the ur-story in less obvious ways, I will consider the implications of Almond's consistent interest in similar characters and themes. A later chapter in this collection considers relationships between the ur-story and another Almond novel, *Heaven Eyes*.

The border boy

Even before his contact with the savage begins, the typical male Almond protagonist has a connection with what is other or outside, beyond walls. While he has male friends with whom he indulges in typically boyish activities like playing violent games and smoking cigarettes, he also has characteristics that separate him from them. He might do very well at school, for instance, and so has hopes of a promising future that will take him beyond his roots and thus away from his friends (Bobby in the *Fire-Eaters*); or he has a talent for some form of artistry, especially writing (Michael in *Skellig*, Kit in *Kit's Wilderness*, Blue in *The Savage*); or he has links to less ordinary or respectable lifestyles (in *Raven Summer*, Liam's parents are artists, unlike their rural neighbours, and in *Secret Heart*, all Joe knows about his absent father is that he ran the Tilt-a-Whirl at a carnival). The protagonist may have a single parent (a mother in *Secret Heart*; a recent widow in *The Savage*) or he may have two, but he never has parents who do not love and respect him and, often, think him wonderful.

The wild thing

The otherness of Almond's representations of wildness varies from the fantastic uniqueness of Skellig, a winged human who might also be a bird or an angel, to the all-too-common reality of the orphans Crystal and Oliver in *Raven Summer*, one a damaged survivor of a fire that took her family and the other a Liberian refugee with a history of violence and even murder in a distant war. Liam, who worries about 'the awful things in the world' reaching his home, sees Crystal and Oliver as representing the results of 'all the wars and savagery all around the world' (*RS[A]*, p. 61). Similarly in *The Fire-Eaters*, the war-damaged 'wild man' (*FE[A]*, p. 14) McNulty, who makes a living eating fire and impaling himself with sharp weapons (as the similarly damaged Crystal cuts herself), and who, according to Bobby's father, comes 'from a mad mad time before your time, from a time of bloody blasted war' (*FE*, p. 54), enters Bobby's life at another moment of potential savagery, the Cuban missile crisis of 1962 when, Bobby's father says, the politicians are 'animals, howling for blood' (*FE[A]*, p. 19). In *Secret Heart*, on the other hand, the representative of wildness is a magical and often invisible but otherwise realistic tiger with 'hot, sour breath' (*SH[A]*, p. 1). And in *Kit's Wilderness*, the savage is an ordinarily human but nevertheless 'wild' boy associated with the nearby 'wilderness', an empty space where the mine once was, and who claims a symbolic kinship with Kit, asserting that the two of them are 'just the same' (*KW[A]*, p. 12). This wild boy, Askew, connects Kit with his family's history of mining and more magically, with the spirits of child labourers dead long ago in the mines – and causes Kit to create a story of an archaic and more literally 'savage' boy who undergoes a similar journey.

That story in *Kit's Wilderness* of a savage emanating from within the protagonist's own wild imagination but connecting him to a wildness in the world outside him is echoed in *Clay* by a life-sized clay figure of a giant man, first modelled and then brought to life by the protagonist and his new friend Stephen Rose. The giant seems to represent the force of evil that Stephen brings out of Davie – or perhaps even creates in him. At one point Davie says, 'I felt Stephen's fingers on me, like he was forming me, like I was his clay' (*C[A]*, p. 61). The same story echoes again in *The Savage*, in which a savage boy first imagined and written about by the protagonist then also comes to life in order to take revenge on the protagonist's enemy.

All three of these savage creations are engendered in and connected with the physical wildernesses they inhabit, as is Skellig, a damaged being at one with the discarded objects in the dilapidated garage he inhabits. There is also a suggestion that Skellig might be intimately connected with Michael: as his friend Mina calls for Skellig, Michael says it feels as if 'she was calling Skellig out from somewhere deep inside me' (*S[A]*, p. 100). There are similar connections between the other boys and the wild things they encounter. In *Raven Summer*, Liam receives an email from Crystal telling him that she feels she has always known him. In *Secret Heart*, the fortune teller Nanty Solo tells Joe that the tiger he encounters responds to 'the taste of something old and animal' (*SH[A]*, p. 87) in him, and Joe thinks of himself as being half-beast and half-human. He also speaks of moving into the wilderness as a matter of going towards 'the furthest fringes of the mind' (*SH[A]*, p. 68), a connection confirmed when Nanty Solo honours those 'who understood that what we imagined could also be something that we touched … who understood that as we stepped into the forest we stepped into the unknown fringes of the mind' (*SH[A]*, p. 145). In the three novels where the wild expresses itself in a creature invented by the protagonist (*Kit's Wilderness*, *Clay*, *The Savage*), there is a stronger focus on the wildness within and ways it might be dangerously and safely expressed. But in all of Almond's novels, the wild outside is a version of the potential wild inside.

The representatives of wildness also have some connection with the past. Skellig connects with the detritus and decay of once-useful objects surrounding him and, through the lightness of his bones, also with Archaeopteryx, the flying dinosaur Mina tells Michael about, and the long history of evolution. Askew connects with the waste-land wilderness where he leads games of death, the mines that once operated there, and also, with Lak, the prehistoric savage in the story Kit writes, and whom Blue's savage in the story he writes in *The Savage* echoes. Clay emerges from the soil of a dilapidated estate and Stephen connects him to an earlier time when there were 'folk like us, folk with power, folk in caves working magic, folk that was half wild' (*C[A]*, p. 143). McNulty the fire-eater connects with the history of the war he fought with Bobby's father, and Crystal and Oliver in *Raven Summer* connect with their equally violent pasts. The tiger in *Secret Heart* connects with both the forest and the dilapidated circus and its history. Despite their obvious differences, these characters all have a similar function. They represent a wildness that is other to the boy's ordinary life. The wildness breaches the walls of the ordinary and forces him to confront both the otherness out there beyond the home that keeps him relatively safe and the dangerous but potentially powerful otherness hidden inside him.

The boyish boys

The presence of other boys and young men, both friends and enemies of Almond's protagonists, introduces an ongoing consideration of the relationships between masculinity and wildness. There are usually two such characters who play significant roles.

The first is usually a good friend of long standing, a boy whom the protagonist grew up with and who ties him to a traditional boy's life of violent games and sports and to traditional ideas about masculinity as toughness and mastery, a form of 'wildness' that the protagonist both shares in and might be in the process of separating himself from. These boys include Leakey in *Skellig*, Geordie in *Clay* and Stanny Mole in *Secret Heart*, who seems torn between his wish to be as animal-like as Joe wants to be – Joe first met Stanny as he was pretending to be a mole (*SH[A]*, p. 67) – and a more traditionally masculine desire to hunt and conquer animals. In *The Fire-Eaters*, Bobby's good friend Joe Connor represents his wild side, but he also encounters a new friend, Daniel, a boy from Kent who teaches him a more dangerous, and, it seems, more admirable, form of wildness: defying unreasonable authority. Stephen Rose in *Clay* is a more satanic version of that rebelliousness: he says he is 'more suited to the wilderness than to the civilized world' (*C[A]*, p. 41), and he tempts Davie into a defiantly ungodly expression of vengeance. In *Kit's Wilderness*, Askew simultaneously acts as both the central representation of wildness and the male friend who gets Kit into boyish trouble; and in another variation in *Raven Summer*, Liam himself is the wilder boy who separates himself from the more conventional and less reckless Max.

The second, more minor character is another boy or older male who represents conventional masculine aggression carried to a further extreme, and therefore, the ways in which machismo is related to the dangerous side of wildness: Coot in *Skellig*; Bobby Carr in *Kit's Wilderness*, called the 'true evil' (*KW[A]*, p. 129); Joss in *Secret Heart,* who has a snakeskin tattoo around his throat, believes in survival of the fittest, and wants to take Joe to 'where it's really, really wild' (*SH[A]*, p. 15); the sadistic Nattrass, Liam's erstwhile blood brother, in *Raven Summer;* the bully Hopper in *The Savage*; and the malevolent Mould, whose earth-related name reveals his likeness to the creature Stephen and Davie create to conquer him in *Clay*. The protagonist's good friend is often associated with and being pulled towards the lifestyle represented by this wilder male, and entices the protagonist to go along with him – a temptation always, eventually, rightly resisted.

Some of these male friends are older than the protagonists, and when they are, there is a hint of homoerotic seduction in Almond's presentation of them. In *The Fire-Eaters*, Joseph Connor kisses

Bobby, and in *Clay*, the slightly older Stephen Rose not only kisses Davie but often caresses him. Along with its other implications, then, the wildness that characters like these represent becomes associated with the transgression of conventional heterosexual and homosocial norms.

The assertive girl

As well as having contested relationships with these other males, the protagonist usually has a significant relationship with a girl his age – often one he has just met. The girl tends to be intelligent, assertive in her opinions and very sure of herself. She insists on the strength of the empathy between the protagonist and herself, and often makes a specific declaration of her love for him.

She is often also an artist, and her art-making represents an alternative way of dealing with wildness. In *Skellig*, Mina, who draws and sculpts clay, introduces Michael to artistic ways of expressing his wildness in opposition to the more conventional ones represented by his male friends. In *Secret Heart*, the trapeze artist Corinna and the circus performance of wildness generally represent a similar opposition to the conventionally masculine expressions of savagery of Stanny and Joss. While Mina and Corinna reinforce Michael and Joe's attraction to magically wild creatures, the actress Allie in *Kit's Wilderness* opposes Askew's wildness – sees him as a brute and a caveman she needs to protect Kit from. Nevertheless, while filled with 'light and life' (*KW[A]*, p. 63) as opposed to Askew's dark and death, she has a different kind of wildness of her own. Her acting of evil may unleash her wild self as much as it controls it, and Kit tells her of a story he might write in which Askew will 'be a dark heavy brute and you'll be a glittering life force and somebody like me'll be in between you both and all confused' (*KW[A]*, p. 171).

While not an artist, Ailsa in *The Fire-Eaters* both encourages Bobby's 'soft' concern for McNulty and stands with Joseph as a representative of the old, uneducated ways Bobby is in the process of moving beyond. In *Clay*, similarly, Maria represents a vulnerability that stands against both Geordie and Mouldy's macho need to battle and the demonic creative powers of Stephen that oppose that need, adding a third choice for Davie; and in *Raven Summer*, Crystal opposes both the too-conventional Max and the too-uncontrollably wild Nattrass. Artist or lover, the girl always represents a path different from the various ones of the protagonist's male friends.

The vulnerable baby

In addition to the older girl there is a younger one, a baby, whose role is primarily to be vulnerable and in need of protection: Michael's sister in *Skellig* and Blue's younger sister Jess in *The Savage*, both of whom are visited and, apparently, protected by the wild creature while asleep; the abandoned baby Liam's family adopts in *Raven Summer*; and not only Askew's sister and the savage Lak's sister in *Kit's Wilderness*, but the baby Kit's Grandpa says is lost inside Askew himself, a baby that 'never had a chance to grow' (*KW[A]*, p. 110). Lak's and Askew's sisters need to be protected by their older brother, and Askew also needs to protect and nurture his undeveloped baby self in order to move past his wildness. In *The Fire-Eaters*, an abandoned fawn nurtured by Ailsa occupies the position usually filled by a human baby, and in *Clay*, the sculpted man Clay, referred to as a creation or child of both Davie and Stephen, occupies that position.

Davie's need to nurture and protect Clay conflicts with Stephen's urge to use him for violent purposes, and the vulnerable youngsters in all the novels represent the protagonist's pull towards a 'soft' concern for others that conflicts with the more conventional need to be 'hard' and masculine. The novels often reach their climaxes when, as a result of actions of the protagonist, the representative of wildness discovers or reveals a softness within. Paradoxically, however, the vulnerable young one can best be protected through the protagonist's connection with the representation of wildness and his softening effect on it.

The repressive teachers

As well as unreservedly loving parents, the protagonists of Almond's novels interact with decidedly less understanding adults, especially teachers. The teachers in most of the novels are given unflattering nicknames by their students (Rasputin and Monkey Mitford in *Skellig*, Burning Bush in *Kit's Wilderness*, Bleak Winters in *Secret Heart*, Prat Parker in *Clay*), and most of them are harsh disciplinarians intent on making their young charges grow up by repressing their real or imaginative wildness. The especially malevolent Todd of *The Fire-Eaters*, his name reminiscent of the German word for death, tells his students that they are half-civilised wild things that need to be taught to conform. The presence of these teachers reinforces the opposition between wildness and normative ideas of acceptable maturity, and thus clearly identifies wildness as a trait of children and the childlike, of childishly transgressive artists or circus performers or madmen. As well as the repressive teachers, there are also a few more sympathetic ones, mostly women, who admire the protagonists' wild imagination.

The events and their resonances

The Almond ur-plot begins with a new arrival: the protagonist moves to a new home (*Skellig*, *Kit's Wilderness*), or meets someone new to his neighbourhood (Stephen Rose in *Clay*, Daniel in *The Fire-Eaters*, Corinna in *Secret Heart*, the abandoned baby, Crystal and Oliver in *Raven Summer*, the savage in *The Savage*). The protagonist is interested in the strangeness of what's new, and forms a contact with it, but an old friend sees the new arrival as a threat to the friendship and tries to pull him back. Meanwhile, the protagonist also becomes aware of the representative of wildness, feels both its alien nature and its connection to himself, and is both thrilled by it and frightened by his attraction to it.

The attraction emerges from the protagonist's sense of his own wildness, a sense Michael acknowledges when he calls owls savages then adds, 'They think we're something like them', and Mina tells him, 'Perhaps they are' (*S[A]*, p. 173.). Kit acknowledges his wildness in accepting Askew's claim that they are connected; Joe acknowledges his in his identification with the tiger; and Blue acknowledges his in saying of the savage, 'sometimes it was nearly like I was him and he was me' (*TS[A]*, p. 31). Often the urge to wildness emerges from a need to rebel against repression and the control of others (*Skellig*, *Secret Heart*, *Raven Summer*), but there are sometimes other resonances. In *The Savage*, the savage seems to represent Blue's rage at his father's death and his wish for a way to combat the bully Hopper, and Clay in *Clay* represents a similar wish to control the bully Mould as well as an excessively egocentric drive to control others generally. In *The Fire-Eaters*, McNulty's acts of self-mutilation seem to represent a heroic but inevitably unsuccessful opposition to authority that explains the rebelliously anti-authoritarian behaviour of both Daniel against a bullying priest and Ailsa against the idea of going to school. Both say they know they will lose but that it is important to fight anyway, for as Bobby tells his father, 'It's always right to protest ... even if you think it's hopeless' (*FE[A]*, p. 167). Bobby understands McNulty, who eats fire when, as he says, 'the world's afire' (*FE[A]*, p. 161), to be a model of Christlike sacrifice, accepting pain in order to protect others from it, and as Bobby prays for the salvation of everyone else, he adds, 'My name is Bobby Burns. Take me' (*FE[A]*, p. 193). Instead, it is McNulty who breathes in the fire and sacrifices himself – and who, the novel implies, may have then saved the world from the fiery holocaust of nuclear war. Or at least he protested, even if it was hopeless.

The contact with the wild being occurs in a wilderness, often in darkness, often underground, sometimes in what might be dreams. Sometimes the wild is a forest, sometimes merely a chaotic, dirty place full of discarded objects, such as the ruined mansion and garden in *Clay* or the garage where Michael finds Skellig or the old hut half-buried in sand that McNulty comes to occupy in *The Fire-Eaters*. Like Kit's wilderness, these are all borderland places, half-civilised, half-wild places where the borderland activity of play – pretend wildness – occurs, and where real savagery is flirted with; in *Secret Heart*, Joe thinks about 'how the lives of people and the lives of beasts could merge out here in the wasteland' (*SH[A]*, p. 65). The circus in *Secret Heart*, pitched on the wasteland, is itself such a border place, a tamed representation of wildness: 'This place come from them that tamed the wild beasts. It come from them that listened to the wild wild beasts inside themselves. All they did was put a tent around it and take it travelin' round and round the world' (p. 95).

These semi-decayed, semi-wild boundary settings represent the actual situation of much of northern England, its industrial past in ruins and its future yet to emerge, and so the experiences of Almond's protagonists can be read as allegories of how such places and their inhabitants might best come to terms with themselves. Kit in *Kit's Wilderness* and Bobby in *The Fire-Eaters* are especially aware of choices between the old life of their ancestors and a move away from the past identified as savage into the wider world beyond: Daniel, the newcomer from the south in *The Fire-Eaters*, thinks that the photograph his father has taken of Bobby's old friend Ailsa and her family at work gathering sea coal reveals them as being 'like something from ancient tales. Half human' (*FE[A]*, p. 100). Almond's characters often associate their own wish to be wild with a past that civilisation has evolved from, even as they continue to move away from what Michael in *Skellig* calls 'the endless shape-changing that had led to us' (*S[A]*, p. 33). They often look at old photographs, for instance – Joe at Nanty Solo's, Bobby at family pictures that are 'like windows into an ancient place' (*FE[A]*, p. 54); and Kit's inheritance of his grandfather's photos represents the obligation these characters come to feel of preserving memories of what once was. The movement into wildness is also, then, an attempt to connect with and recover the past and then bring it forward into the future, to meld its supposedly outmoded values into the ever-developing new civilisation.

In the wild borderland, children and wild adults tend to engage in the borderland activity of play: more or less safely enacting wildness. Sometimes the enactments are quite literally representations. In *The Fire-Eaters*, the wild McNulty has tattoos of beasts and dragons and Bobby's friend Joseph is in the process of completing a large dragon tattoo, and in *Raven Summer*, Crystal has tattoos of a phoenix on her arm and of wounds on her shoulder blades (signs, as in *Skellig*, of her loss of angelhood). Also in *Raven Summer*, Liam paints his face as a monster to delight the baby (*RS[A]*, p. 142), echoing Corinna's painting of children's faces as animals in *Secret Heart* – especially Joe as a tiger. In that novel, Joe also wears the skin of a tiger in order to inhabit the tiger's spirit: 'Beneath the pelt, beneath the curious tent of skin and striped fur, Joe Maloney danced a tiger dance, was transformed by tigerness, became a tiger' (*SH[A]*, p. 150).

The child's play associated with wilderness places in all the novels generally represents violence. Askew spins his knife in the game of death, Lak, Stanny Mole and Geordie wield knives, and Bobby receives a knife as a gift from Joseph. According to its first sentence, *Raven Summer* 'starts and ends with the knife' (*RS[A]*, p. 3) that Liam uses first in war games and then in a violent attack on an enemy. Children play wilderness war games in *Kit's Wilderness*, *The Fire-Eaters* and *Raven Summer*, and there is a less playful war in the wild between boys from Pelaw and Felling in *Clay* (*C[A]*, p. 17).

The wild place also usually includes a cave or grave or other dark hole in the ground connected both with games of violence and with ideas of death. *Kit's Wilderness* centrally involves Askew's den, a deep hole where the children play their game called Death, and later, a deserted mineshaft and a cave occupied by the imaginary Lak and his family. In *Raven Summer*, similarly, Nattrass plays dangerous games over a gravelike pit. In *The Fire-Eaters*, there are descriptions of a bomb shelter, and McNulty connects shelters with graves: 'Dig down to where the dead live! Cover yourself with the earth!' (*FE[A]*, p. 161). In *Sacred Heart*, there is a cave at the centre of the wild forest where Joff beheads a panther and to which Joe returns the tiger, and in *Raven Summer*, the climactic events take place in and near a dark cave where Liam brings Oliver and Crystal as a retreat from the world's savagery and then must confront the savagery in Oliver's past, in Nattrass's present and finally, in himself. The cave is a place of refuge, a retreat from the dangers of the world beyond the wilderness and behind the wall that might well be deathlike. But it is also a place where wildness can be most centrally confronted.

Embracing and entering the darkness, the protagonist finds himself caring for the wild thing and trying to help it, often with the understanding that doing so will also be helpful in some important way to himself. Michael believes that helping Skellig stay alive will somehow also save his baby sister. Kit understands that Askew's game of death and later, bringing Askew out of his darkness, are related to keeping his own grandfather and the history of mining he represents alive. Bobby connects helping McNulty with saving his father from a threatened illness. Davie tries to make Clay more caring as a way of resisting his own urge to savage vengeance, and Blue seems to have invented the savage boy as way of expressing both his anger at being bullied and his grief over his father's death. Liam embraces the abandoned children that enter his life as a response to his own worry about how violence in the world might affect himself; and Joe's treatment of the tiger – allowing the wild its wildness rather than attempting to triumph over it as Joss does – represents a way of dealing with his own wish to be wild.

In other words, the protagonist's interactions with the wild thing lead him to confront his attitudes towards a related series of apparent opposites: wildness and civilisation, the animal and the angelic, imaginative magic and normal reality, egocentricity and creativity, otherness and familiarity, danger and safety, being soft and being hard, the male and the female, the rural and the urban, immersion in the past and a focus on the future. Joe sums up the response to these opposites in *Secret Heart*: 'The choice was easy. The eerie wasteland or the gates and walls of school? He chose the wilderness' (*SH[A]*, p. 52). Having chosen the wilderness, each protagonist must learn to distinguish dangerous and healthy ways of being wild.

As each novel heads towards its climax, then, the main character finds himself in a wild place in the dark, accompanied by the representation of wildness, and witnesses graphic evidence of wildness: the owls feeding Skellig in the dark attic, the beheaded panther's severed head that results from Joss's savagery in *Secret Heart*, McNulty's sacrificial inhaling of the fire in *The Fire-Eaters*, the savage's threatening of Hopper in *The Savage*, Nattrass's potential murder of Oliver in *Raven Summer*, Kit's own potential murder by Askew in *Kit's Wilderness* and Davie's own potential murder by the monster in *Clay*. Then the protagonist (with, sometimes, another character he has bonded with) asserts a oneness with wildness in a form that aids the representative of wildness and gives it peace.

The bond often occurs in the transcendent moment of a dance. In *Skellig*, Michael, Mina and Skellig 'turned together, kept slowly turning, like we were carefully, nervously, beginning to dance. ... It was like we had moved into each other, had become one thing' (p. 120). Kit imagines dancing with a group of cavemen in *Kit's Wilderness*, Blue dances with the savage in a moment when he knows what it is like to be 'truly wild' (p. 75), and Joe dances alone as he feels at one with magical invisible birds and animals (p. 28) and then again with Corinna in a moment of whirling unity with other creatures (*SH[A]*, p. 165). Other moments of transcendent unity involve characters sensing other hearts beating within them. Michael says, 'I touched my heart and felt the baby's heart beating bedside my own' (*S[A]*, p. 97), and as Joe dreams of the tiger, 'He felt a tiger heart drumming in his chest' (*SH[A]*, p. 72); Nanty sums up the significance of this communion with wildness when she says, 'The heart is beating in you as it should, then far beyond it is the secret one, like some creature panting in a deep dark cave' (*SH[A]*, p. 87).

These experiences of communion allow the protagonists and, perhaps, others to come back out of the dark and into the light again – as Kit says in *Kit's Wilderness*, 'out of the ancient darkness into the shining valley' (*KW[A]*, p. 3). In *Raven Summer* Liam's mother explains how that happens: 'We have to nurture the parts of us that aren't savage ... . We have to help the angel overcome the beast' (*RS[A]*, p. 74). The angel overcomes the beast as wild, hard characters reveal their inner softness: Askew's concern for his sister, Joe's perception of the soft heart under his friend Stanny Mole's desire for hard manliness or Blue's realisation of the growing softness in his savage – 'He still felt like the savage but like something else as well' (*TS*, p. 38) – or the acknowledgement that Clay cannot kill Davie because, as Stephen says, 'there's too much of Davie in you, Clay' (*C[A]*, p. 213).

The transformation of dark and death into light and ongoing life, wildness into angelhood, clearly has Christian resonances. The Almond ur-plot is essentially a story of incarnation – becoming one with the wild natural world, embodied as a beast – that leads to salvation, often by means of a passage through a deathlike darkness in a sepulchre-like place. The Death game in *Kit's Wilderness* enacts a resurrection, an emergence from a gravelike or tomblike cave, that might well stand as a model for the plots of all the novels. As the almost-pun in the title of one of them seems to suggest, the secret at their heart is a sacred one.

The angel also overcomes the beast by reshaping it into some form of art. In *Kit's Wilderness*, Kit's story of the caveman Lak, who mirrors Askew, leads Askew to follow Lak's urge to protect his sister and rejoin his family; and in his ability to draw, Askew himself can turn his wildness into something more positive. Askew says, 'Your stories is like my drawings, Kit. They take you back deep into the dark and show it lives within us still' (*KW[A]*, p. 15), but Michael's story and his own pictures also show Askew how to move out of the dark. Blue's story of another savage boy in *The Savage* also allows him both to express and purge his own savagery, and in *The Fire-Eaters*, Daniel's photographs reiterate a teacher's acts of bullying in ways that expose and help stop their savagery. As a thrilling but safe performance of wildness, a version of Bakhtin's carnivalesque that both celebrates and helps purge the desire for what exists beyond walls, the circus in *Secret Heart* represents another useful form of art.

But art is not merely or always beneficial. Sometimes, as in Allie's stage portrayal in *Kit's Wilderness* of a dangerously self-involved girl or, especially, in the creation of Clay, art expresses violent wildness without necessarily mediating it. Sometimes, as the various photographic and cinematic depictions of violence by Liam's mother and Nattrass in *Raven Summer,* or in McNulty's self-damaging but possibly world-protecting re-visioning of war as fire-eating and self-mutilation in *The Fire-Eaters*, the art is intractably ambivalent, a borderland activity that might defang violence or might merely be allowing and even encouraging its expression. For Almond, artistic creativity is always a borderland activity, necessarily engaging wildness but necessarily also engaging it enough to be as potentially dangerous as it is potentially healthy.

Simpler and more complex variations

What I have described thus far reveals a strong focus on similar characters and themes in a number of Almond's novels. Some of his other books have less clear-cut but still-present connections to what I have identified as an ur-story. For instance, Almond's novel for younger readers, *The Boy Who Climbed into the Moon*, is a whimsical tale about a boy's trip upwards into the light rather than down into the dark; even so, it still involves its protagonist's encounters with exotic representations of otherness and his coming to terms with his own capacity for wild ideas. The graphic novel *Slog's Dad*, illustrated by Dave McKean, does something similar; as the narrator tells of his friend Slog's belief that his dead father will return to visit him once more, the images reveal a variety of ways in which Slog imagines his father risen heavenwards: as a paper cut-out held aloft, as an angel descending with birdlike wings (somewhat like Skellig), as a balloon painted with a primitive face that detaches itself from a scarecrow and climbs, as a muscular superhero with a red cape. The actual man Slog encounters in the midst of these imaginary wild possibilities and believes to be his father is a figure who transcends the borders of respectability in two opposite ways, who defies logic in being alive again and in having regrown the legs he lost to disease before he died, but who neverthe-less still smells of the undesirable garbage it was his unrespectable job in life to collect. Slog's Dad is a wilderness figure of both imaginative and societal outsiderliness.

If *Slog's Dad* and *The Boy Who Climbed to the Moon* seem to be too simple to have more than an indirect relationship to the novels I discussed earlier, *The True Tale of the Monster Billy Dean telt by hisself*, published simultaneously in editions that represent it either as another Almond novel for younger readers or as his first one for adults, may be too complex to be read as a version of the ur-story. It does, however, include some central elements of that story: a young male protagonist, 'a littl boy in a littl lockd room with waste & wilderness arl arownd' (*BD[A]*, p. 10) – a wasteland created by an attack by an unnamed enemy in an ongoing war – who enters into that wilder world and interacts with its variously wild inhabitants. Among them is a girl of Billy's own age who is yet another artist – and he himself has artistic leanings as a maker of books and the writer of the often misspelled text in which he appears and which the novel consists of, as well as a concern about 'becomin somethin els sumthin stray-njer sumthin wilder sumthin that seemd much mor strong & bold than littl Billy Dean' (p. 23). Other than that girl, though, Billy has no contact with people of his own age; and especially, there are no male friends to represent various choices Billy must make. Instead, though, there are adults who seem to represent versions of the choices offered to the boys in the other novels. There is Mrs Malone, who encourages Billy in his magically successful efforts to transcend the border between life and death and contact the dead during séances: 'you belong to me, William Dean. And to the dead & the bereaved, who hav wayted for you' (p. 139). Under her tutelage, Billy identi-fies himself as one of a group of 'harf wild boys and girls that yell in tongues and move easily between the livin and the dead' (p. 213) – and who, like the characters in the other novels, bring the dead back and restore the past. Then there is Mr McCaufrey, the butcher, who offers instead a view of the glories of accepting life as it is and the glory of its interconnections as they are: 'When you eat the beest the beest eats you. ... All things flow into each other' (p. 125). Finally, there is Billy's own father, an often-absent authority figure, a representative of the traditional patriarchal power of the Church and repressor of his own irrepressible wildness, whom Billy yearns for and must learn to separate himself from. In the end, too, as in the ur-story, Billy chooses to leave the wasteland and its wilder temptations, and opt for a saner life nearby, yet once more near the border – although again, with serious differences from the other novels, as Billy finds release from the wasteland through the Oedipal act of killing his father – with, not surprisingly, a knife.

At first glance, the story of Almond's most recent book, the graphic novel *Mouse Bird Snake Wolf* with illustrations by Dave McKean, seems quite different from those of the earlier novels. For one thing, it has three young protagonists, not one. For another, gods appear in it – albeit mostly sleeping ones – a presence that makes it seem more like an allegorical fable than the more reality-based kind of stories Almond tells elsewhere. But its narrative about how the three children begin to fill up the gaps and holes the lazy gods have left in their world by inventing the animals of the title also resonates intriguingly with the ur-story. After wandering away from home to a wilder place 'beneath a gnarled old tree' – a reference to the biblical tree of knowledge? – the three children discover the wild animals they create by looking inside themselves, so that their creative acts allow that wildness to emerge into the world outside. Furthermore, what first appears a positive act of freeing self-expression turns out to have negative implications: the animals they create are increasingly dangerous, and the last of them, a particularly malevolent wolf, devours its two creators – a lesson about over-indulgence in the expression of wildness similar to ones expressed earlier. Finally though, as also happens in the earlier novels, the wild can be controlled by those able to resist it; the remaining child can will the wolf gone and his companions back again. As in the novels, in other words, *Mouse Bird Snake Wolf* explores the borders between the wild within and the wild without, and between wildness and the factors that control and therefore allow it.

Where the ur-story seems most distant in Almond's work is in his few books with female protagonists – a difference which in itself reinforces the significance of the relationship between his views of wildness and masculinity. While *My Name is Mina*, about what happens to a central female character in *Skellig* before the events of that novel, describes a trip to a dark place underground, it echoes little else of the ur-story – and indeed, in its representation as Mina's journal, tends to read more like a scrapbook of not especially related materials than as a plot-oriented novel with relationships to an ur-story. And while Almond's novel for younger readers *My Dad's a Birdman* has a more traditionally linear plot and involves a girl and her father who make wings and become something like pretend, flightless versions of Skellig or Slog's Dad, there is no journey into the dark – nor, indeed, any obvious wildness; the grief over what appears to have been the death of Lizzie's mother is a darkness merely hinted at in an atmosphere of cheerful absurdity. Almond's picture-book story in *Kate, the Cat and the Moon* of how a girl turns into a cat in the dark of night and wanders through her family's dreams does engage the ur-story's obsession with wildness, but is much simpler than the ur-story – as is Almond's play *Wild Girl, Wild Boy*, in which Elaine's grief over her father's death manifests itself in the form of a boy who emerges from and draws her into the dark wilderness of her father's allotment – a story retold about a boy and with more complexity in *The Savage*.

But while *Heaven Eyes*, Almond's one novel for older readers before *My Name is Mina* that centrally involves a girl, seems more different from Almond's novels about boys than any of them seem from each other, it, too, offers a complex version of the expected connection to a wild and exotic other in a dark place redolent of the past. As I describe in more detail in a later chapter in this book, its central character's gender seems to lead to a highlighting of different aspects of the same concerns. Nevertheless, *Heaven Eyes* does express those concerns.

Uniquely the same

Readers familiar with children's fiction are not likely to be very surprised by the general thrust of what I have described here as a shared story in so many of Almond's novels. Almond's ur-plot possesses many of the most common characteristics of texts written for children – the ones I outline in my book *The Hidden Adult: Defining Children's Literature*. Most obviously, his novels are versions of the central home–away–home story of children's fiction: the journey beyond the walls of a safely ordinary home to a more dangerous and unsettling place – the place, as the title of Maurice's Sendak's canonical picture book proclaims, where the wild things are. Furthermore, and like so many children's novels, Almond's versions of the story engage a series of binaries which are key to adult perceptions of the condition and needs of childhood, binaries that relate to and emerge from a consideration of what those opposed locales, safe home and wild away, mean: imagination and common sense, magic and normal reality, childishness and maturity, self-expression and self-control, machismo and soft-heartedness, egocentricity and concern for others, nostalgia for the past and hope for the future, and above all, of course, wildness and civilisation. And like many if not all of the children's novels that most deeply engage both child and adult readers, Almond's novels tend to be ambivalent in the attitudes they arrive at in relation to those binaries. While Almond's novels all have the conventionally expectable happy ending of children's literature, one involving a return home to the safe embrace of loved ones, they always qualify the happiness with a sense of what might have been lost by returning or what might need still to be gained. They are as little interested in dismissing adult repression in favour of untrammelled liberty as they are in dismissing childlike wildness for the safety of conventional ideas of maturity. They want it all, and they want it both ways: a mature childishness and safe wildness, a childlike maturity and a wild way of being safe. And like children's fiction generally, and in spite of their dwelling on the horrors of war and violence and good times gone, they are unfailingly optimistic about the possibility of achieving that wished-for state. That is what makes the happy endings happy.

In the light of all that, though, it might be easy to conclude that Almond is not a very good writer. We tend to expect praiseworthy writing to be more original, more creative, less expressive of estab-lished conventions and less conventionally repetitive of the same central concerns. Might the repetitive nature of these novels be a sign of their weakness? Personally, I think not. I think, in fact, that their repetitiveness is a key to what makes them so compelling.

For one thing, what is repeated is compelling in itself. It is what has driven children's literature throughout its history, and what continues to drive it. The obsessions of Almond's novels are the central concerns of many adults who care about, think about and, especially, write about childhood – and therefore, for good or ill, what many adults want children to think about their childhood, and what children do often, then, as a result of that, think about their childhoods. Almond's genius is to offer intensely compelling versions of what works best as children's literature. His books manage to express the key and power-ful conventions of writing for children in ways that make them very powerful indeed.

It appears, also, that he can do so because what is conventional is significant to him personally. If Almond has merely been producing what usually works best as children's literature as a cynical way of sustaining a career, he has a huge talent for hiding it. As his stories for adults in *Counting Stars* reveal, Almond retains a strong interest in his own childhood experience, and an ability to be simultaneously nostalgic and clear-eyed and puzzled about it. What is repeated in his novels seems to be so because is it is deeply meaningful to Almond himself; and as the many awards his novels have received suggest he clearly knows how to make it deeply meaningful to many readers, both children and adults.

Nor is his work really all that obviously repetitive. Considering the extent to which his novels share common situations, concerns and character types, what is most remarkable about them is not their similarity, but their differences from each other. They represent a variety of different kinds of fiction, from primarily realistic writing (historical in *The Fire-Eaters*, contemporary in *Raven Summer*) to horror (*Clay*) to the ghost story (*Kit's Wilderness*) to outright magic realism (*Skellig*, *Secret Heart*); and they represent what are at heart the same or related matters in terms of a wide range of not obviously related issues, from the spontaneity of childhood play to the anarchy of uncontrolled artistic creation and to the anarchy of uncontrolled but actual war. Each one offers a quite different experience from the rest.

Yet for all that, what they share with each other enriches rather than diminishes them. It allows them to be read in terms of their connections to each other, and that makes each one more complex and more interesting than it is when read on its own. Not only do the connections between the novels reveal how orphans are akin to monsters or angels, or how childhood play is like and unlike all-out war, but the connections also allow Almond to explore similar problems from quite different perspectives. For instance, while the protagonists of both *Kit's Wilderness* and *The Fire-Eaters* are relatively civilised boys confronting wildness in their male friends, Liam, the protagonist of *Raven Summer* is a relatively wild boy confronting it; and meanwhile, his friend Max is a less wild boy like the protagonists of the other two novels. The difference expands and enriches readers' understanding of the central issues. Similarly, art, depicted so positively in *Skellig* and *Kit's Wilderness*, reveals its dangers in *Clay* and *Raven Summer*. And my own understanding of the decidedly un-savage Daniel in *The Fire-Eaters* as a decidedly different version of wildness clearly emerges from my sense of how this novel might relate to all the rest.

In other words, my knowledge of their connections with Almond's other work allowed me to see Daniel and the novel he appears in as a variation on Almond's other novels. In *The Hidden Adult*, I suggest that a significant quality of children's literature is that 'its texts are internally repetitive and/or variational in form and content, and tend to operate as repetitions and/or variations of other texts in the genre'.[2] As well as operating as variations of texts for children by others, Almond's texts are variations of each other. Read in relation to each other they display what the novelist Milan Kundera views as the central quality of variational writing: 'The journey of the variation form leads to ... the infinity of internal variety concealed in all things.'[3] In being similar, they reveal their intriguingly complex differences.

In being similar, also, they reveal their uniqueness as different expressions of the characteristic working of one distinct and distinctly interesting mind. In *Dickens and his World*, a critical study published in the middle of the last century, J. Hillis Miller said that his purpose was 'to assess the specific quality of Dickens' imagination in the totality of his work, to identify what persists through all the swarming multiplicity of his novels as a view of the world which is unique and the same'.[4] While quite different from Dickens, the multiplicity of Almond's novels similarly expresses a view of the world which is wonderfully unique and also, wonderfully, the same.

Notes

1. 'David Almond', *Barnes and Noble Meet the Writers*, http://media.barnesand noble.com/index.jsp?fr_chl=4f1e67180775c0199816531cf6d28855b 99bed39 (accessed 3 May 2010).
2. Perry Nodelman, *The Hidden Adult: Defining Children's Literature* (Baltimore, MD: Johns Hopkins University Press, 2008), p. 243.
3. Milan Kundera, *The Book of Laughter and Forgetting*, trans. Michael Henry Heim (Harmondsworth: Penguin, 1981), p. 164.
4. J. Hillis Miller, *Charles Dickens: The World of His Novels* (Cambridge MA: Harvard University Press, 1958), p. viii.

3

Ontology, Epistemology and Values: Philosophy and Cognitive Science in David Almond's *Skellig* and *My Name is Mina*

Roberta Seelinger Trites

How do children learn philosophical concepts? Some children learn them directly, from parents and teachers and spiritual leaders who engage them in questions about what it means to be alive, what it means to reason, what it means to be ethical. Still more children learn about philosophy indirectly, from living the lives they live – and consuming the texts to which they are exposed. Although many children do not engage openly in debates about metaphysics and values, they frequently experience in children's literature concepts that engage them in thinking about values – and in ontology and epistemology – that is, in what it means to *be* and what it means to *know*; in what it means to be a sentient and rational being; in how we are constructed by the world we live in, and how we choose to live in it.

For example, in David Almond's *My Name is Mina* (2010), Mina asks, 'Is there a God? Was there ever emptiness?' (*MNIM*, p. 16). *My Name is Mina* is the prequel to Almond's *Skellig* (1998), in which Mina tells her friend Michael, 'Sometimes we have to accept that there are things we can't know ... . Sometimes we think we should be able to know everything. But we can't. We have to allow ourselves to see what there is to see, and we have to imagine' (*S*, p. 140). Mina and Michael fundamentally question what it means to be alive and what it means to know. They also worry whether they should help someone who might be homeless when their parents don't even know what they are up to, a situation that creates a recurring ethical tension throughout *Skellig* about what these children value and how much responsibility they bear for others.

Throughout, I rely on standard definitions of epistemology, ontology and values from the *Stanford Encyclopaedia of Philosophy*, which offers the following definitions. *Ontology* is 'the study of what there is'; ontological problems are those that 'deal with whether or not a certain thing, or more broadly entity, exists'.[1] *Epistemology*, in its strictest sense, 'is the study of knowledge and justified belief' but also involves broader 'issues having to do with the creation and dissemination of knowledge in particular areas of inquiry'.[2] Ontology thus pertains to how we understand being, while epistemology involves how we know what we know. *Values* is the field involved with how humans evaluate, categorise and prioritise that which is good.[3] The study of ethics, then, is a subdiscipline of the study of values.

Concerns with epistemology, ontology and values also undergird the work of cognitive scientists, who seek to understand not only how the brain works, but how we *know* and what we do with that knowledge. As F. Elizabeth Hart notes, cognitive studies focuses on 'the mind's substantive indebtedness to its bodily, social and cultural contexts' and on those figural processes (such as metaphor) and categorisations that 'contribute to recasting human reason into a set of highly imaginative – not logical but figural – processes'.[4] As George Lakoff and Mark Johnson define cognitive science, it is the 'discipline that studies conceptual systems', and they argue that '[o]ur experience of the world is not separate from our conceptualization of the world. Indeed, ... the same hidden mechanisms that characterize our conscious system of concepts also plays a central role in creating our experience. ... [T]here is an extensive and important overlap between those mechanisms that shape our concepts and those that shape our experience.'[5] For example, Lakoff and Johnson reject all notions of the Cartesian split between body and mind because – as they put it – 'the mind is inherently embodied, reason is shaped by the body'.[6] They argue that philosophical questions emerge from three things: 'a reason shaped by the body, a cognitive unconscious to which we have no direct access, and metaphorical thought of which we are largely unaware'.[7] It is these three components of cognitive science that help explain how deeply philosophical David Almond's novels are. In particular, *Skellig* and its prequel, *My Name is Mina*, demonstrate how significant both embodied reason and the relationship between the cognitive unconscious and metaphorical thought are to children's literature in general and Almond's *oeuvre* in particular. This chapter will thus proceed in two sections: first I will analyse embodied cognition in *Skellig* and *My Name is Mina*, that is, I will examine how these texts grapple with what Lakoff and Johnson would describe as 'reason shaped by the body'. Then I will demonstrate how Almond employs metaphorical thought to interrogate complex philosophical questions about being, knowing and values. Ultimately, David Almond's novels are philosophically imbued works that also help us understand the significance of cognitive science to children's literature.

Defining embodied reason

In the novel *Skellig*, Michael finds in the garage of his new home a man he initially assumes is homeless but who proves to be a creature that may be an angel, a new phase in evolutionary history or something else altogether. Michael nonetheless understands the creature Skellig and his ontological status entirely in terms of embodiment, as does the only friend to whom the boy shows Skellig, Mina (the girl next-door). Michael establishes a set of epistemological questions when he relies on his perceptions to question how he has gained knowledge about Skellig; that is, the text makes clear that he knows what he knows by emphasising knowledge as he gains it through his five senses. For example, he knows Skellig has wings because he first feels them on Skellig's back, '[l]ike thin arms, folded up. Springy and flexible', and because he sees them with his own eyes (*S*, p. 30). Furthermore, Mina also underscores the cognitive importance of perception in *My Name is Mina* when she writes in her journal: 'Look at the world. Smell it, taste it, listen to it, feel it, look at it. Look at it!' (*MNIM*, p. 31). Indeed, Michael's first perception of Skellig relies on perception, specifically on vision: 'that's when I saw him' (*S*, p. 8). He subsequently doubts his own perception, thinking that night, 'I'd never seen him at all. That had all been part of a dream' (*S*, p. 10). Skellig later underscores how significant vision perception is to Michael when the man asks the boy sarcastically, 'Had a good look? ...What are you looking at, eh?' (*S*, p. 30). That last question is, indeed, the text's pivotal ontological question: what *is* Michael looking at? Skellig is remarkable, with fingers and knuckles 'twisted and swollen' by arthritis, 'hundreds of tiny creases and cracks all over his pale face' (*S*, p. 29). Skellig tells Michael that 'Arthur Itis ... is the one that's ruining me bones. Turns you to stone, then crumbles you away' (*S*, p. 31). Readers might well wonder if Michael has simply found an old gargoyle in the garage and is imagining it into being.

Michael invites Mina to meet Skellig. The initial scene that involves the three of them serves the almost mechanical purpose in the text of assuring the reader that Michael is neither imagining nor inventing this creature; Skellig has an ontological reality that Mina, too, can perceive. 'I'll see whatever's there', she whispers to Michael as they enter the garage (*S*, p. 74). When Michael looks at Mina as she first observes Skellig, the boy emphasises her embodiment: 'I looked back at Mina's dark form looking down at us, her pale face, her mouth and eyes gaping in astonishment' (*S*, p. 75). She is both body and mind; she is, as Lakoff and Johnson would have it, 'an embodied mind' because her cognition is inevitably housed within a body.[8] Michael and Skellig, too, are embodied minds in the same sense; their minds and bodies cannot be separated. Eventually, Skellig reveals his wings: 'They were twisted and uneven, they were covered in cracked and crooked feathers. They clicked and trembled as they opened. They were wider than his shoulders, higher than his head' (*S*, p. 94). Michael touches them with his fingertips and palms and feels 'the bones and sinews and muscles' that support the wings (*S*, p. 95). When Mina asks Michael why he is touching them, Michael's answer reflects his attempt to understand how he knows what he knows.

'What you doing?' she whispered.
'Making sure the world's still really there,' I said. (*S*, p. 95)

Michael and Mina nurse Skellig back to health with aspirin, cod liver oil, beer and Chinese food. Skellig calls beer 'Nectar ... the drink of the gods' (*S*, p. 75) and Chinese food 'the food of the gods' (*S*, p. 29), implying that he may well be a fallen god himself. He is an eating, breathing, thinking being who sometimes eats live rodents and vomits pellets of their bones, just as owls do. He may be human or animal or angel, but he is an embodied, sentient being. The text gives the reader no determinant answer as to Skellig's ontological status; rather, readers are given information about his and others' perceptions, embodiment, language and thought – and are left to draw their own conclusions. Thus, readers are invited to conclude that embodied perception is a key component of cognition.

Mina is specifically embodied as 'little and she had hair as black as coal and the kind of eyes you think you can see right through' (*S*, p. 25); she frequently sits in trees. She describes herself in *My Name is Mina* as 'very skinny and very small and she had jet-black hair and a pale face and shining eyes' (*MNIM*, p. 43). Her doctors believe that she should be medicated to 'make her feel better', but her mother understands, 'They'll stop her from feeling anything at all. She's not some kind of robot. She's a little girl that's growing up' (*MNIM*, p. 44).

Mina's mother thus makes a direct link between the embodiment of physical growth and psychological growth. She tells her daughter that as she grows, 'she'd feel stronger more often and not feel so small' (*MNIM*, p. 43). That is, growth involves both body and mind. This second text is direct in discussing cognition in terms of the mind and human thought when Mina insists in her journal that her mind 'is not in order. My mind is not straight lines. My mind is a clutter and a mess. It is my mind, but it is also very like other minds. And like all minds, like every mind that there has ever been and every mind that there will ever be, it is a place of wonder! THE MIND IS A PLACE OF WONDER!' (*MNIM*, pp. 11–12). As *My Name is Mina* draws to a close, Mina and her mother stare at the stars, and her mother tenderly cradles her daughter's head in her hands. 'I can nearly hold your whole head in my hands,' she tells Mina; 'Your head holds all those stars, all that darkness, all these noises. It holds the universe' (*MNIM*, p. 282). She then rests her daughter's head against her own and says, 'Two heads, two universes, interlinked' (*MNIM*, p. 282). Again, the text is connecting embodiment and cognition, this time with a recognition that human society depends upon our ability to recognise each other as embodied minds that are dependent on one another. In other words, Mina's mother is teaching her daughter something about her own values: that it is a good thing to recognise and appreciate that other people have their own intricate and complex thought processes. The philosophical implications are rich: our ontological status depends on our embodied minds, as does our epistemology. But even more important, our ability to recognise each other as embodied minds allows us to treat each other ethically, with respect for each other's values. Because Mina is learning to value the complexity of other people's minds, she can accept the complexity of Skellig's when she meets him – and she values him enough to help him. Mina must, however, first understand her own cognitive complexity. As Mina later writes in her journal, 'Does everybody feel this excitement, this astonishment, as they grow? I close my eyes and stare into the universe inside myself' (*MNIM*, p. 287).

In *My Name is Mina*, Mina writes about Michael's embodiment almost entirely in terms of action and emotion (as opposed to writing about him in terms of thinking): he 'stare[s] glumly' 'at the yard in his new home and 'kick[s] it hard' (*MNIM*, pp. 13, 31); he bounces his ball in the yard, against the garden wall, and against the garage (*MNIM*, pp. 262–3). 'He glares at the street as if he hates it' (*MNIM*, p. 263). She notices his '[c]lenched fists. Hard eyes' – and she agrees with her mother that he needs a friend now that he has moved into a new neighbourhood (*MNIM*, p. 294). The character Skellig does not appear in *My Name is Mina*, but in *Skellig*, the mystical creature also demonstrates a relationship between embodied action and emotion. Three times, Skellig holds hands with children and dances with them in a circle in ways that enliven them: twice with Mina and Michael, once with Michael's baby sister who is dying but becomes miraculously revived by Skellig's dance. In the first dance, Skellig 'seemed stronger than he'd ever been. He took my hand and Mina's hand', and the three circle in and out of light and darkness in a moonlit attic until they are whirling so fast that 'Each face spun from shadow to light, from shadow to light, from shadow to light, and each time the faces of Mina and Skellig came into the light they were more silvery, more expressionless. Their eyes were darker, more empty, more penetrating. ... It was like we had moved into each other, like we had become one thing' (*S*, pp. 119–20). Eventually, Michael perceives 'ghostly wings' growing on Mina's back (*S*, p. 120). Skellig calls the two children 'a pair of angels' and tells them that he has been healed by 'the owls and the angels' (*S*, pp. 166, 120). Later, he dances with Michael's baby sister and perhaps heals her, and in his final meeting with Michael and Mina, they dance again in a circle: 'We began to turn. Our hearts and breath were together. We turned and turned until the ghostly wings rose from Mina's back and mine, until we felt ourselves being raised, until we seemed to turn and dance in the empty air' (*S*, p. 167). Although Skellig expresses few emotions other than pain and frustration early in the novel, by the time he has regained enough health to initiate action himself, his actions create emotional catharsis for those who move with him.

Michael, Mina and Skellig all demonstrate the impossibility of the Cartesian split. That is, none of them can *know* without embodied experiences that affect their rationality and *being*. As French philosopher Maurice Merleau-Ponty writes in his refusal to accept the Cartesian split, 'I'm conscious of the world through the medium of my body.'[9] Sensory perceptions affect Michael's, Mina's and Skellig's thoughts – which are clearly embodied – and the abilities and limitations of their bodies subsequently cause them to make the value judgements they do. Michael and Mina, for example, perceive Skellig's embodied suffering and consciously decide to come to his aid. As they help him heal, he heals others – including them and Michael's baby sister. *My Name is Mina* actively expresses how important it is for humans to recognise that we are extraordinary beings, despite the pain that surrounds us. As Mina puts it: 'this horrible world is so blooming beautiful and so blooming weird that sometimes I think it'll make

me faint!' (*MNIM*, p. 31). Mina tells Skellig he is beautiful twice
(*S*, pp. 85, 94). She is acknowledging that he is beautiful because he
exists as an embodied being, both viscerally and cognitively.

The cognitive unconscious and metaphorical thought

Certain concepts from cognitive science have specific applicability
within children's studies. For example, cognitive scientists explore
both the *brain* and *thought* as interrelated phenomena; thinking cannot happen independently of a biologically situated brain. They also
acknowledge that most cognition is *unconscious* thought, rather than
conscious. They even assert: 'It is a rule of thumb among cognitive
scientists that unconscious thought is 95 percent of all thought –
and that may be a serious underestimate.'[10] Cognitive scientists
argue that human thought – both conscious and unconscious –
depends heavily upon *categorisation*, which they understand as the
brain's primary form of cognition and an 'inescapable consequence
of our biological make-up'.[11] For example, when Mina divides
the world into the value-driven descriptions 'blooming beautiful'
and 'blooming weird', she is categorising, without even realising
that she is. Categorisation, in turn, affects how our brains manage
information in the form of *concepts*. How we know what we know
depends on our ability to separate categories from each other: chair
from child; anger from joy; beautiful from weird. Concepts, in turn,
lead to *conceptual structures*, or conceptualisations, with which our
brains can understand complicated concepts such as 'emotions' as
one category and 'anger' or 'joy' or 'grief' as more specific categories
within that structure – and our cognition allows us to understand
that categories such as 'joy' and 'happiness' are more interconnected
than 'joy' and 'anger'.

Moreover, cognitive science has demonstrated how dependent
upon *embodiment* our conceptual structures are. At an early age, we
develop the ability to create categories based on our bodies: 'here' is
closer to our bodies than 'there'; 'being full' is a concept we understand both from eating and from using our sense of sight and sense
of touch to perceive containers being filled.[12] As a result of defining
concepts in terms of our bodies, we systematically create and rely on
embodied metaphors: that is, metaphors that explain concepts in terms
of our experiences and perceptions. For example, many speakers of
English equate metaphors of vision with metaphors of understanding: 'Yes, I *see* that' or 'The argument *looks* different from my *point
of view*.'[13] Understanding and vision are not the same thing, but we

frequently *map* one of those concepts onto the other, creating a metaphor that is both *embodied* and *conceptual* (because both the vehicle and the tenor of the metaphor are conceptual, and at least one of the two terms arises from an embodied experience, such as seeing). In other words, a standard metaphor involves something (the tenor) that is described by something unrelated (the vehicle). In all of these examples 'understanding' is the tenor that is described in metaphorical terms by the vehicle 'sight'.

A similar mapping occurs in the *Skellig* books. For example, when Michael takes Mina into the garage to be witness to the phenomenon he has found there, he tells her, 'I'm worried that you won't *see* what I think I *see*' (S, p. 74, emphasis added). On one level, Michael is worrying that Mina won't share the same visual perception that he has, but on a far more significant metaphorical level, he is worrying that Mina won't understand, that Mina won't accept that Skellig is real. Michael connects directly the concepts of 'thinking' and 'seeing' when he says 'what I think I see' (S, p. 74). Later, Mina and Michael talk to Mina's mother about various types of visions, including William Blake's. Here, too, humans structure the concept of the spiritual and mystical using an embodied metaphor of sight, *visions*. Mina's mother shows them Blake's drawings of his visions and then says, 'Maybe we could all *see* such beings, if only we knew how to … . But it's enough for me to have you two angels at my table'; 'Yes,' she continues, 'Isn't it amazing? I *see* you clearly, two angels at my table' (S, p. 132, emphasis added). The perception of seeing and the cognitive act of understanding are structurally fused in this woman's dialogue. Moreover, characters in this novel often say, 'See?' as shorthand for 'do you understand?' (S, pp. 22, 37, 58), and on the very first page when Michael describes discovering Skellig, his narration establishes the conceptual connection between the embodied perception of seeing and the embodied concept of understanding: 'I'd soon begin to *see* the truth about him, that there'd never been another creature like him in the world' (S, p. 1, emphasis added). Lakoff and Johnson argue that humans cognitively organise concepts based on our bodies' perceptions.[14] Our metaphors, in turn, arise from these perceptions as conceptual metaphors – that is, when one concept structures another, as vision here structures understanding.[15]

Another set of conceptual metaphors in *Skellig* and *My Name is Mina* involve a quotation from William Blake that hangs next to Mina's bed: 'How can a bird that is born for joy / Sit in a cage and sing?' (qtd S, p. 50). Mina uses the metaphor of the caged bird to explain why she does not attend school: 'schools inhibit the natural curiosity, creativity, and intelligence of children. The mind needs to be opened out into the world, not shuttered down inside a gloomy classroom' (S, p. 49). The metaphor is a double one that can be expressed as basic metaphors: CHILDREN ARE BIRDS and SCHOOLS ARE CAGES, which Mina reiterates in *My Name is Mina* (*MNIM*, p. 18). When Mina is assigned a writing task for her school's high-stakes testing day, she stares out the window at the birds who are free, unlike her. The headteacher gazes on the children from the hallway through the glass door of their classroom, emphasising how caged the children are. Mina, however, has already understood language in terms of imprisonment and power, having written in her journal, 'I'll try to make my words break out of the cages of sadness, and make them sing for joy' (*MNIM*, p. 19). She writes, 'My stories were like me. They couldn't be controlled and they couldn't fit in' (*MNIM*, p. 15). Her teacher, whom she calls Mrs. Scullery, has told her 'that I should not write anything until I had planned what I would write. What nonsense! ... Does a bird plan its song before it sings? OF COURSE IT DOES NOT! It opens its beak and it SINGS so I will SING!' (*MNIM*, pp. 12–13). And, indeed, Mina learns that nonsensical language can help her break free from the prison cage of school. During the standardised test, she answers the prompt, 'Write a description of a busy place' with a nonsense essay entitled 'Gliberrtysnark' (*MNIM*, pp. 160–1). It opens, 'In thi biginin glibbertysnark woz doon in the woositinimana. Golgy golgy golgy than, wiss wandigle', and continues to describe the glibbertysnark's adventures in a busy place (*MNIM*, pp. 161–2). The teacher and headteacher, of course, both fail to understand the nonsense, and so Mina's mother elects to homeschool her. Mina is 'VERY VERY VERY PLEASED' that she has been 'TAKEN OUT OF SCHOOL!' (*MNIM*, p. 163). No longer its prisoner, she sits in a tree, birdlike, observing a nest of blackbird's eggs as they first hatch and later grow to hatchlings. Her mother tells her, 'I can imagine you as a bird', and Mina imagines that the blackbirds think she is 'some kind of weird bird' herself (*MNIM*, pp. 80, 24). She learns about the archaeopteryx, the winged dinosaur from whom all birds evolved – and who makes a reappearance in *Skellig*. She meets the owls who live in the attic of her grandfather's house in *My Name is Mina*, and those owls also reappear when Mina and Michael take Skellig to shelter him in that attic and the owls begin to feed him. At various points in *My Name is Mina*, she thinks about bats, goldfinches, skylarks, chickens and starlings; references to eggs and to angels fill the pages of both books. Michael's teacher talks about Icarus and his wings melting in *Skellig*, and both children talk to their parents about whether or not shoulder blades have been left over, after evolution, from the place where wings once grew.

At one level, CHILDREN ARE BIRDS and SCHOOLS ARE CAGES operate as fairly traditional (and obvious) symbolism. The children, after all, live on the none-too-subtly-named 'Falconer Road'. Almond extends the traditional use of bird symbolism, however, both linguistically and philosophically. Linguistically, Almond uses a cluster of words surrounding the idea of flight to evoke cognitive freedom. Mina suggests in her journal, 'Sleep while you fly. Fly while you sleep' (*MNIM*, p. 202). She loves afternoons with her mother in which 'ideas grow and take flight' (*MNIM*, p. 87). In *Skellig*, Michael's English teacher tells him to 'let your imagination fly' (*S*, p. 155). He also dreams that his sister is a baby bird in a nest; when he is awake and she has had her recuperative surgery, he observes her arching 'her back like she was about to dance or fly' (*S*, p. 180). Mina also reminds the reader again that schools are 'CAGES and PLACES TO BE AVOIDED!' (*MNIM*, p. 123). At one point, Mina climbs out of her tree feeling disoriented, 'like I was coming out from a poem or a story, or like I was a poem or a story myself. Or like I was coming out from an egg!' (*MNIM*, p. 191). She believes that 'words should wander and meander. They should fly like owls and flicker like bats', and some pages of her journal 'will be like a sky with a single bird in it. Some will be like a sky with a swirling swarm of starlings in it. My sentences will be a clutch, a collection, a pattern, a swarm, a shoal, a mosaic. They will be a circus, a menagerie, a tree, a nest' (*MNIM*, p. 11). She despises people who are 'bird trappers ... who trap the spirit, people who cage the soul' (*MNIM*, p. 180). This interconnected set of metaphors demonstrates how conceptual categories interconnect and limit each other in a process cognitive scientists call *entailment*.[16] That is, when we use metaphors to conceptualise, the metaphors we employ limit how we can think about that concept. Thus, if we think about the imagination 'taking flight', we at least temporarily limit how we are thinking about imagination and so are not likely to simultaneously think about it in other terms, say by way of contrast, thinking of imagination as spontaneous combustion or fertile soil. Since the following concepts all belong to the conceptual category of birds – flight/flying, cages/traps, emerging from eggs – these entailments work together in these two novels to link linguistically the philosophical concepts of children and freedom. Almond's use of this categorical entailment is consistent and intricate. While some readers of *Skellig* may miss the point that children need freedom, no reader of *My Name is Mina* possibly could. Mina makes the point directly in her

journal: 'CHILDREN HAVE TO BE LEFT ALONE SOMETIMES!
... SOMETIMES CHILDREN MUST BE LEFT ALONE TO BE
STILL AND SILENT, AND TO DO' (*MNIM*, p. 111).

Another network of entailments in these two novels involves the
underworld, Persephone, death, and the use of 'dead' as an adjective,
as in 'dead easy and dead stupid' (*MNIM*, p. 92). When Michael first
hears Skellig in the garage, he hears a gentle scratching sound, and
then 'dead quiet' (*S*, p. 4); his baby sister's face is 'dead white' before
she is healed, and her hair is 'dead black' (*S*, p. 11). The use of 'dead'
as slang for 'very' is not accidental: Mina is working through her grief
that her father has died; Michael is facing his grief that his sister might
die – and their experiences with Skellig seem like a brush with death.
'I thought he was dead,' Michael says upon first meeting Skellig, 'But
I couldn't have been more wrong' (*S*, p. 1). Furthermore, in *My Name
is Mina*, Mina attempts to journey into the underworld by exploring
an abandoned mine, and she thumps on the earth in the spring to
awaken Persephone. When Michael suggests naming his newly healed
baby sister 'Persephone', his father rejects the name, and they give
her instead the more life-affirming name, 'Joy' (*S*, p. 182). Ideas about
death and the underworld intertwine to invoke ontological questions
about what it means to be a living body – and the adjective 'dead'
itself becomes the linguistic intensifier that underscores the importance of this type of philosophical questioning. Thus, the text explores
ideas about what it means to be 'dead' – as opposed to 'alive' – both
linguistically and philosophically.

Both *Skellig* and *My Name is Mina* also employ a network of
entailments involving the metaphor THE LIVING BODY IS A
CONTAINER. Mina's mother, after all, has told her that her brain
'holds the universe' (*MNIM*, p. 282); that is, Mina's brain is a container
that holds ideas. People in the hospital 'lay exhausted, *filled* with pain'
(*S*, p. 66, emphasis added); Mina's teacher accuses her of being '*full*
of nothing but stupid crackpot notions' (*MNIM*, p. 155; emphasis
added); Mina is happy when someone tells her to live her life well,
'Live it to the *full*' (*MNIM*, p. 72; emphasis added). This entailment
ultimately involves various ontological questions: 'What is the human
body? What is thought? How are we filled with knowledge about our
bodies' being? How do we think about our bodies as containers?' But
these uses of the words *filled* and *full* also demonstrate how linguistic
entailments shape human thought. It is almost impossible *not* to think
of our bodies as containers, in part because we use this metaphor of
'filling' them so frequently, whether we are talking about being 'full'
after we eat or 'filled with new life' when women are pregnant. But

here, Mina's ability to conceptualise ontological status emerges from what she knows and how she knows it; she has an epistemological condition that is influenced by her embodiment.

Thus, the linguistic entailments in *Skellig* and *My Name is Mina* also serve the philosophical issues at work in these novels. Although *Skellig*'s ontological status is never defined, the novels return time and again to questions about what defines the living human body, how things are created, and what happens after death. For example, Mina observes that most household dust is actually particles of dead human skin: 'lots of people's skin mingles together and dances in the light, and the skin of the living and the skin of the dead mingle together and dance in the light!' (*MNIM*, p. 73). Moreover, she thinks of herself as a container when she observes that '[t]he human body is 65 percent water. Two-thirds of me is constantly disappearing and constantly being replaced. So most of me is not me at all!' (*MNIM*, p. 124). Mina also wonders how new things are created. As she writes, she thinks, 'Look at the way the words move across the page and *fill* the empty spaces. Did God feel like this when he started to *fill* the emptiness? Is there a God? Was there ever *emptiness*?' (*MNIM*, p. 15; emphasis added). Later in the novel, she again equates writing, language and creative power: 'Maybe writing was a bit like being God. Every word was the start of a new creation' (*MNIM*, p. 237). More than the other characters in these two novels, Mina puts into words the nature of what it means to create something and how we know what that feels like. Ultimately, she is questioning the ontological status of human creation.

The most basic philosophical question in both novels may be the one that Mina and Michael both ask Skellig, 'What are you?' (*S*, pp. 78, 167). When Michael asks the question, Skellig answers: 'Something like you, something like a beast, something like a bird, something like an angel' (*S*, p. 167). Mina speculates, however, that 'the only possible angels might be us' (*MNIM*, p. 29), implying the sameness of angels and humans. As for birds, they are 'quite extraordinary enough without having souls' (*MNIM*, p. 77); 'If there is a God,' Mina writes, 'could it be that he's chosen the birds to speak for him?' (*MNIM*, p. 66). She emphasises this point in her journal: 'THE VOICE OF GOD SPEAKS THROUGH THE BEAKS OF BIRDS' (*MNIM*, p. 66). Although Mina tells Michael in *Skellig* that her father is in heaven 'watching us' (*S*, p. 50), she writes in the prequel that 'I don't really believe in Heaven at all, and I don't believe in perfect angels. I think that this might be the only Heaven there can possibly be, this world we live in now, but that we haven't quite realized it yet' (*MNIM*,

p. 29). Moreover, Mina tells Michael that Blake believed souls could 'leap' out of the body and back into it, relying on the container metaphor that the body is a container in which to hold the soul. Mina defines the soul leaping out of the body-as-container using a dance metaphor: 'It's like a dance', she says (S, p. 152). That dance, of course, is reflected in Skellig's circular dancing that seems to meld the souls of the dancers together.

Skellig and My Name is Mina are no more determinant about who we are as humans and how we know what we know than the texts are in defining Skellig's ontological status. And yet the very asking of the questions leads to a significant set of value judgements: we may not know who we are, but we need to care for those who need us, such as Skellig and Michael's sister and the baby birds that Mina and her mother defend from a marauding cat. 'Sometimes we have to accept that there are things we can't know', Mina tells Michael (S, p. 140), and yet both texts clearly imply that children should be given the freedom to observe life, analyse it, and decide for themselves how to live it. We may not entirely understand our own being and how we know what we know according to these novels, but we are called to understand our own values and lead ethical lives, nonetheless.

Conclusion

What, then, is the relationship between philosophy and cognitive science – and why does this intersection matter to children's literature? On the most basic level, cognitive science teaches us that human development includes the ability to categorise, conceptualise, and create metaphorical structures that have epistemological significance. Humans' developmental ability to understand metaphor begins early in childhood and is explained by Christopher Johnson's *theory of conflation*: young children conflate sensorimotor experiences, like warmth, with non-sensorimotor experiences, like the emotional warmth of being held, which in turn feels like being loved.[17] Although by the time children are of school age, they can differentiate between the domains of being held physically and being held metaphorically, neurotypical children will have already begun understanding and employing metaphors like, '*warm* smile' or 'friend I *hold* dear in my heart'.[18] Children's novels are one mechanism by which children experience the *conflation* involved in *embodied metaphors*, as David Almond's multiple metaphorical uses of vision, birds and death demonstrate. Furthermore, children's novels also provide critics the opportunity to analyse how metaphorical networks have epistemological implications during youth, especially as these networks create entailments that influence how children conceptualise.

But perhaps more significant, in philosophical terms, is the way that cognitive science provides a middle ground between philosophical debates about empiricism and relativism. Hart writes about this debate in terms that capture the philosophical tension as it bears on epistemology. Empiricism, relying as it does on concepts of perception and scientific data, tends to valorise the primacy of ontology as a field of study in affirming *being* as the central goal of knowledge. Relativism, on the other hand, relies so heavily on our understanding of humanity as culturally constructed that epistemology – that is, the study of *knowing* – gains prominence in philosophy informed by relativism. Hart advocates a third position, through cognitive linguistics, one that prioritises *experientialism*. As she demonstrates, Lakoff and Johnson argue that concepts form our experiences; that is, what we know influences our being, and our being is influenced reciprocally by how we know. Within linguistics, then, Lakoff and Johnson have tried to mediate a 'third position', in which the ontology of the rational human being co-creates the epistemology of the socially situated human being.[19]

> We are philosophical animals. We are the only animals we know of who can ask, and sometimes even explain, why things happen the way they do. ... Philosophy matters to us, therefore, primarily because it helps us to make sense of our lives and to live better lives. .. Since everything we think and say and do depends on the workings of our embodied minds, cognitive science is one of our most profound resources for self-knowledge.[20]

And as they also observe, in order to be articulated, all philosophy depends on metaphorical thinking: 'The fact that abstract thought is mostly metaphorical means that answers to philosophical questions have always been, and always will be, mostly metaphorical.'[21]

Theirs is a recognition of the relationship between body and mind, between conscious mind and unconscious brain, and between language and perception. This 'third position', as Hart calls it, seems to me crucial to the study of children's literature because childhood is, by its very definition, an embodied state.[22] That is, while earlier metaphysicists could afford to ignore childhood as a time when humans were not yet fully rational, poststructural relativists have not necessarily been able to account for the newborn infant, born with a distinct personality but not yet exposed in meaningful ways to social construction.

Lakoff and Johnson, however, provide a way to account for the child both as embodied in infancy/childhood/adolescence, while simultaneously being shaped conceptually by the ideological pressures of the world in which s/he grows. In other words, poststructuralism does not always account fully for the biological definition of infancy/childhood/adolescence; nor does essentialism or empiricism fully account for the cultural factors that define how the individual is formed by social pressures. But in investigating how language shapes our concepts, and how concepts, in turn, shape the human ability to conceptualise, Lakoff and Johnson allow for the type of corporeal philosophy that Elizabeth Grosz calls for in *Volatile Bodies* when she writes:

> human bodies have irreducible neurophysiological and psychological dimensions whose relations remain unknown and ... human bodies have the wonderful ability, while striving for integration and cohesion, organic and psychic wholeness, to also provide for and indeed produce fragmentations, fracturings, dislocations that orient bodies and body parts toward other bodies and body parts.[23]

Cognitive science allows for childhood studies to integrate the study of the body and the mind in ways that acknowledge human development, cognitive development and philosophical inquiry.

In conclusion, David Almond relies on language – specifically, on embodied metaphors – to explore what it means to be both a sentient, rational being and to live in a world that, despite not always being rational, nonetheless affects our social construction. His works are deeply philosophical – and fairly controversial in their refusal to privilege one side of the debate between empiricism and constructionism. Is Skellig an evolved creature whose existence can be empirically proven? Or is he a social construction, the result of two children's need to have a life they *can* save when they can't save a father (Mina's) or a sister (Michael's) from dying? The text never makes that clear. Certainly, the children experience Skellig as empirically real, but they also explain him as an angel in terms of the religion that has socially constructed them. The ambivalence here is the fulcrum of Almond's philosophical wisdom in allowing young readers to explore these mysteries for themselves.

To underscore the relevance of cognitive science to the philosophical questioning in Almond's novels, I cite one of Mina's teachers, who says, 'our brains make stories naturally ... they find it easy' (*MNIM*, p. 236). In this passage, Almond openly acknowledges the cognitive function of story creation. The brain is hard-wired for story-telling, so brains find it 'easy'. This teacher adds 'that stories weren't really about words ... They were about visions. They were like dreams' (*MNIM*, p. 237). Almond's language here and throughout both novels is poetic, but it is poetry that serves the purpose of engaging children in metaphysical and existential questions: what does it mean to *be*? And what does it mean to *think* and to *know*? And most important, how do we choose to enact the values that emerge from the socially constructed knowledge that emerges, in part, from the stories we create and those that we read?

Notes

1. Thomas Hofweber, 'Logic and Ontology', in *Stanford Encyclopaedia of Philosophy* (30 August 2011), http://plato.stanford.edu/entries/logic-ontology/ (accessed 17 January 2014).
2. Matthias Steup, 'Epistemology', in *Stanford Encyclopaedia of Philosophy* (14 December 2005), http://plato.stanford.edu/entries/epistemology/ (accessed 21 January 2014).
3. Mark Schroeder, 'Value Theory', in *Stanford Encyclopaedia of Philosophy* (29 May 2012), http://plato.stanford.edu/entries/value-theory/ (accessed 21 July 2012).
4. F. Elizabeth Hart, 'The Epistemology of Cognitive Literary Studies', *Philosophy and Literature* 25(2) (2001): 315.
5. George Lakoff and Mark Johnson, *Philosophy in the Flesh: The Embodied Mind and Its Challenge to Western Thought* (New York: Basic Books, 1999), pp. 10, 509.
6. Lakoff and Johnson, *Philosophy in the Flesh*, p. 5.
7. Lakoff and Johnson, *Philosophy in the Flesh*, p. 7.
8. Lakoff and Johnson, *Philosophy in the Flesh*, pp. 37–8.
9. Maurice Merleau-Ponty, *Phenomenology of Perception*, trans. Colin Smith (New York: Humanities Press, 1962 [1945]), p. 82.
10. Lakoff and Johnson, *Philosophy in the Flesh*, p. 13.
11. Lakoff and Johnson, *Philosophy in the Flesh*, p. 18.
12. George Lakoff and Mark Johnson, *Metaphors We Live By* (Chicago: University of Chicago Press, 2003 [1980]), p. 51.
13. Mark Johnson, *The Body in the Mind: The Bodily Basis of Meaning, Imagination, and Reason* (Chicago: University of Chicago Press, 1990), p. 108.
14. Lakoff and Johnson, *Metaphors We Live By*, p. 1.
15. Mark Turner, *Reading Minds: The Study of English in the Age of Cognitive Science* (Princeton, NJ: Princeton University Press, 1991), pp. 158–9.
16. Lakoff and Johnson, *Philosophy in the Flesh*, p. 47.
17. Christopher Johnson, 'Metaphor vs. Conflation in the Acquisition of Polysemy: The Case of See', in Masako K. Hiraga, Chris Sinha and Sherman Wilcos (eds), *Cultural, Psychological, and Typological Issues in Cognitive Linguistics* (Amsterdam, PA: Benjamins, 1999), p. 155.

18. Lakoff and Johnson, *Philosophy in the Flesh*, p. 46.
19. Hart, 'Epistemology', pp. 320–1.
20. Lakoff and Johnson, *Philosophy in the Flesh*, p. 551.
21. Lakoff and Johnson, *Philosophy in the Flesh*, p. 7.
22. Hart, 'Epistemology', p. 320.
23. Elizabeth Grosz, *Volatile Bodies: Toward a Corporeal Feminism* (Bloomington: Indiana University Press, 1994), p. 13.

4

The Possibilities of Becoming: Process-Relational Theology in the Works of David Almond

Karen Coats

In David Almond and Dave McKean's hauntingly beautiful and original creation fable, *Mouse Bird Snake Wolf*, a host of gods and goddesses create a world full of wondrous things before they tire and become more interested in taking tea and naps than in finishing their work. Three children, Harry, Sue and Ben, enjoy their world, but they notice its unfinished quality, finding its gaps and empty spaces both appealing and frightening, and they call out to the gods to make more things. When the gods remain silent, they take it upon themselves to create the things they think the world needs by imagining and sculpting their creatures from found objects and then bringing them to life with their words and their sense of the way the creatures should sound and move: little Ben creates a mouse, Sue a bird, and Harry a snake. While Ben is happy with the new creatures they have made, Harry and Sue want a bigger challenge, and together, against Ben's protests, they imagine a wolf.

Their imagined creation is indeed beautiful, but as their snarls and drooling and yells bring it to fierce and terrifying life, it devours them. The indolent gods once again ignore Ben's appeals, and he sets about unmaking the wolf, reducing it back to the 'clay and sticks and petals and nuts and grass' from which it was created (*MBSW*, n.p.). He rescues his friends, but as the children awaken, they feel the residual effects of their work, and they are changed: 'They were silent. They had been inside their wolf; now their wolf was inside them, like a dream. They felt it, running through them. They heard it, howling and snarling deep inside them' (*MBSW*, n.p.). The gods too are changed by the children's work: when they awaken, they have an experience very like that of the children:

> But then they fell silent, and there came a sound from deep inside themselves, and from the gaps and spaces that they'd left below: astonishing snarling, extraordinary howling. And the gods listened and were entranced, and they all knew, as they sipped their tea and nibbled their cake, that the new and marvellous beast would soon find its way out again into the world. (*MBSW*, n.p.)

The richness of this short fable lends itself to multiple interpretations, from the mundane to the numinous. Certainly one could view this as a cautionary tale on either a small or large scale. The conventional imagery of a wolf that devours children is reminiscent of Red Riding Hood, especially since one of the gods, grumpy from being awakened, scolds the children for messing about in the work of creation, and thus, as with little Red Riding Hood's, the story becomes a record of disobedience and its consequences. But it could also be interpreted as a warning for adults who are irresponsibly idle; while the gods indulge in self-congratulatory indolence, the children make mischief that cannot be completely undone. On a grander scale, the idea that humans are capable of creating things that, while technically brilliant and even beautiful, can have unintended consequences, including large-scale destruction, makes this an even more urgent cautionary tale for a nuclear age.

While these interpretations are valid and compelling, I would like to offer yet one more that positions this story as perhaps the clearest and most overt expression of an ideological thread that can be traced throughout Almond's oeuvre. In nearly all of his books, Almond rends the veil between the past and present, the seen and the unseen, the actual and the possible, to reveal their interconnectedness, and insists that each of his main characters has a vital role to play in the process of creating ourselves and the world, that we are all interrelated agents of our own becoming. Because his characters often do things that seem impossible in our present experience of the world, most critics follow his characters in labelling these events 'magic', and situate his works as exemplars of magical realism. But there is a world-view that posits that the events Almond describes are not necessarily magical in the sense that they are impossible according to natural law, but instead are merely possibilities that have not yet been actualised. By exploring the ways in which Almond's texts are aligned with some of the central tenets of this world-view, I hope to make clear how his books provide an implicit but very clear demonstration of the strain of modern ecumenical theology called process theology.

Process thought: from philosophy to theology to Almond

Process theology is built upon process philosophy, a world-view which has scattered antecedents throughout the history of ideas, but which found its most complete articulation in the work of Alfred North Whitehead. Whitehead began his career as a mathematician, but increasingly turned his attention to philosophy as he became dissatisfied with existing ontological paradigms that focused on unchanging logical axioms and timeless substances as the inherent nature of things. A full explanation or even a decontextualised summary of his system would take us too far into the weeds of philosophical terminology and far-reaching theological debates for my purposes here, so instead I will undertake the reciprocal task of describing the major aspects and commitments of process philosophy and theology that I find relevant to the underlying views of the cosmos, the ways of being, and the understanding of how humans could potentially function in the world that seem to inform Almond's fiction while interpreting his work through a process-theological framework.

As I analyse how Almond's work participates in this world-view, I must emphasise a very strong disclaimer: I in no way want to suggest that Almond himself subscribes or adheres to a process view as Whitehead articulated it. In Don Latham's book-length study,[1] as well as in interviews, can be found much information and discussion about Almond's personal religious beliefs, but my particular commitments as a critic impel me to leave such personal revelations well alone in my interpretation of fictional texts. Poststructural theory and psychoanalysis have made much of the death of the author as well as his or her largely unconscious embeddedness in complex cultural systems, and I find that this frees critics to examine how the texts speak for themselves, or at least lend themselves to interpretations that foreground the reader's intentionality and concerns as much as the author's. That said, it would be unethical to impose a reading on a text that violates its integrity by ignoring or interpreting certain textual elements in such a way that contorts them in the interest of conformity to a theoretical perspective. In keeping with a process view, then, I will describe how I came to believe that an understanding of process theology enriches our reading of Almond's work.

When I first read *Skellig*, *Kit's Wilderness*, *Heaven Eyes*, *Slog's Dad* and *The Savage*, I had no experience with or knowledge of process philosophy. I did know, however, that Almond was doing something with his characters that I had not seen before. Almond's children were not playing with magic as a device or slipping through portals to imaginary worlds to engage in wish-fulfilling fantasy adventures. Instead, they were having sustained, thoughtful encounters with the supernatural, which was as real and tangible to them as the natural world. They were experiencing what Rudolf Otto called the numinous – the experience of being in the presence of the holy, in both its aspects as *tremendum*, which indicates a feeling of awe mixed with fear, and *fascinans*, its power to compel and to draw one into personal communion with a being that is wholly actual yet wholly other.[2] What's more, their experiences had the power to invoke in me as a reader a sense of wonder that was not the same as mere pleasure in a well-made story or escapist fantasy, but felt more like the power of numinous *possibility*. At that point, I didn't know what to make of this experience.

In pursuit of another project, I began to research philosophies of embodiment which led me to Benedict Ashley's magisterial work, *Theologies of the Body: Humanist and Christian*. Ashley, a Catholic philosopher and theologian, traces historical, scientific, theological and ideological conceptions of the body through to a radical-process interpretation of science and a process theology of evolutionary embodiment. In his work I found one of those satisfying cognitive connections that produce an almost audible 'snick' of recognition: I knew what he was talking about because I had seen this world-view enacted in *story*, and the feeling I intuited *there* was being explained to me *here*. Ashley begins his work with an acknowledgement of embodiment that, though grounded in common sense and experience, has nonetheless fallen out of much of our philosophical and religious thinking, which tends to favour the conceptual over the embodied:

> I exist and live as a body in a world of bodies. We bodies contact each other and by this contact we create the world-space. To be a body, however, is to exist only in process: forming and decaying, appearing and disappearing, recurring and undergoing modification, development and growth.[3]

This is a concise expression of the founding premise of process philosophy, a 'philosophy that takes the human experience of change seriously – ultimately seriously'.[4] Most philosophies, including philosophies of science conceived prior to the discoveries of the theories of relativity and evolution, concern themselves with eternal verities and absolute physical laws that determine or predicate outcomes; they are taken up with questions about the qualities of substances, rather than the dynamism of relational flows between actual entities. Even contemporary humanist philosophies depend on deterministic conceptions of biological heredity, cultural construction and ideological enclosure when they seek to account for human bodies, subjectivities and societies. These philosophies, then, can only offer anaemic and ultimately unsatisfying accounts of genuinely creative emergence, not only of new bodies and new concepts, but of new modes or processes of emergence itself.[5] A being like Skellig, then, '[s]omething like you, something like a beast, something like a bird, something like an angel … Something like that', can only ever be imaginary in such philosophies, a wish-fulfilling dream as he is for Michael's mother. In process philosophy, however, he can be conceived of as a yet unrealised actuality in an ongoing evolutionary process (S, p. 167). Similarly, Slog's dad returned from the dead can be viewed sceptically by Davie as a vagrant angling to get hold of a Saveloy with everything, but he could also be a body transformed by processes we don't yet understand or have access to, but are not unheard of in human history, given the resurrections of Lazarus and Jesus.

And this is the very point at which process philosophy is transformed into a theology. Whitehead sought to articulate an internally consistent, philosophically rigorous world-view that took into account the common sense of human experience and intuition. This common sense, for Whitehead, includes not only those facts that proceed from scientific understanding, but also our aesthetic, ethical responses to the world as well as our intuition of the numinous and of creative possibilities that are not determined by the past. Rather than seeing time, space and matter as impassive substances or elements, he uses the language of dynamic *events* with *characteristics*, the chief characteristic of all events being change. Our common sense and limited experience of the physical world certainly support the idea of change as either mechanistic reproduction or entropy: plants produce seeds which develop into their own kinds, which in turn produce more seeds, and then die, and animals and humans undergo a similar cycle of life, reproduction and death. But what of events that differ from their pasts? How does process theology account for progress and anomaly? How would it account for Skellig?

God in the midst of change

Whitehead did not accept the idea that the past is entirely deterministic or that the universe was exclusively mechanistic, only capable of reiterative processes; in his determination, the evidence of evolution throughout history simply doesn't support such a world-view. Likewise, a metaphysics of unchanging substances cannot account for novelty and dynamic responsiveness either, which are clearly evident in the history of the world. In order for his system to be internally consistent, then, Whitehead needed an organising principle that would contribute an ideal subjective aim for each entity to realise as its fulfilment – a future that would convey value on present decisions. Molecules, understood this way, are conservative, their ideal subjective aim being consistent repetition unless they are acted upon by some external force. Human subjects, on the other hand, are capable of dynamic cognitive and emotional responses as well as consciousness. They can therefore make active decisions to integrate past experience, facts, and natural laws into present experience in such a way that present experience is not fully determined by those causes, but is at least partially directed towards a future ideal of what they could become. Further, Whitehead contended that this ideal subjective aim must be located in goodness and continual enrichment rather than any sort of ultimacy or absolutism; for him, perfection is not to be understood according to the Greek idea that any change in a perfect form is a devolution, but instead his idea of the perfect is 'that which is capable of indefinite enrichment'.[6] Since genuine novelty cannot emerge from a deterministic past, and entropy is as likely in a system of chance as any form of progress or development, Whitehead felt that atheistic and agnostic world-views could not account for the source of ideal aims that would lead to continuous becoming; therefore he needed the concept of God to complete his system. In Whitehead's system, God is the source of all subjective aims, and as an actual entity that contains all of those aims, he acts as their limit as well.

Whitehead argues further that the God of a consistent and rational world-view cannot be wholly other to reality in his attributes, nor can He be called in as an explanation for irrational or para-rational events when other explanations fail: 'God is not to be treated as an exception to all metaphysical principles, invoked to save their collapse. He is their chief exemplification.'[7] If this is the case, then, and evolutionary change is an inherent characteristic of all actual entities, then God himself, as an actual entity, is changed or, as Whitehead would say, *enriched* by the activities of human beings in the world. Likewise, the characteristic of creativity, if it resides in God, must reside in his creatures as well, insofar as they are made in His image. This is clearly illustrated in *Mouse Bird Snake Wolf*, where the creative actions of the children work their way not only into the world, but also into the dreams of the gods, who are not the same when they awaken, because they have been introduced to a new thought. Harry, Sue and little

Ben are responding to the notion of world in process. As William Hocking put it:

> There are certainly some regions of reality which are *unfinished*. We are endowed with wills only because there are such regions, to which it is our whole occupation to give shape and character. In such regions the will-to-believe is justified, because it is no will-to-make-believe, but a veritable will to create the truth in which we believe.[8]

Over and over again in Almond's books, we meet characters who create the truths in which they believe. Michael offers perhaps the mildest expression of this when he asks Skellig to 'think about' his baby sister getting better (*S*, p. 56). As the book progresses, his belief that the fate of his sister is enmeshed with the recovery of Skellig as well as with his own heartbeat becomes more and more definite until it in fact passes from belief to truth.

With other characters, Hocking's insight is more literally realised. In *Kit's Wilderness*, for instance, Kit brings Lak's mother into existence in the cave with John Askew, while in *Heaven Eyes*, the children watch as the saint they have unearthed from the Middens bears Grampa's soul away. Also in *Heaven Eyes*, Wilson Cairns breathes life into his clay creatures, as do Davie and Stephen Rose in *Clay*. Blue brings the savage part of himself to actual life in *The Savage*. Slog, in *Slog's Dad*, sees his dad in the rumpled man on the park bench.

Clearly, each of these incidents is more readily interpreted by the common-sense view that they are merely imaginative acts of story-telling, but Almond takes care to situate his characters in here-and-now reality. His settings, while fictional, are also clearly recognisable, with landmarks and features common to the environs around the River Tyne. Moreover, all of the mysterious sightings and circumstances are witnessed by more than one child, as if to verify that what might appear imaginary is in fact part of the actual world of the story. When Michael asks Skellig if he can bring Mina to see him, Skellig asks, 'Someone to tell you I'm really here?' (*S*, p. 55). The Savage leaves actual bruises and smudges on the people he touches, and John and Kit are constantly checking with one another to assure themselves than they have both seen the ghost children, Silky, and Lak's mother. Davie asks questions to try to trip up the man claiming to be Slog's dad, but the man doesn't falter.

This insistence that what seems impossible is in fact real blurs the line not merely between fact and fiction, or between magic and realism, but between fiction and possibility, which is what initially led me to consider an interpretation of Almond's work from a process perspective; indeed, if the claims of process theology have validity, a creature like Skellig is not only possible in our evolutionary future, but he is likely, given the point of view of a process-informed Christology.

Christ – and Skellig – in process theology

David R. Griffin, in *A Process Christology*, suggests that '[i]n actualizing God's *particular* aims *for him*, Jesus expressed God's *general* aim for his entire creation'.[9] That is to say, the things that Christ was able to do during his time on earth and which were verified by multiple witnesses, such as healing the sick, turning water into wine, walking on water and raising the dead, are exemplary of the teleological aims of the evolutionary process guided by the subjective aims God has for his creatures. Process thinkers do not posit human being as we now experience it, with its self-reflective consciousness and capacity for invention and innovation, as the pinnacle of evolution, but instead see the project as ongoing. And many (though by no means all) process theologians follow Griffin in contending that '[t]he aims given to Jesus and actualized by him during his active ministry were such that the basic vision of reality contained in his message of work and deed was the supreme expression of God's eternal character and purpose'.[10] If that is the case, it is possible to see in Skellig the next movement in human evolution – a being that is still embodied, with all that entails with regard to pain, entropy and a need for care, but which also, given that loving care, is capable, like Christ, of releasing healing energies into the world, travelling in the astral plane, and operating without regard to physical laws such as gravity. In fact, none of the seemingly impossible or magical things that Almond's characters do, such as breathing life into beings formed of clay, healing the sick, defying gravity, rising from the dead or floating above the ground, represents an act not found in the historical record of Christ's actual life on earth.

I think it is important to note at this point another disclaimer, and that is that just as I make no claims for Almond's knowledge or intentional use of process theology, I do not want to give the impression that my interpretations of certain features of his texts reduce them to allegories, or worse, mere illustrations of a particular position. It should go without saying that good stories are composed of events, characters and motifs that can be interpreted in multiple ways. Interpretive work can open up new possibilities for understanding multivalent signs, but good stories are not the same as straightforward explanations, definitions or even illustrations of philosophical or theological principles.

As I was working through this project, for instance, I posed the question of why Almond often works with constellations of three characters, namely, two boys and a girl: Mina, Michael and Skellig; Kit, John and Allie; Erin, January and Mouse; Ben, Sue and Harry. Because I was considering the texts from a theological reference point, I played with the idea of an interpretation that mirrors a traditional Trinitarian view of a transcendent creator, an incarnate redeemer, and a spiritual comforter and guide, but quickly realised that such a view is not a defensible one, nor does it need to be, because Almond is writing fiction, not theological allegory. The power of three characters who each bring a different aspect to a strong communitarian bond forms an interesting intertextual pattern, but the number three isn't necessarily significant, as shown when Erin, January and Mouse adopt Heaven Eyes as their fourth, and bring her home to an even larger community. Thus my caution, to both myself and my reader, is to remember that, while Almond's texts do seem to have a strong affinity with the principles of process theology, they should not be read as completely coincident with them. What's more, process theology is not monolithic within itself, particularly with regard to its take on Christology. My reading of *Skellig* as a possible next step in human evolution, as well as other examples in Almond's works viewed from this particular perspective, thus has the limited utility of reconceptualising what common-sensically appears as magic as the possibility of what we might become if we were to accept or entertain the premises of process theology.

Whitehead himself, for instance, never developed an explicit theory of Christ, but he did find the existent views of God in his time unacceptable. He complained that God had been conceptualised as 'the image of an imperial ruler, … a personification of moral energy … an ultimate philosophical principle', none of which matched the

> brief Galilean vision of humility [that] dwells upon the tender elements in the world, which slowly and in quietness operate by love and … finds purpose in the immediacy of a kingdom not of this world. Love neither rules, nor is it unmoved; also it is a little oblivious to morals. It does not look to the future; for it finds its own reward in the immediate present.[11]

Whitehead's God is never coercive, but instead acts as a loving lure, much like the sun in Aesop's fable, which process theologians often use to illustrate their perspective of how God works in the world.

In the fable, the North Wind and the Sun have a contest to see who is stronger. The challenge is to see which one can make a traveller remove his cloak. The Wind blows with all its harrowing force, but this only causes the man to wrap his cloak more tightly around himself. The Sun merely shines down, and its warmth affects the man such that he removes his cloak. Thus the Sun in seen as working through the power of persuasion rather than force, and this is how most process theologians view the power of God.

The lure of God in free will and creation

Besides illustrating the power of God, however, the story also includes the response of the traveller, which is equally important in process thinking for enriching the world. Lewis Ford explains it this way:

> Each event requires the persuasive power of God to provide the lure or possibility or initial aim to be realized, but it also requires the creaturely power to actualize that aim by integrating together the totality of efficient causes derived from the past. Without God there would be simply chaos, for the individual occasion would lack any ordering principle to initiate its process of integration, but without the world, God's aims for the world would never be realized, since God acts solely by the power of persuasion, which can be effective only so far as it elicits response. This means that *every* creaturely activity is also a divine activity, incarnating God's purposes in the world, to greater or lesser degree. Only those actions that are fully responsive to God's aims, to be sure, *reveal* God's actions in the world, for only they realize his intentions without distortion. Other events may thwart or frustrate or only partially realize the divine intent, but they still necessarily involve divine action, though with diminished effectiveness.[12]

This is the way process thinkers conceive of both free will and the existence of evil. The power of God lies in the persuasiveness of his subjective aims for every occasion; in this He functions as their limit as well as their lure. The aims themselves would lead us to the perfection of continual enrichment, but the decisions we make towards fulfilling them are conditioned by the distortions and diminishments of past experiences as well as by our freely determined degree of responsiveness to the lure itself.

Stephen Rose's creative power in *Clay* demonstrates how evil results from distorting God's intentions. Stephen is undeniably gifted, but he refuses to accept any limiting principle. We know, then, that Stephen's actions are a distortion of divine aims because they are logically inconsistent with them. God created beings with free will, and He limits Himself to persuasive power so that He doesn't violate that free will. Stephen hypnotises his aunt, depriving her of her free will, and he creates a being that can only ever do the bidding of its master. Thus he rejects the possibility of his creature's becoming and uses his creative powers in a diabolical way.

Davie, on the other hand, worries about the question of artistic creation and its limits. His teacher, Prat, responds:

> 'But is human creativity equal to the creativity of God?' he said. 'That question has led many down a darkening and ever more terrifying path. … We cannot, like God, create a soul. We cannot, like God, create life. But who is to say what the limits of our creativity may nevertheless be?' (C, p. 80)

This is why Davie ultimately decides to destroy Clay. As he takes the creature on a walk through his town, he points out all of the members of his community in implicit acknowledgement of their individuality, their actualisation as family members, athletes, fans, gardeners, that is, as people who exercise their free will, live out their lives and die according to a natural order that serves as a limit. Clay has none of these qualities, and is incapable of acquiring them, incapable of ever aspiring to a free will that would enable him to freely respond to an aim that would direct his becoming. As a result, Davie knows that he does not belong in the world.

Re-creating the past

On the other hand, we see the working-out of free will in the movement between past determinants and future possibilities, as well as the view of God as a slow and loving lure toward the immediate purpose of realising His aim with regard to any actual situation, in both *Kit's Wilderness* and *Heaven Eyes*. John Askew and Erin Law are trapped in the tragedies of their past and present circumstances. Askew's father is abusive, and this present circumstance is exacerbated by the fact that John's future seems wholly conditioned by his past. The game of Death that he devises is an attempt to find some way out of the circle of hopelessness by finding a true guide through the morass of tragedy figured by the abandoned pit and by a memorial that suggests that John is in fact already dead – that his possibilities are all already lost. The children who play the game, however, are all pretenders, as Allie points out, until Kit arrives. Kit actually enters into the nothingness of his own death, and emerges with the ability to see the dead children and Silky as well as a way to connect with John.

Like John, Kit is trying to sort out his present in reference to his family's past and a present that includes pain, his in the form of the impending loss of his grandfather. The difference is that his mother and his grandfather's stories offer him an alternate set of past events to consider as he actively constructs his present. Instead of condemning John outright for his rough appearance and dangerous reputation, Kit's mother says, 'Oh … One of that lot … But we mustn't be guided only by appearances, or the family that produced him' (*KW*, p. 20). That is, neither past circumstances nor present facts are wholly determinative of future possibilities. But neither are they irrelevant. Kit's grandfather remembers Askew's grandpa as a hero as well as an artist who carved a tiny pit pony from coal that he still has, and suggests that John's talent is an inheritance from past generations. Further, he remarks, 'And aye, they've always been a queer crew, but when you needed a mate, they was always there' (*KW*, p. 35).

Kit takes this value of loyalty and connection to heart and works slowly and patiently to win John's trust. His method for working out his own feelings and connecting to John involves a creative appropriation and revisioning of the distant past in light of John's difficult present. He uses these creatively realised pieces to form a story that can lure John into a new understanding of his possible future. In this way, he is, as Ford notes in the passage quoted above, enacting a divine activity in his work of integrating the causes of the past in the service of a future aim. The work has to proceed slowly because John is under no compulsion to follow the lure. Time is therefore drawn out in the novel, with most chapters beginning with some indication of its passing, either day to day or through the deepening of the winter season. The theme of the slow but generative merging of time and relationship is emphasised even further by the geography lessons of Pangaea that Allie resists but that Kit finds evocative. Their teacher, Dobbs, even expresses his commitment to process thinking and the interconnectedness of all things in his frustration over Allie's inattention:

> 'You may think that tectonic plates have nothing to do with you, Miss Keenan!' he yelled. 'But that's just because the plates in your own skull have yet to join up with each other. You're an infant world, girl. You're semiformed. You're a tectonic gap.' (*KW*, p. 81)

Kit has to regress to an infant world himself to reshape John Askew's present in a way that lures him to a positive future, selectively interweaving actual occasions and causes with a vision that, while dark and difficult, gives John hope.

The lure of generative darkness

But Kit himself also feels the lure of the pit, of experiencing 'the strange joy of dropping down together into the darkness that we feared' in order to experience 'the joy of coming out again together into the lovely world' (*KW*, pp. 27–8). This affirmation of the positive power of primordial darkness as an integral and generative facet of process theology is elaborated by Eulalio R. Baltazar. In *The Dark Center: A Process Theology of Blackness*, Baltazar maintains that the religious basis of Western colour symbolism rests on the equation of reason and rationality with light and vision, resulting in a view of reality that is decidedly presentist, because the only truth or being we can really know is what is currently visible to us. Both metaphysical and empirical philosophies agree that the past and the future are places of unknowability – that is, they are dark to us, and the dark is traditionally cast as a place of fear, nonbeing, ignorance and unreason. Under such a vision that equates knowledge and progress with light, we must flee from darkness, as Kit's teachers encourage him to do. But Allie in her way, and John and Kit in theirs, value the darkness, finding its unknowability generative. The unknowability of the past allows Kit to reconstruct it, the unknowability of the future causes Allie to desire it, and the unknowable bits of the present – the mystery of Silky, the ghost children that John and Kit can see, Lak's mother in the cave – function as lures to the children towards an understanding where love, not reason or rationality, overcomes abuse and death.

Erin's experience with darkness in *Heaven Eyes* is similar to John's and Kit's; her trip to the Black Middens finds its climactic moment when she gets lost, literally and emotionally, in the slime-filled basement, where the memory of her mother, usually so comforting, becomes a reinvocation of her death instead, leaving Erin in a place 'beyond words, beyond laughter, beyond tears. No hope. No joy. No life. Death grew all around and drew me in' (*HE*, p. 104). It is significant, then, that Anna, 'with her lovely eyes that saw through all the trouble in the world to the heaven that lies beneath', is the one who finds Erin and lures her out of her personal hell (*HE*, p. 228). In fact, it is most significant that Anna is called Heaven Eyes by the man who rescued her, because she functions as the lure that leads first him and eventually all of the children of Whitegates past their damage and into their possibilities. Her loving presence is enough to help even Maureen become better at her job of shepherding the children towards their own becoming.

While subsequent process thinkers continue to debate Whitehead's conception of God, and even whether or not it is a necessary concept at all for his system, process theologians have been attracted to his ideas because they settle two seemingly intractable debates: the conflict between an omniscient, omnipotent God and a genuinely free will, and the idea that if God created everything *ex nihilo*, then he must have created evil as well. In traditional literary and religious symbolism, darkness is associated with evil, sin, hell, and a lack of enlightenment. But the way Almond uses darkness, including mystery, night, coal pits, the Black Middens, the deepness of dreams, the pain of mistakes and bad decisions, and mysterious and almost grotesque figures such as the saint in *Heaven Eyes* and Skellig, accords with the process view Baltazar elaborates. While Baltazar's primary aim is to recover darkness in its positive valence as an intellectual and ideational antidote for racism, his discussion has far-reaching consequences for understanding the ways of being and the way we acquire knowledge about the world that inform Almond's texts. Baltazar argues:

> Darkness is the source of life and energy at all levels of being. As the source of green life is a dark soil and as the source of light energy is the dark center of the sun, so the source of life for theology is the darkness of mystery and myth and the source of the life of grace for Christians is the saving darkness of faith which hides the Divine Darkness. But both Western theology and the Christian life have undergone a bleaching process, driven by fear of their respective dark centers.[13]

Almond is clearly not afraid of those dark centres; indeed, his characters – Kit, John, Allie, Erin, January, Heaven Eyes, Blue, Harry, Sue, little Ben, Slog, Michael, Mina and Skellig – all find the source of grace by following the lure of God into a darkness out of which they emerge remade.

The sources of care

The use of such naturalistic metaphors calls attention to another aspect of process theology that finds significant expression in Almond's texts, namely its strong emphasis on environmental care and the importance of interpersonal relationships. Ashley frames it this way:

> As a body-self I find myself empowered to make a practical, active response to my situation in the world by taking control over the parts of my own body and over the bodies that environ me. I was created out of world-processes that I find still going on within me. I in some measure

direct their flow. In the flood of change I am a gate which can swing open or shut to redirect the current. As I emerge from the processes which have created me, I find myself able to be a creator. ... In the blind torrent of creative change I awaken, and I find you opening your eyes. As our eyes meet we realize that we can and must take charge together of a world in process.[14]

When Michael and Mina begin to care for the decrepit Skellig and when they protect the fledglings from danger, when Erin, January and Mouse meet the enigmatic Heaven Eyes, and when Kit takes responsibility for the emotional healing of John Askew, they enter into a process that combines evolutionary embodiment and the processes of history with a participatory theonomy, that is, the participation of people in God's divine purposes because this is the work we were created to do; we are each called to assist in the creative process of helping the world become what it was intended to be. In each of these stories, a dominant theme of redeeming individual brokenness through dynamic interrelatedness emerges; characters heal themselves through the process of reaching out to and healing others. In the process, they remake both their worlds and themselves.

My final disclaimer, then, has to do with process theology itself. Ultimately, I can make no truth claims for this particular world-view, and it is certainly not my intention to convert anyone to this way of thinking; it is but one among many vying for our attention as we seek to understand the relation between minds, bodies, and our experience of the numinous. As I have noted, process theology did not begin as a theology at all, but as an attempt to formulate an internally consistent philosophy that could account for evolutionary change and creative emergence in light of biological inheritance and the limitations of a mechanistic view of the universe. It has gained uptake among religious thinkers, but many traditional Christian theologians dismiss it as heretical. However, the defence of its consideration lies within process thinking itself, as it posits that a continual refreshment of consciousness through the introduction of and reflection on new ideas and relationships between people and the natural world is the natural state of individuals; it is what we are called to do by the lure of God. Process theology further describes how all things are dynamically interrelated, and asserts that God places in our hands the responsibility of re-creating the world that has created us. This in and of itself presents an appealing ethics of care for the environment and other people which we see enacted consistently by the characters in Almond's fictional worlds. Mina is perhaps Almond's best representation of a process thinker, protesting the very idea of seeing overdetermined ends in beginnings as her teacher, Mrs. Scullery, asks her to do. 'Do I plan a sentence before I speak it? OF COURSE I DO NOT! Does a bird plan its song before it sings? OF COURSE IT DOES NOT!' she says (*MNIM*, p. 13). In fact her entire journal reflects the basic methodology of process thought as outlined by Gray: first, that facts are useful limitations of reality but not definitive; second, that a careful consideration of relationships between humans as well as between non-human things, undergirded by careful observation and research, should be undertaken before any decision to act; and third, that the results of any action are bound to be unpredictable, which results in originality. As Mina charts and reflects on her activities and decisions, as she interacts with the natural and the human world, she reveals her fundamental nature to be that of open-ended process, ever responsive to the lure of her own becoming.

As a philosophy and a theology, process has a distinct, jargon-laden terminology that seeks to engage and correct philosophies that came before it. My explorations here have only scratched the surface, and my efforts to cut through some of the more technical aspects have certainly reduced their nuanced complexity, particularly as I have limited my discussion to those points relevant to Almond's evocative and multivalent work. But the basic tenets of the philosophy – creativity, interrelatedness, free will, responsiveness to the past, and the lure of the divine – find exquisite expression in Almond's books. Indeed, reading Almond's fiction through a process-relational theological framework has the persuasive power to transform storytelling magic into numinous possibility.

Notes

1. Don Latham, *David Almond: Memory and Magic* (Lanham, MD, Toronto and Oxford: Scarecrow Press, 2006).
2. Rudolf Otto, *The Idea of the Holy*, trans. John W. Harvey (Oxford: Oxford University Press, 1958).
3. Benedict M. Ashley, OP, *Theologies of the Body: Humanist and Christian* (Braintree, MA: Pope John Center, 1985), p. 3.
4. James R. Gray, *Modern Process Thought: A Brief Ideological History* (Lanham, MD: University Press of America, 1982), p. 231.
5. See Ashley, *Theologies of the Body*, p. 331.
6. Lewis S. Ford, *The Lure of God: A Biblical Background for Process Theism* (Minneapolis, MN: Fortress Press, 1978), http://www.religion-online .org/showbook.asp?title=2217 (accessed 31 August 2013), Ch. 1, para. 32.

7. Alfred North Whitehead, *Process and Reality* (New York: Harper & Row, 1957), p. 521.
8. William Hocking, *The Meaning of God in Human Experience* (New Haven, CT: Yale University Press, 1912), p. 140.
9. David R. Griffin, *A Process Christology* (Lanham, MD: University Press of America, 1990), p. 220; original emphasis.
10. Griffin, *Process Christology*, p. 218.
11. Whitehead, *Process and Reality*, pp. 520–1.
12. Ford, *Lure of God*, Ch. 4, para. 11; original emphasis.
13. Eulalio R. Baltazar, *The Dark Center: A Process Theology of Blackness* (New York: Paulist Press, 1973), p. 3.
14. Ashley, *Theologies of the Body*, pp. 4–5.

5

'A sense sublime': Religious Resonances in the Works of David Almond

Valerie Coghlan

Introduction: Almond's worlds

A lurking capacity for the extraordinary to nudge at the ordinary permeates David Almond's writing – something akin to Wordsworth's pantheistic 'sense sublime of something far more deeply interfused' resonates throughout much of his work. His books' metaphysical qualities suggest comparison with authors of adult magic realism, and Almond acknowledges the influences of Gabriel García Márquez and Italo Calvino on his writing,[1] which is characterised by a stylistic lyricism and frequently occurring allusions to some presence or force that transcends the everyday life of his characters. Romanticism, and in particular, the influence of William Blake, infuse his writing: '[i]n Almond's work, children meet angel-like birdmen and characters frequently discover an ability to shift shape into wild animal form, motifs which are markedly Blakean'.[2]

Despite this, his prose is plain and unadorned by any overt intention to do more than recount, often in first-person narratives, how matters unfold. Even when events that seem magical or supernatural happen, as they quite often do in Almond's texts, he has a knack of describing them as matter-of-fact occurrences, while avoiding a reductive note that would negate the lurking sense of the mysterious. When Ailsa Spink finds a seemingly dead fawn she 'just kept telling God to heal it', and next day when she wakes 'it had its eyes open and it was looking up at me' (*FE*, p. 102). This seemingly miraculous recovery is summed up by Ailsa in a manner typical of Almond's depiction of the intervention of the extraordinary into the ordinary world: '"You got to believe, don't you?" she said, "Or nowt'd ever happen"' (*FE*, p. 103).

The required leaps in suspension of disbelief often asked of readers of fiction are not always openly evident in Almond's work. He does not bring his characters, or his readers, into an alternative world: events stay rooted in very ordinary settings into which the fantastical intrudes with consequent disruption or distortion of the accepted norms. While their universe may tilt, his characters are frequently required to accommodate this within the quotidian life of home and school, friendship or enmity. His settings tend to be gritty; he appears to suggest that it is normal, even if unexpected, to find in a dirty garage a being that could be an angel (*Skellig*), or that a seemingly ordinary jackdaw might lead two children to find an abandoned baby (*Jackdaw Summer*). Sometimes, readers are left to decide for themselves whether certain things really did occur, or if they were the result of perceptions or misconceptions on the part of protagonists. Did Davie really see Clay, the golem-like creature fashioned from earth, walk about, or did Stephen hypnotise him into thinking it? (*C*, p. 271). Did Joe actually observe a tiger walking in the night or was it something arising out of his unconscious? (*SH*, p. 72–3), and the possibility that Ailsa was mistaken about the fawn is offered as an option: 'Yak said deer play possum sometimes. Daddy said we must've been mistook' (*FE*, p. 102). While his narrators and protagonists are not unreliable in the sense that they deliberately mislead readers, they constantly bring complexity and lack of certainty to events, leaving gaps destabilising the reader's perceptions of the unusual, and possibly supernatural, events which occur. Almond himself says that their realism is 'the primary thing about my books',[3] and that his characters are 'straightforward, ordinary people in ordinary places, but inside them are extraordinary things'.

Religion as influence

This melding of realism with the supernatural – the ordinary with the extraordinary – Almond suggests is a result of his upbringing as a Roman Catholic:

> Maybe that's something else to do with being brought up as a Catholic: you're taught to think about the other world, but you grow up in this one, and you realise there couldn't be anything better. So you find the miraculousness in reality.[4]

The Roman Catholic Church is particularly adept at incorporating the quotidian with the metaphysical. Many of its doctrines and traditions are also the bedrock of other Christian denominations, but, along with strong evangelical Protestantism, Catholicism demands an unwavering adherence as a means of salvation for the soul – something that is often difficult, even for those who try hard to do so, to shrug off. The Jesuit saying 'Give me the child until he is seven and I will give you the man' and the often quoted 'Once a Catholic, always a Catholic' are rooted in the Church's requirement for adherence to its principles in the formation of the young. Catholicism also feeds human imagination through a rich repository of Bible stories, and even more so, by means of ritual that is colourful and powerful, especially at saints' days and festivals. Many who have left the Roman Catholic Church still talk of the splendour of Corpus Christi and May Day processions, of the mystery of Passiontide and Easter ceremonies, of the austerity of Lenten fasting and of the mystical transformation embodied in the Eucharist – ceremonies and ritualistic obligations that feature in Almond's books. The Catholic Church, with its symbols and its rituals, were part of the everyday lives of Almond and his contemporaries in Felling, near Newcastle-upon-Tyne, where Almond grew up; its residue is found in the sense of possibilities, things that might occur by means of miracles and supernatural interventions, present throughout his writing. In the short story 'Loosa Fine' (*Counting Stars*), Almond's first-person narrator talks of an annual parish pilgrimage to Lourdes:

> To those like me who had never been, Lourdes seemed to be both out of the world and a simple extension of our parish, some warmer and brighter suburb of Tyneside. It was a place of miracles populated by people like ourselves and filled with familiar landmarks. (*CS*, p. 134)

Almond's literary Catholicism is firmly centred on working-class communities in north-east England, notably his home-town of Felling. *Counting Stars*, Almond's autobiographical short-story collection, shows the teenage David both accepting the Church's role in the life of his community while questioning its authority and gradually moving away from it. In the title story, David realises as he grows older that an elderly teacher in his school, Father O'Mahoney, by emphasising the sinfulness of counting stars as it questions what it is outside the power of mortals to know – 'It is a blasphemy for man to feign knowledge of what can be known only to God' – was attempting 'to stifle the liberating effects that education might have on our minds'. He was deliberately 'keeping his flock in a state of obeisance and fright before his worn-out religion' (*CS*, pp. 13–14).

Many of the themes, tropes and characters featured in Almond's children's novels are prefigured in *Counting Stars*. These are most evident when they challenge readers to consider how seemingly supernatural occurrences may perturb the accepted boundaries of normalcy within a society, even when that society adheres to the metaphysical manifestations inherent in their religious practices. The opening story, 'The Middle of the World', shows a family's religious faith intertwined with beliefs that are more elemental than those accepted by their church. David and his siblings visit the graves of their father and infant sister, Barbara (6), who, even though they are dead, are nevertheless assured of their places in the family as though they still lived. Mam, in the story 'Where Your Wings Were', slips her fingers beneath David's shoulder blades, telling him that '[t]his is where your wings were. You left them behind when you came here' (*CS*, p. 174). Barbara, in angelic form, visits David in a dream, leaving him with the assurance that one day he too will have his wings back. In *Skellig*, following the birth of his sister, Michael's Mum echoes this: '"shoulder blades are where your wings were, when you were an angel," she said. "They say they're where your wings will grow again one day"' (*S*, p. 36). Michael makes a connection between the mysterious winged man he and Mina found in the garage and his mother's story, and, makes a further connection as he holds his baby sister: 'I touched her skin and her tiny soft bones. I felt the place where her wings had been' but '[t]hen we went in the car to the hospital' (*S*, p. 37). The practicalities of life take over as Michael and his parents take the ailing baby back to hospital. Here, as in his subsequent novels, Almond leaves the reader the option of making further connections. Following an interview with Almond in which he talks about his religious upbringing, journalist Sarah Crown suggests that 'the ease with which Michael and Mina accept the wonder at the heart of their story has its roots in a religious upbringing that required him to accept and embrace the mystical'.[5]

The north of England, where David Almond grew up, has always been strong in its traditionalism and its loyalty to the Roman Catholic Church. Almond often refers in interviews to his Catholic upbringing and its influence on him; while he is no longer a practising Catholic, unlike many who reject the church of their childhood, he does not seem to hold any anger or resentment towards it:

> When you stop being a Catholic you have no religion to fall back on, but you do have a sense of possible transcendence. And it seems to me

that this is the transcendence. Heaven is here. The more I live, the more gorgeous and wonderful the world is, but it is also terrifying and constantly endangered.[6]

In interviews Almond is prepared to discuss the influence of religion in his own background, and religious practice and belief on the part of his characters are evident in a number of his books. This is unusual in Anglophone children's literature where anything to do with religion is only infrequently mentioned and, and even more rarely, features in any significant manner, especially in British writing. Critical comment also overlooks religious or spiritual subject matter, its presence or absence, in children's books. Peter Hunt is one of the few critics to focus on this, remarking that

> religion of all kinds has been virtually silenced in mainstream children's literature, and this has left both a philosophical and sociological void, perhaps uneasily filled by myth and fantasy. Secondly, religion has taken on strong negative connotations.[7]

It is hardly surprising that religion is rarely a topic in children's books when even a quick survey of the indexes of critical works on adult English literature shows few entries under 'religion' or 'spirituality' or any other related topics. For example, the latest edition of *The Oxford Companion to English Literature* (2009) contains no entries on these or related topics, although there are British writers for adults whose work has overtly religious references, or who grapple with spiritual themes without referring directly to religious practice. Like Almond, these authors are or were mostly Roman Catholic; for example Graham Greene, Muriel Spark, Evelyn Waugh and David Lodge.

Transcending boundaries

Hunt reasons that:

> the overwhelming majority of mainstream children's books in English moved from a religiously-driven, primarily Evangelical literature to a literature in which humanistic, non-redemptory values are celebrated. The books have also moved to a position in which religious activity is feared or not understood, or in which religion has become an empty cultural gesture. Ultimately they have moved us to the complex question of how fiction relates to faith and where the boundary between the two lies.[8]

The strictures of this boundary, but more interestingly its porosity, are very evident in Almond's writing. Almond is by no means a 'religious' writer, that is, someone who promulgates a particular belief-system, and in many instances his characters challenge their accepted faith as they mature or step outside its restrictions. Sometimes this is in a relatively minor way, or, at other times, this may be a major transgression of the boundaries, like Davie's theft of the Eucharistic elements, something that is a most grievous sin in Catholic eyes (*C*, pp. 140, 143).

Almond shows the normality of religious practice and belief as part of life for many in the communities he describes, but then goes on to probe where 'normality' might begin or end for his characters. The boundary between faith and fiction suggested by Hunt is evident in *Slog's Dad* (2010). Again, a young Davie is the narrator. The father of his friend Slog was a man given to singing hymns, including the Catholic favourite, 'Faith of Our Fathers'; so, on the principle of 'once a Catholic, always a Catholic' it would seem he died in the Catholic faith. When he appears to his grieving son after his death, does Slog really see him, or does Slog's intense grief make him imagine that a man sitting on bench is his dad? (*SD*, pp. 44–7). In common with earlier books by Almond it transmutes what is 'acceptably' supernatural into what is outside the bounds of 'normality'. Hunt contends that 'if readers believe in magic, they must believe in the occult, and the occult … is the obverse of the spiritual'.[9] Responding to the banning of books portraying magical events, Hunt argues that this is because their censors (especially those representing religious organisations) believe in the occult and cannot accept it as a device in works of fiction. Almond, has, in a sense, a foot in both camps, but does not come down on the side of realism, religion or magic. Instead, he locates his narratives in realistic, and in many cases real, settings – the north of England of his childhood – but then challenges the accepted parameters of realism. David Almond implies that magic, even if it is not the obverse of the spiritual as suggested by Hunt, is its travelling companion.

A loss of innocence

Most of Almond's protagonists come from loving homes, where, even if not overtly Catholic or religious, the traditional Catholic value of family at the core of society is central. While the protagonists in *Heaven Eyes* live in Whitegates, a children's home, they too desire a family. Erin, the narrator, and her friend January Carr, long for their mothers, Mouse for his father and Heaven Eyes, the child they find living in abandoned docklands with an old man, 'Grampa', wants

Erin to be her sister. Erin realises that Whitegates provides a surrogate family where 'most of us love each other and look out for each other' (*HE*, p. 5), and where, in doing so, 'we could find a tiny corner of the Paradise that we'd all lost' (*HE*, p. 5); this they sometimes remember in circle time when '[w]e were asked to try to imagine how things were for us before we were in Whitegates' (*HE*, pp. 5–6). Again the echoes of the Christian story of the Fall of Mankind are overt; in *Skellig* readers are left to make their own judgement on whether or not the strange being in the garage is a fallen angel, and in *Heaven Eyes* Paradise is lost, but regained, albeit not as an ideal, but through a new, more realistic understanding on the part of the Whitegates children.

In Almond's work the trajectory from innocence to experience is clearly delineated. As noted earlier, a number of commentators see this as gesturing towards William Blake's writing, and in particular to *Songs of Innocence and of Experience*.[10] Keith O'Sullivan contends that 'Blake's construction of childhood contains no real sense of nostalgia for the loss of innocence – even though the unavoidable movement towards experience sees the blissful naïveté of youth give way to the harsh realities of adult responsibility.'[11] Almond holds to the notion that innocence is not entirely shattered as experience is gained; there is, however, no sense of longing for past childhood innocence on the part of any of his protagonists. While Almond's characters possess a fundamental morality, they are not idealised as entirely innocent either; the process of gaining experience is ongoing, although Latham, discussing *Skellig*, suggests that the capacity 'to recognize the presence of angels in the world is usually lost in a move to adulthood'.[12]

Like Philip Pullman, Almond presents the Fall as a transitional state that keeps on recurring; Pullman, whose 'His Dark Materials' trilogy acknowledges Milton's version of the story of the Fall, comments on the universality of the experience and his own treatment of it:

> I try to present the idea that the Fall, like any myth, is not something that has happened once in a historical sense but happens again and again in all our lives. The Fall is something that happens to all of us when we move from childhood through adolescence to adulthood and I wanted to find a way of presenting it as something natural and good and to be welcomed … celebrated, rather than deplored.[13]

Growth and redemption

Almond also offers the view that while human nature is fallible, redemption is achievable – part of the bedrock of Catholic teaching – but redemption does not lead directly to Paradise. While Christian teaching is predicated on salvation by means of forgiveness of sin and ensuing redemption, Almond's characters are not 'saved' either literally or allegorically, but they are given hope that in future things will be better. January Carr, for example, is united with his mother, but the other children in *Heaven Eyes*, including Heaven Eyes herself, still live in Whitegates at the conclusion of the book. And, Almond here suggests, it is the power of story that offers hope: '[t]here are moments of great joy and magic. The most astounding things can lie waiting as each day dawns, as each page turns' (*HE*, p. 215).

Almond's characters still have a great deal of growing to do, suggesting that his texts fall within Roberta Seelinger Trites's framework of the *Entwicklungsroman*, novels of development, ending before the protagonists reach adulthood, rather than the more commonly used *Bildungsroman*.[14] They conform to Trites's definition of *Entwicklungsroman* as 'very self-consciously problematiz[ing] the relationship of the individual to the institutions that construct his or her subjectivity'.[15] Almond uses the Roman Catholic Church – an institution that demands a major role in the construction of subjectivity – as a formative influence on some of his characters, and severance from it as a marker in their maturation process. In all of Almond's books tropes which resonate with Christian, and especially Catholic, teaching are evident; in particular, time in the wilderness, sacrifice and redemption.

Wasteland and wilderness

Almond was introduced to the poetry of T.S. Eliot at school when a teacher read *The Waste Land* to his class. Almond 'was gobsmacked. I thought it was absolutely wonderful.'[16] While Eliot – who interrogated religious belief through his poetry – wrote *The Waste Land* in response to what was occurring in inter-war Britain, elements of its questioning, even if not of its nihilism, can be seen in Almond's novels. However, the properties of Almond's 'wastelands' or wildernesses are more akin to landscapes suggested by William Blake and William Wordsworth in their liminality and metaphysical attachments. They are places not usually frequented by adults, away from authority and where protagonists undergo a transformative experience, functioning, as John Stephens suggests, as a transitional space: 'The Waste Land of myth and legend is often a symbolic site in children's literature, functioning as a gateway for physical and emotional transitions.'[17]

The nature of the 'wilderness' experienced varies in Almond's novels, but always it is not only a state of mind, but also a very definite physical place; he mingles pantheistic resonances with allusions to Jesus Christ's time of temptation in the wilderness; it is a place of trial, literally a testing ground. It is often a liminal area in its physical location and in its function as a place where characters are mentally and emotionally on the threshold as they journey towards adulthood. The Bible emphasises the need for human souls to go through cathartic experiences so they may be worthy of regeneration, and frequently this happens in a place apart: prophets cry in the wilderness, the Israelites sojourn in the desert, and most notably, Jesus Christ spent forty days and forty nights undergoing and resisting temptation in the wilderness. Often, Almond employs such a 'wilderness time' to bring about growth in his characters, most of whom are on the cusp of adolescence, or are adolescents – protagonists tend to become a little older in some of his later books. Almond does not use time in the wilderness to develop his characters into fully-fledged adults, and nor do they always resist temptation. Boy characters in particular still have a lot of growing-up to do, but are better equipped to fulfil the roles they will later assume, thus positioning the novels within the model of the *Entwicklungsroman* proposed by Trites.

Counting Stars contextualises the young David's 'temptations' as a means of moving him into a space where he can gain a more mature perspective on family, place and faith. 'The Time Machine' shows him 'seduced' by the kiss of Corinna, a young woman who works in a funfair, into pretending that he has experienced time travel when he enters an attraction that purports to offer punters the chance to visit another era (*CS*, pp. 66–7). He falls in love with Theresa as he returns from kissing the cross on Good Friday in 'The Subtle Body' (*CS*, p. 88). Here, the move from innocence to sexual experience is nuanced, as characters break from the chrysalis of a caring but limiting society, where the sexually restrictive teachings of the Catholic Church are predominant, to an awareness of Tibetan religion which, in contrast, is seen as exotic and liberating. David's desire for Theresa is counterpointed by Catholic signifiers: a picture of Christ exposing his heart as David smells Theresa's body and feels the brush of her hand against his; they are overlooked by a statue of the Virgin Mary on the mantelpiece and plaster angels on the wall; they drink sherry that tastes like altar wine. But David has become interested in the teaching of a Tibetan monk, T. Lobsang Rampa, from which he learns of out-of-body experiences. As David and Theresa walk literally and metaphorically away from Felling into the hills above the town they leave behind its restrictions and those of the church of their upbringing, talking of 'the wideness of the world, the narrowness of our homes' (*CS*, p. 100), and, entangled together in the grass, they are not only physically moving away from their upbringing, but emotionally and spiritually too. The hills are metaphorically positioned as a liminal space between home and the wider world; they are a vicarious if not an actual wilderness and a place where David and Theresa feel liberated from the strictures of upbringing.

The garage in which Michael and Mina find the 'fallen angel', Skellig, is also a vicarious wilderness. Here 'wilderness' is characterised by the attributes of a literal wasteland; it is a place where rubbish has been dumped, but by association with Skellig, it becomes a magical space where the children are literally asked to make leaps of faith, to decide without adult intervention what they are going to do about Skellig, and to assume responsibility for looking after him. Instead of angels ministering as they did to Christ in the wilderness and to David in 'Where Your Wings Were' in *Counting Stars*, in *Skellig* it is the children who minister to an angelic being.

In *Kit's Wilderness*, Almond's second novel, the title signals the importance of wilderness, both as an actual piece of local wasteland where strange things occur, and as a signifier of Kit's emotional state. It is 'an empty space between the houses and the river, where the ancient pit had been' and where 'the game called Death' (*KW*, p. 5) is enacted by a group of children led by John Askew, a troubled boy with a difficult home life. A little later this ground is portrayed in a more benign light as 'the wide space of beaten grass where dozens of children played' (*KW*, p. 9), but it functions metaphorically as well as literally by pointing up the anguish of John Askew's parents: Askew's father 'howled into the empty wilderness' for his missing son following Askew's disappearance (*KW*, p. 139), and his despairing mother walks with her baby 'aimlessly through the frozen wilderness' (*KW*, p. 157). In *Kit's Wilderness*, *Clay* and *Jackdaw Summer* the attraction for a teenage boy of an untamed space, away from adult intervention, is evident. In each novel something transcendent takes place – more overtly in the first two books – that results in the protagonists moving towards greater maturity, and, it is implied, they are redeemed from transgressions which they may have committed or been about to commit.

Magic spaces

Secret Heart is the most metaphysical of Almond's books; here the blurring between reality and magic is constant. The space traversed by Joe Maloney as he escapes from school, from a gang of bullies and from worries about his mother is a dystopian wasteland. Joe, who is an outsider with his peers and who possesses visionary abilities, lives in the aptly named Helmouth, 'a place at the city's edge before the wasteland started' (*SH*, p. 13). The wilderness is beyond all this, separated from town and wasteland by the ultimate symbol of modern life, the motorway. This wilderness is a testing ground; Joe resists temptation when his friend Stanny Mole tries to persuade Joe to accompany him and the older, devilish Joff:

> 'We'll walk all day,' Stanny said. 'Way past this. We'll walk to where it's wild, really, really wild. We'll have our combats on. Knives and catapults and snares in our pockets. We'll kill something for lunch. We'll strip a tree to make the shelter. Joff'll drink and talk about his army days and we'll listen to the night. There's nowt like it, Joe.' (*SH*, p. 15)

But no matter how much Stanny and Joff try to persuade him to go with them 'out into those places of wildness and vision and dream' (*SH*, p. 68), Joe resists, knowing that

> if he ever did go there, it must be with someone who saw what he saw and felt what he felt, someone who was a true partner, a true friend. Someone who understood what it meant to move from Helmouth towards the furthest fringes of the world, towards the furthest fringes of the mind. (*SH*, p. 68)

Instead the bleaker wasteland offers transformation for Joe; he knows 'how the lives of people and the lives of beasts could merge out here in the wasteland. He knew what it was to be Joe Maloney but also more than Joe Maloney' (*SH*, p. 65). The edge of the wasteland is the site for a travelling circus that opens up another world to Joe when it comes to Helmouth – this is a world that has the possibility for the merging that he desires. But the arrival of Hackenschmidt's Circus takes Joe beyond the wasteland; with Corinna Finch, a circus girl, Joe finds someone who can indeed see what he sees and feel what he feels, and with Corinna he enters the wilderness, both literally and spiritually, guided by the subliminal tiger that lurks at the edge of his consciousness and with which he identifies – his secret heart. In the wilderness they find the body of a decapitated panther, and Joe knows that '[t]his could have been his own work, if he had come out here carrying knives and hatchets with Stanny Mole and Joff' (*SH*, p. 159). He and Corinna instead have visions, which clearly signify Blake's poem, 'The Tyger', as they watch to see if the prowling tiger will actually kill Stanny and Joff in reparation for the death of the panther:

The tiger prowled, prowled, its great tail held out behind, its head held high. … It was always there now, always in view, as if it became more certain of itself, grew more confidently into its new life. … Animals stepped out from the forest, half-seen, half-understood things, things half in and half out of the deep darkness; beasts with four legs but with heads that seemed human; beasts that stood erect but with broad horns growing from them. (*SH*, p. 161)

The tiger, although conjured from Joe's subconscious where 'memory of tiger was running through his blood' (*SH*, p. 73), seems vivid and corporeal as it stalks around the sleeping figures. Stanny, who, it is implied, still has the innocence required to see the mystical tiger,[18] is terrified by its threat when he wakes (*SH*, p. 163).

Sacred and profane sacrifices

Scenes of near-death in the context of blood-sacrifice as reparation for evil committed occur in several of Almond's novels. In *Kit's Wilderness* the troubled Askew dreams of violently killing his abusive father (*KW*, p. 191), in *Clay* Stephen threatens the bully, Martin Mould, at knifepoint (*C*, p. 79) and in *Jackdaw Summer* the bully Nattrass is held at knifepoint by Oliver before Liam actually stabs him (*JS*, pp. 198–205). In these scenes death is averted, although Stephen subsequently kills Mould; each incident happens in a place apart, a wilderness that is real but is given mythical resonance by events enacted there.

These are violent, Old Testament-like moments, but the New Testament notion of vicarious sacrifice occurs in several of Almond's novels, most obviously in *The Fire-Eaters* and *Secret Heart*. While there are many themes and religious resonances in *The Fire-Eaters*, set in 1962 at the time of the Cuban missile crisis, sacrifice and redemption are the most central. Bobby is on the cusp of adolescence, moving beyond his close-knit world of Keely Bay to the Sacred Heart secondary school. Latham comments on Bobby Burns's 'sacrificial nature' (*FE*, p. 102), remarking on his willingness to sacrifice himself to restore good health to his ailing father, and on the fire-eater McNulty's 'symbolic act of self-sacrifice in breathing in the fire that is threatening to engulf the world' (*FE*, p. 102). But Bobby also offers himself as a sacrifice for the impending disaster:

As we walked, sometimes Ailsa and I murmured our prayers together. We wished and wished: *Don't let it happen. Keep us safe.* Sometimes when

I reeled and slipped and lost connection with the world around, I thought
it must be the beginning of my death. I thought this might be how it
felt when my own prayers began to work, when I was taken as sacrifice.
(*FE*, p. 228)

In *Secret Heart*, during Joe's visits to the ruined Blessed Chapel, he
offers prayers for his mother and drops a five-pence coin through a
slot in its old stones. Later he meets Corinna, from Hackenschmidt's
Circus, whose name is the same as that of the older girl David meets in
the 'The Time-Machine' *(Counting Stars)*, suggesting perhaps that she
is a younger version of the overtly sexualised Corinna from the funfair. Both invite the young male protagonist to enter a world hinged
between reality and fantasy, and both are aware of the vulnerabilities
of the boys concerned. Corinna brings Joe to Nanty Solo, a blind old
woman, who has paranormal powers. Nanty Solo recognises in Joe 'the
taste of something old and animal' (*SH*, p. 88), and urges him to pick
something from her box of relics: '[b]its of a world that was here before
and that's here still for them that knows how to see' (*SH*, p. 88). What
Joe picks is identified by Nanty as the bone of a tiger. She presses a
fragment of it onto the tip of his tongue, while instructing him to swal-
low, and whispering 'Amen' (*SH*, p. 91). Later, when, terrified, Stanny
Mole has fled from the wilderness and Joff, the devilish tempter, Nanty
Solo invites him to eat the tooth of a unicorn, resting it on his tongue
as a priest would rest a wafer at a Holy Communion. This confirms his
redemption and acceptance again by Joe. The Eucharistic allusions are
obvious, but Nanty's Communion is pagan, and, although the story she
tells Joe about 'the first of all nights' (*SH*, p. 93) has a biblical resonance,
'[i]n the beginning' (*SH*, p. 92), it is contextualised in terms of the
demise of Hackenschmidt's Circus. Now the circus is about to close,
it is the last days, Friday, Saturday and Sunday; Almond underlines the
Easter allusions with an apocalyptic sense of finality, of a world ceasing
to exist, with the ending of the circus. The circus tent symbolises the
world as Nanty talks about the old days 'when the [tent] canvas was
so new that it blocked out all the light', but, she explains, the canvas
will become worn and wind will rip it, and 'there will be nothing but
emptiness above the place, just as there was all that time back, the time
there was no tent at all' (*SH*, p. 187). Then Almond turns Nanty's hier-
atic utterances to wry laughter, before shifting again to a language that
melds the spiritual with the worldly as Corinna and Joe leap from the
high-wire platform 'into the empty air, through memories and dreams,
through other worlds and other lives, and the net sighed as it caught
them in this world, in this life and kept them safe' (*SH*, p. 188).

Ritual and redemption

The clash, as well as the intertwining of pagan and Christian elements, is clearly enunciated in *Clay* (2005). *Secret Heart* may be the novel that most directly gestures towards quasi-religious rituals and mysteries but there is no mention of formal religious practice; however, the setting and plot of *Clay* intersect with Catholic ritual and belief throughout. *Clay* is set in Felling, and the old priest who acts as a wise counsellor to Davie in *Clay* is Father O'Mahoney, who is presented as a clone of the priest in *Counting Stars*. The strange occurrences following Stephen's arrival are all the more enigmatic because they take place within a close Catholic community: they are framed in the context of traditional Catholicism. Mysterious things happen, or appear to happen when Clay, fashioned golem-like from earth, gains life. The Eucharistic elements of bread and wine, stolen by Davie, are the impetus for this, a travesty of the belief that these elements give new spiritual life to participants in a Mass. Davie is an altar boy, but is beginning to reject the religion of his family, signalled in the opening paragraphs where he pokes free a piece of communion wafer stuck to his teeth while sharing cigarettes and stolen altar wine with his friend, Geordie, after they have helped to serve Mass (*C*, p. 1). Stephen, an older boy who has recently left a seminary under mysterious circumstances, is the catalyst for Davie's actual move from a state of comparative innocence to transgressing in a manner that he could not have even dreamt of before Stephen's arrival. Stephen comes from a troubled home; in the seminary he learned arcane skills that led to his expulsion; he is determined to do deeds that Davie and his mate Geordie only joke about. He kills bullying Martin Mould while Davie and Geordie only fantasise about this without any intention of doing so, joking that '[y]ou'd go straight to Heaven for getting rid of a thing like Mouldy' (*C*, p. 4). Almond creates a tension between good and evil, but neither is clear-cut. Davie is no saint, he too kills, but it is a dog, and Stephen possesses a creative energy, which Falconer suggests is 'essentially positive and life-giving until it is fettered or shut off, at which point it distorts and darkens into something suppressed or exorcised as evil'.[19] She continues by suggesting that 'Stephen believes that modern day religious practices derive from more powerful and ancient shamanistic rituals.'[20]

Crazy Mary is Stephen's 'distant aunt' with whom he lives when he comes to Felling. At the conclusion of *Clay*, Davie again performs the role of an altar boy when he gives Crazy Mary the wine-stained cloth and fragment of bread he stole to put life into Clay, but he does not go to confession and Mass to ask for forgiveness as a good Catholic might.

The implication is that such actions are now both behind him and beyond him. The ending is open, and the outcome of Davie's experience is uncertain. Almond has remarked that '[s]tory is a kind of redemption',[21] so it is no surprise that Davie finds peace and possible redemption in telling his story (*C*, p. 296), and Kit (*Kit's Wilderness*), Erin (*Heaven Eyes*) and Bobby (*The Fire-Eaters*) also achieve catharsis through story.

'A sense sublime'

That 'Almond and Pullman invite their readers to challenge orthodox Christian morality' is suggested by Falconer,[22] who maintains that Almond offers 'ways of bridging the increasing divide between secular and faith communities, in their exploration of the psyche's fundamental spiritual instincts'.[23] On Almond's part, this desire to explore has led to him pushing through the boundaries of his traditional Roman Catholic upbringing, while maintaining a strongly spiritual element in his work. His writing is grounded in humanistic values, but extends beyond these in many of his books to incorporate a spiritual dimension, generally giving readers the option of interpreting this as they choose, but leaving them with a sense that his work embodies something akin to Wordsworth's ontological invocation of 'a motion and a spirit, that impels / all thinking things, all objects of all thought, / And rolls through all things'.[24]

David Almond's writing is characterised by a generosity and openness to different manifestations of traditionally religious, pagan, mythical and humanist thinking. There is a wordless state that resonates with something beyond the knowable, at times ineffable, that inhabits many of Almond's books. It is a 'sense sublime' that lingers in readers' imaginations at the conclusion of his novels, just as he leaves readers with the more literal impression of Joe and Corinna as *Secret Heart* concludes, when '[t]hey walked on, leaving their images to stroll for years in the children's minds' (*SH*, p. 123).

Notes

1. Don Latham, *David Almond: Memory and Magic* (Lanham, MD, Toronto and Oxford: Scarecrow Press, 2006), p. 6 and *passim*; Rachel Falconer, *The Crossover Novel: Contemporary Children's Fiction and Its Adult Readership* (New York and London: Routledge, 2009), p. 137; Nolan Dalrymple, 'Navigating Borderlands of Fiction, Magic and Childhood: Finding David Almond', *Bookbird – A Journal of International Children's Literature* 48(4) (2010), 1–4.

2. Dalrymple, 'Navigating Borderlands of Fiction', p. 2.

3. Jennifer M. Brown [Interview], 'David Almond and the Art of Transformation', *Shelf-awareness*, 13 May 2010, http://www.shelf-awareness.com/issue.html?issue=1185#m9201 (accessed 31 March 2014).

4. Sarah Crown, 'A Life in Writing: David Almond', *Guardian*, 21 August 2010, http://www.theguardian.com/culture/2010/aug/21/david-almond-skellig-writing-books (accessed 31 March 2014).

5. Crown, 'A Life in Writing'.

6. Nicolette Jones, 'David Almond: Story is a Kind of Redemption', *Daily Telegraph*, 25 October 2008, http://www.telegraph.co.uk/culture/books/3562549/David-AlmondStory-is-a-kind-of-redemption.html (accessed 31 March 2014).

7. Hunt, Peter, 'The Loss of the Father and the Loss of God in English-language Children's Literature (1800–2000)', in Jan De Maeyer *et al.* (eds), *Religion, Children's Literature and Modernity in Western Europe 1750–2000* (Leuven: Leuven University Press, 2005), pp. 295–303.

8. Hunt, 'The Loss of the Father', p. 295.

9. Hunt, 'The Loss of the Father', p. 303.

10. Latham, *David Almond*; Falconer, *Crossover Novel*; Dalrymple, 'Navigating Borderlands of Fiction'.

11. Keith O'Sullivan, 'Binding with Briars', in Valerie Coghlan and Keith O'Sullivan (eds), *Irish Children's Literature and Culture: New Perspectives on Contemporary Writing* (New York and London: Routledge, 2011), pp. 99–113, p. 100.

12. Latham, *David Almond*, p. 40.

13. Robyn Butler (Chair of debate), 'Question of Faith. Phillip Pullman debates religion with the Archbishop of Canterbury, Dr Rowan Williams', *Daily Telegraph* (17 March 2004), http://www.telegraph.co.uk/culture/3613962/The-Dark-Materials-debate-life-God-the-universe....html (accessed 31 March 2014).

14. Roberta Seelinger Trites, *Disturbing the Universe: Power and Repression in Adolescent Literature* (Iowa City: University of Iowa Press, 2000), p. 18.

15. Trites, *Disturbing the Universe*, p. 20.

16. Jones, 'David Almond'.

17. John Stephens, *Language and Ideology in Children's Fiction: Language in Social Life* (London and New York: Longman, 1992), p. 174.

18. Latham, *David Almond*, p. 89.

19. Falconer, *Crossover Novel*, p. 146.

20. Falconer, *Crossover Novel*, p. 147.

21. Jones, 'David Almond'.

22. Falconer, *Crossover Novel*, p. 28.

23. Falconer, *Crossover Novel*, p. 188.

24. William Wordsworth, 'Lines Composed a Few Miles above Tintern Abbey', in *Lyrical Ballads* [1798], http://www.poetryfoundation.org/poem/174796 (accessed 31 March 2014).

6

Birdmen from the Depths of the Earth: Radical Landscape in the Fiction of David Almond

Nolan Dalrymple

> One of the things I remember about growing up in Felling was that it really was right on the edge of the urban and the rural landscape. The rural landscape was quite a rough rural landscape, it was damaged by coal mining, it was scarred by industry. It wasn't Gloucestershire. ... So it was definitely about that semi-urban, semi-rural thing. ... I find it incredibly touching, that blend of the rural and the urban.[1]

David Almond's treatment of these conflicting elements is radical in two key ways: first, he subverts and recasts dominant images of the north-east of England, the setting of all of his fiction;[2] furthermore, the landscape encountered by his child characters reveals itself to be fundamentally different from their expectations and its apparent nature. In Almond's North-East, children discover repeatedly a marriage of rural wildness and urban civilisation, undercutting those images which have come to typify landscape of the region; this radical vision is perhaps most evocatively presented in Almond's wildernesses and wastelands.

Urban settings almost invariably contain areas of untamed wilderness, alongside spaces of wasteland: the legacy of industrial decline. Frequently, such wastelands function like a portal for Almond's child characters, ushering them forth into the unspoilt wilderness beyond. Natural spaces, such as his grandfather's allotment, are central to Almond's imaginative reworking of his own childhood memories, and he writes of the 'freedom in walking away from the centre, in climbing closer to the lark-filled sky'.[3] Furthermore, Almond describes the act of writing itself as a desire to 'explore the gardens of the mind, crawl through wilderness, emerge with scratched skin and muddied knees'.[4] The metaphors he employs here draw upon typically Romantic imagery associating creativity with the natural landscape and other wild spaces. Just such a space is found in *Skellig*, in the garden which adjoins Michael's family's new house. This wild space, in the heart of urban Tyneside, becomes a kind of haven for the young boy, as troubling events unfold around him.

Early in the novel, Michael resents the garden, as he resents almost everything related to a move he associates with the arrival of the new baby and the attendant shift in his role within the family. The novel is focalised through Michael who describes, with his new friend, Mina, going 'back to the wilderness we called a garden and she [his mother] went back to the flaming baby' (*S*, p. 4). The garden is 'another place that was supposed to be wonderful', but in fact comprises 'just nettles and thistles and weeds and half-bricks and lumps of stone' (*S*, p .5). However, once he has discovered the mystical figure of Skellig, also closely allied to the natural world, Michael begins to seek refuge in the wilderness of the garden. He and Mina visit the owls that inhabit the decaying shell of Mina's grandfather's house, then run 'through the lanes to our wilderness' (*S*, p. 41). In an effort to distract Michael from worries about the health of his baby sister, Michael's father sets him to working on 'getting some of that jungle cleared', cautioning him to 'watch out for the tigers' (*S*, p. 43). After Michael has introduced Mina to Skellig, the two children stand in 'the wilderness' and contemplate his extraordinary nature; later, after a bitter argument with Mina, Michael heads 'straight through into the wilderness' where he squats and tries to hold back his tears (*S*, pp. 76, 103).

The wild landscape of the garden plays an important part in Michael's growing affiliation with the wildness of Skellig, and his desire to share the creature's 'oblivious heart' (*S*, p. 132). Although ultimately the wilderness of the garden is tamed, for a time it provides a necessary space where Michael can face some metaphorical tigers, and lose himself in the natural world. Almond's gardens, here and in *Clay* (2005), depart from typical images of the region which tend to portray a binary opposition of wild and civilised aspects of the region's landscape; instead they epitomise his celebration of wilderness as lying at the heart of the North-East, and at the heart of both childhood and children's fiction.[5]

Almond's second children's novel, *Kit's Wilderness* (1999), also features a wild space at the centre of the children's world, as suggested by the novel's title. Its significance is foregrounded from the opening of the first chapter:

> In Stoneygate there was a wilderness. It was an empty space between the houses and the river, where the ancient pit had been. That's where we played Askew's game, the game called Death. (*KW*, p. 5)

Again, this is no pre-industrial arcadia, but rather a wilderness which has reclaimed a formerly industrial site. This emphatic, declarative opening sentence, finely honed by Almond during the writing process, clearly places the wilderness at the centre of Kit's world; combined with the novel's title, it suggests an affiliation with the wild landscape.[6] Key events of transformation for the children of Stoneygate occur in the wilderness. After Askew's game of Death, the group 'strolled back together through the wilderness with the dead one in our midst'; it is also 'alone at the edge of the wilderness' that Askew first attempts to recruit Kit into his inner circle, and following the meeting, though full of trepidation, Kit 'dreamed I followed him through the night across the wilderness' (*KW*, pp. 8–9, 13). Later, after Askew has been expelled from school for leading others into his dangerous games, Kit is warned by the headmaster not to 'follow him into the wilderness' (*KW*, p. 77). This, however, is exactly what Kit must do in order to connect with his grandfather and his heritage.

For the children of the town, life in Stoneygate is lived in close proximity to the natural landscape. Kit's family home is located 'at Stoneygate's edge, one of a long line that faced the wilderness and the river', and the local girl who becomes his closest friend, Allie Keenan, lives 'behind us in one of the houses by the green at Stoneygate's heart' (*KW*, pp. 17, 27). When Kit's grandfather takes him to see the house where Askew lives, 'towards the fringes of Stoneygate', the confluence of the urban and rural landscapes within Stoneygate is made even more clear (*KW*, p. 23).

> Grandpa cast his eyes across the steepening landscape, pointed to where the disappeared pits once were.
> 'Now it's proper countryside again,' he said. 'A great place for you to live and grow. Great place for young life to flourish.'
> And he closed his eyes and smiled and listened to the larks, dark tiny specks that belted out their songs from high up in the sky.
> The Askews lived in the final street, a potholed cul-de-sac of old pit cottages before the hills started. (*KW*, pp. 23–4)

I explore Almond's treatment of the post-industrial landscape in more detail in due course; here it is important to note that the natural wilderness so central to Stoneygate is located in the midst of, rather than simply adjacent to, the urban and industrial landscape, unlike, say, the landscape of fellow north-east author Robert Westall's *Falling into Glory* (1993).[7]

For Kit, like Michael in *Skellig*, the wilderness provides refuge and solace. As he discusses the game of Death with Allie and loses patience with her frivolity, he feels tears running from his eyes as he proclaims that '[p]eople *do* die', and hears how 'the words were carried away across the wilderness on the breeze' (*KW*, pp. 40–1). It also provides an unlikely solace for Askew's violent father, who Kit hears 'howling across the wilderness' (*KW*, p. 188). The wilderness at the heart of the novel is a primal place, seeming almost prehistoric later in the book where Kit describes an evening scene where '[a]ll across the wilderness the fires glowed and hunched figures leaned towards them' (*KW*, p. 101). It is also deep within this wilderness that Kit encounters the physical manifestation of Lak's mother, a member of the Neanderthal family featured in the story he writes for school. Importantly, however, this figure emerges within the drift mine, which reminds the reader of the powerful intersection of the industrial within the natural landscape. Though ancient, the wilderness is not pre-industrial, suggesting both the eternal presence of industry within the region, and also the propensity of the wild North-East to reconcile both modern and ancient influences in the wake of post-industrialisation.

Refuge and escape

In *Heaven Eyes* (2000), the two children, Erin Law and January Carr, dream of escaping their derelict, urban neighbourhood to live within the natural landscape. Early in the novel, Erin describes one of the pair's numerous attempts at running away from Whitegates, the children's hostel where they live, into the nearby moors:

> Another time we wandered right up the riverbank towards the moors and slept on the heather beneath the glittering sky. We saw shooting stars and talked about the universe going on for ever and ever. We talked about wandering for years like this, two vagabonds, free as the beasts and birds, keeping away from the city, drinking from streams, feeding on rabbits and berries. (*HE*, pp. 10–11)

Much of the novel concerns a further attempt by the children, along with a third companion, to escape again from the oppressive

Whitegates, 'a three-storyed place with a garden laid to concrete and a metal fence around it', and the urban dereliction surrounding them, but the place into which they escape and seek refuge is itself a product of industrial decay (*HE*, p. 4). As they leave, they move 'into the waste ground … where all the warehouses and terraced streets had been knocked down' and 'over great piles of rubble, all that was left of the warehouses and workplaces', before embarking downriver in search of the freedom of the sea; however, they end up landing on the mud of the Black Middens in a landscape of 'teetering warehouses, collapsed, walls, dark alleyways' (*HE*, pp. 29–32, 55). Though offering some temporary respite to the children, this place, inhabited by the mystical girl, Heaven Eyes, and her threatening Grampa, also contains dangers resulting from its industrial heritage. Heaven Eyes warns of 'places to tumble out the world and not get found again', and Erin herself is almost lost amongst 'the dilapidated quays, the broken buildings, the ruins of the past' (*HE*, pp. 89, 97). She looks back over the journey that has brought them here.

> I remembered walking down to the raft again for the first time with January when we felt so light and free. We spun out on to the river and hugged each other. Freedom. Freedom. A new beginning. So how had we come so quickly to this dark dilapidated dangerous place? (*HE*, p. 98)

Eventually, the group returns to Whitegates, 'uphill, away from the river through the wasteland', only to discover that their odyssey has in fact occurred within sight of the home (*HE*, p. 181).

In this episode, the existence of the marvellous and surprising within the everyday landscape serves to transform the children's perspectives on their ordinary world, and to inspire them to reassess the value of their urban north-east home. Erin comes to see that 'the most marvellous things could be found … a river's-width away' and '[t]he most extraordinary things existed in our ordinary world and just waited for us to find them' (*HE*, p. 181). Importantly, such extraordinary things are to be found within the urban landscape. In her study of fear in Almond's fiction Geraldine Brennan points to the appropriateness of this landscape for the writer of adolescent fiction, noting how '[c]hildren on the brink of puberty play among remnants of the past in wastelands which are poised between one useful life and, perhaps, another as yet unspecified'.[8]

Towards the novel's close, January and Erin head to 'the waste land', and look across to the city's 'brick and steel and stone' with its 'scents of petrol, seaweed, sea, fish, rot, flowers, dust' (*HE*, p. 207). Although they still dream of escaping into the natural landscape of the moors, of 'striding through bracken, skipping over little streams, lying beneath the sun on soft green turf, surrounded by the calls of curlews and the scent of peat', they also come to a realisation of the value of their urban lives (*HE*, p. 208).

> 'Might be awful,' I said. 'But I love it just the same.'
> 'Love what?'
> 'Being alive, being me, in this world, here and now.'
> He grinned.
> 'It's bloody great, eh?' he said. 'Bloody great.'
>   We stood up and wandered across the waste land towards the estate. (*HE*, pp. 208–9)

The boundary between urban and rural landscapes also features prominently in *Secret Heart* (2001), a novel in which numerous settings emphasise the intersection of the two. Joe, the novel's young protagonist, lives in Helmouth, a place with more than merely a name in common with images of desolation:

> Helmouth. It was called a village, but was just a place at the city's edge, before the wasteland started. A mess of new houses and old houses and cracked pavements and roads. … They kept saying there'd be great things coming – a swimming-pool, a leisure centre, a shopping centre, a new estate. But it was like Helmouth had been left behind, like it had been forgotten about. … In Helmouth, everything just came to nothing. (*SH*, p. 13)

The landscape of Helmouth and its environs is an archetypal Almond space; the village is a marginal place, on the fringes of the industrial city, and is bordered by an area of wasteland which adjoins a place of wilderness beyond. It is the wasteland and wilderness which attract Joe, first through the appearance of a circus which sets up its tent on the waste ground, and later by the experiences which lead him into the wild places beyond. Like the children in *Heaven Eyes*, Joe clambers 'through the ruins of old terraced houses' (*SH*, p. 44). Importantly, both the wasteland and wilderness are located within sight of 'the motorway where the traffic droned in a haze of fumes and sunlight' (*SH*, p. 14). These two landscapes, urban and rural, exist in a symbiotic relationship. The circus brings a force of nature in the form of a tiger into this derelict industrial space, in order that those who live there may remember their relationship with the wild and natural landscape. It is an act that seeks to enrich the urban world.

The 'wise woman' Nanty Solo speaks of this to Joe, describing how, '[i]n the beginning ... the tent was raised in a green field outside a great city ... . And people left the city and walked out into the green field' (*SH*, pp. 92–3). Later, she relates it specifically to Joe and Helmouth:

> 'We brought the tiger out, Joe Maloney. We carried it out of the dark-ness into the light. We carried it across the earth. .... We brought it to the open spaces beside great cities, to tiny villages beyond high hills, we brought it to places like Helmouth. And how they rushed to see this wonder! ...'
>
> 'Don't worry,' she whispered. 'Yours is the bravest soul of all. The tiger has chosen you to carry it out of the glowing blue tent and into the for-est again.' (*SH*, p. 148–9)

Although it does carry Joe into the forest again, and he is able there to commune with the natural world and become, for a time, a wild part of a wild place, the tiger's significance lies in the way that it remains within him, as part of his secret heart, on his return home.

The wilderness in this novel is always linked to the urban. When Joe and the circus girl Corinna hear the scream of the slaughtered panther, they notice how the sound 'echoed across the slopes, across the motorway, across the ruined fringes of Helmouth ... echoed into their hearts and beyond their hearts' (*SH*, p. 141). This wilderness also attracts Joe's friend, Stanny, and the older man Joff. At the start of the novel, Stanny tries to persuade Joe to join them on an expedition into the wilderness that lies beyond the boundary of the motorway.

> 'We'll walk all day,' Stanny said. 'Way past all this. We'll walk to where it's wild, really really wild. We'll have our combats on. Knives and catapults and snares in our pockets. We'll kill something for lunch. We'll strip a tree to make the shelter. We'll light a fire. Joff'll drink and talk about his army days and we'll listen to the night. There's nowt like it, Joe.' (*SH*, p. 15)

This planned pilgrimage into the wild landscape really constitutes an act of aggression against the natural world, culminating in the bru-tal slaughter of the wild panther by Joff. It is pure 'boy's own adven-ture' material, in contrast with Joe's engagement with the wild which sees him become at one with the spirit of the tiger and the natural landscape of 'ancient scorching grasslands and ancient forests' which it carries 'deep into the heart of this English wood' (*SH*, p. 156). In this novel, as elsewhere in Almond's fiction, north-east children develop very close affiliations with wild animals and birds; indeed Joe transforms into the tiger at points. Such intense anthropomorphism features as a common trope in twentieth-century British children's literature, and is not unique to either Almond's work or north-east fiction more generally.[9] What is distinctive here, however, is the way that children in Almond's North-East always develop a deep sense of the wildness within them in order to shed new light on the landscapes in which they live.

Wild things emerge from the heart of the urban landscape in *Clay*, too. Braddock's Garden is the central location in the novel, the place where Davie and his friends congregate and also the site of Stephen Rose's mystical ceremonies involving the creature, Clay. The garden is a wild place, in the midst of the industrial landscape of Felling. Stephen Rose is closely associated with the wild from the outset, as his grandfather Rocky is rumoured to have 'ended up living in a tent in Plessey Woods, all horrible and hairy and running away if anybody come near' (*C*, p. 20). A similar fate is imagined by Davie for Stephen himself, whom he imagines 'hiding out, practising his arts in Plessey Woods, or in Kielder Forest or the Cheviots, or in some distant empty wild place that has no name' (*C*, p. 293). Stephen associates himself with a primal, mystical tradition, linked to the wild landscape:

> 'Saints used to live in caves like this,' he said. 'In the desert. In the wilderness. They tested themselves.'
> …
> 'At Bennett [seminary school],' he said, 'a priest once said that mebbe I was more suited to the wilderness than to the civilised world.'
> 'Felling's the right place for you, then,' said Geordie. (*C*, p. 53)

Although Geordie's comment is jovial, it contains a truth about the wilderness at the heart of Almond's fictionalised Felling. This space, Braddock's Garden, is important to the adolescents in the novel, particularly Davie. Yet again Almond uses the wild setting to provide a place of refuge, and Davie's girlfriend Maria bemoans the proposed redevelopment of the area in order to build a new housing estate, which will destroy 'a bit of Paradise' (*C*, p. 112). Typically, Braddock's Garden is no unspoiled wilderness, but an overgrown quarry. In this novel again, the natural landscape exists side by side with the urban. The creature Clay is himself constituted of earth and various plant materials, and he comes to symbolise the wilderness itself given life to walk out into the town. As Rachel Falconer notes, central to the novel is the fact that the boys' creation, Clay, is 'a natural monster … rather than sewn from corpses or animated by electricity'.[10]

Before we finish the man's chest Stephen presses a wizened rose hip
there to make a heart. ... We put a conker inside the skull for a brain. ...
Sycamore seeds make eyes, ash keys make the ears, dried-out hawthorn
berries make nostrils, twigs and grass stems make his hair.
  'We plant him like a garden,' Stephen says. (*C*, p. 176)

Just as the wilderness of Braddock's Garden has reclaimed the former industrial site of the quarry, so too this walking embodiment of
the natural landscape is in turn subsumed within Davie's father's town
garden as he is slowly 'washed into the sandy border, and earth returns
to earth' (*C*, p. 293). There is a cyclical unity in this, which reaffirms
the interdependence of the rural and the urban within the landscape
of Almond's fictionalised North-East.

Savage spaces

The wild landscape also comes to life and walks through the town
in Almond's later work, *The Savage* (2008), a collaboration with artist
Dave McKean. This remarkable text, a blend of prose and graphic
novel forms, tells the story of Blue Baker, a young boy struggling to
come to terms with both his father's sudden death and the bullying
he is experiencing at school. He finds the act of writing therapeutic, and produces the story of 'The Savage', which tells the tale of a
wild boy living in the woods near his home-town. In magic-realist
style, the boundary between the two stories of Blue and the savage
begins to blur, confounding the reader's expectations. It seems that
Blue's writing is able to call the savage into the real world, where he
intervenes on Blue's behalf with the bully Hopper, and visits Blue's
home. The book is rich in interpretative possibilities for both reader
and critic, inviting questions about the power of storytelling, and
suggesting a psychoanalytical reading of the savage's function for the
character of Blue. Through the figure of the savage, Blue is able to
regress into a wild state, and vicariously confront both internal and
external conflicts.
  Although the savage is associated with the wilderness of Burgess
Woods, his existence is sustained by forays into the urban landscape.
In his characteristically unconventional spelling, Blue describes how
'he lived on beries and roots and rabbits and stuff like old pies that
he pinched from the bins at the back of Greenacres Rest Home',
and that his 'wepons were old kitchen nives and forks and an ax that
he nicked from Franky Finnigin's alotment', tools gleaned from the
town (*TS*, p. 9). He inhabits a place of dereliction, 'under the ruined

chapel in Burgess Woods', a place linked to the industrial heritage of the area by Blue's description of how he 'chucked [his victims'] bones down an aynshent pit shaft' (*TS*, p. 7, 10). Despite being, in Blue's eyes, 'truely wild', and feasting on raw chicken with 'blud ... trikling down over his chin', his 'delishus brekfast' is washed down with 'a bottle of Fanta that heed pinched from the back of The Grey Horse' (*TS*, p. 11, 20). Through the character of the savage, Blue attempts to reassert the presence of the wild world within his home town. People in Blue's fictionalised version of Almond's fictionalised north-east town, Saltwell, seem to have lost touch with the wild landscape to the extent that they are unable to believe in the savage's existence even when they experience it first-hand.[11]

> The savage was mainly active at night. ... Sometimes people coming back from late-night parties or lock-ins at The Grey Horse came across the savage, but nobody ever really believed what they had seen. They told themselves they were mistaken. They thought they were dreaming or drunk. How could there be a savage like that living in an ordinary sleepy little town like ours? (*TS*, p. 30)

As the story of the savage and the frame narrative of Blue's experiences both progress, Blue finds himself regressing and attuning to his inner primal nature, just as the savage evolves emotionally. While engrossed in creating the story, Blue reports that he is 'grunting and growling as I wrote', eventually baring his teeth and snarling at his teacher before running off to commune directly with the savage in his cave (*TS*, pp. 67–8). Boy and savage meet, symbolic of the civilised and primal aspects of Blue's psyche vying for dominance, as suggested by Blue's description of the wild boy as appearing 'like a reflection, and he was just like me, only weirder and wilder and closer to some magic and some darkness and some dreams' (*TS*, p. 73). The culmination of both narratives comes as the savage acknowledges Blue as a kindred spirit, and places chicken feathers in his hair. Together they grunt and stamp the earth, and Blue experiences 'how it felt to be the savage, to be truly wild' (*TS*, p. 75). At this point, Blue hears his father's voice comforting him, before he returns to his home. Having regressed into savagery, Blue is able to return to the civilised world, carrying elements of the wilderness with him, his new-found fortitude now firmly rooted within him, just as 'the chicken feathers were in my hair and the savage was in my heart and my dad was in my soul' (*TS*, p. 76). Blue joins other north-east children from Almond's fiction, such as Michael in *Skellig*, Joe in *Secret Heart* and Davie in *Clay*, all of

whom discover their deep affinity with the wilderness at the heart of
Almond's north-east landscape.

Angels, birdmen and tigers

Almond's North-East is a place of transformation; through birds and
animals, children here are able to commune directly with the natural
landscape, often as a result of mystical and magical experiences.

Secret Heart employs such supernatural motifs throughout. Very
early in the novel, Joe sees skylarks rising from the ground into the air,
and hears them 'singing in the sky and singing in his heart', an image
which is recalled later in the text as he talks with the magical figure
of the circus owner, Hackenschmidt, and closes his eyes as '[s]kylarks
burst out singing deep inside' (*SH*, pp. 13–14, 112–13). The secret
heart of the novel's title refers to the affinity with the natural, animal
landscape within Joe, a connection he comes to realise as he gradually
becomes at one with a mystical tiger-presence which creeps into his
world. The connection between boy and beast appears immediately
at the novel's opening:

> The tiger padded through the night. Joe Maloney smelt it, the hot,
> sour breath, the stench of its pelt. The odour crept through the streets,
> through his open window and into his dreams. He felt the animal wild-
> ness on his tongue, in his nostrils. (*SH*, p. 1)

In such images, Almond asserts the ubiquitous presence of the
wild, natural north-east landscape coterminous with the industrial
and urban. Such transformations frequently occur in the derelict
wasteland, where Joe is able to evoke the presence of wild animals.
At one point, Joe eats a concoction known as 'Nature Stew', which
has been prepared by his friend, Stanny Mole (a boy who also takes
on characteristics of his animal name); after eating the skylark's egg
it contains, Joe feels himself begin to transform into a bird (*SH*, pp.
25–8). His ability to shape-shift is elaborated in the following passage:

> He knew how the lives of people and beasts could merge out here in the
> wasteland. He knew what it was to be Joe Maloney but also more than
> Joe Maloney. Out here by day he could rise into the blue like a skylark.
> At night he could flicker through the darkness like a bat. He emptied
> his mind now of being just Joe Maloney. He felt weasel fur growing on
> the backs of his hands. He felt claws where his fingers were. He hissed
> and he was a snake slipping through ancient cellars beneath the ancient

chapel. He crouched on all fours and his face and teeth sharpened as he took on the shape of a fox. Nobody knew that he knew how to do these things. They were secret, things that grew from his secret heart. (*SH*, pp. 65–6)

Whilst clearly this can be read as a figurative representation of feelings of instability as the adolescent body morphs towards physical maturity, this 'half-beast, half-human thing, a thing that can sprout horns or fur or feathers', there is also something specifically of the North-East in Joe's experience (*SH*, p. 119). Not only is he of the North-East, but it is also suggested that the ultimate transformation which occurs in the novel could only happen here; the tiger has searched fruitlessly until now – arriving here and finding Joe. As he moves from first experiencing simply 'the memory of the tiger … running through his blood' (*SH*), through being disguised as the creature by his friend Corinna, on to swallowing the piece of tiger bone given to him by Nanty Solo, and ultimately to becoming the tiger and bringing its presence to life 'here in this Helmouth Garden' (*SH*), so Joe's journey is also a quest affecting the landscape of Helmouth, which is transformed from a place of dereliction at the margins of existence into the site of a momentous event for the whole world.[12] In this north-east garden, Joe takes on the form of the tiger, an act with which he is able to '[r]efresh the world' (*SH*, p. 201). Such rebirth can perhaps be read as symbolic of the regeneration occurring in Tyneside during the time of the novel's composition.

North-east children have an affinity with wild creatures in *Clay*, too. As the two youngsters walk through Felling, Davie's girlfriend, Maria, describes how sometimes 'she felt closer to animals than she did to people … grown-up people, anyway' (*C*, p. 108). In *The Fire-Eaters* (2003), Bobby and his friends are described by the sadistic Mr Todd as 'half civilized … wild things', which he attempts to tame using violence (*FE*, p. 92). Such images, of course, draw upon established motifs within children's literature which associate children with nature and the uncivilised. However, they can also be positioned within a larger set of images associated with the North-East, which contribute to its construction for younger readers as a wild zone. Significantly, when children commune with wild creatures in Almond's work, they do so through magical acts which evoke ideas of the mystical and transcendent. This is particularly evident in Almond's use of bird imagery.

The novel which features birds most extensively is *Skellig*. Its central figure, Skellig, is a supernatural, winged angel-like creature with a close affiliation to birds. The children, Michael and Mina, take Skellig

to the attic of Mina's grandfather's ancient house in order to care for
him, a place which is the domain of a family of wild owls. The owls
parallel the two children; just as Mina approaches Michael in order to
make amends following an argument, so too 'the other owl descended
and perched in silence beside its partner' (S, p. 106). Similarly, just
as the children nurture Skellig back to health, so too the owls bring
him offerings from their nightly kills (S, p. 109). Mina describes
the fledgling owls as '[b]eautiful tender savages', and impresses upon
Michael how the adult birds will 'defend their chicks to the death',
qualities which could equally apply to the children themselves;
Michael is racked with anxiety over his baby sister's illness and he
invokes the beautifully savage Skellig to protect her (S, pp. 162–3).
The baby's imperilled existence is also symbolised using bird imagery: the fledgling blackbirds face the dangers of the garden just as the
baby's illness becomes more acute, and just before Skellig intervenes
on her behalf. With figures such as Skellig, Almond seeks to rework
and expand images of savagery and primitiveness which have so long
been associated with the North-East, and to recast them as inflected
with qualities of beauty and tenderness.[13]

Though not directly acknowledged as such, the figure of Skellig
is highly suggestive of angels, and these supernatural creatures also
permeate Almond's North-East. In the short story 'Where Your Wings
Were' in Counting Stars, the narrator receives dreamlike visitations
from an angel, which are sensual and almost erotic experiences for the
adolescent boy. One particularly powerful episode seems to anticipate
a scene in the later Skellig:

> One night, after she'd been with me for hours, her wings began to beat
> more quickly and I felt myself being lifted. I held on tight, gazed into
> her perfect face as we began to fly through the gentle winds of the dark.
> … I knew she was there only by the continued rhythmic beating of her
> wings. (CS, pp. 177–8)

Ultimately, this angel leads the narrator towards an experience of
transcendent, divine truth, as he meets his deceased sister and learns
from her that his shoulder blades really do mark the place where his
wings were in an earlier incarnation as an angel. This is radical knowledge, Blakean in its evocation of the sacred within the profane, and its
revelation proves transformative for the adolescent Catholic boy who
has learnt 'that God slept, that even angels weren't always good, that
I'd have my wings back one day, and that dreams were only dreams'
(CS, p. 181).

What such birds and birdlike creatures offer to Almond's north-east children is the possibility of flight. The ability to fly is a common motif in fantasy writing for children, often symbolic of the desire for escape from the constraints of childhood.[14] I have written previously of how ideas of escape are bound to representations of the north-east landscape in children's fiction, not least in Robert Westall's writing. In Almond's fiction, the ability to fly is certainly associated with the breaking of boundaries and the experience of new horizons for his north-east children, but is more concerned with the act of soaring within the regional landscape rather than moving beyond it. Typically, Almond seeks to show that the transition from innocence to experience need not equate to outgrowing the region; indeed, there is nothing limited or limiting about Almond's North-East. In doing this, Almond challenges those established images of the region portraying the North-East as a starting point from which young people's exit velocity lifts off. Bestowing the children in his fiction with birdlike abilities is one of the ways Almond emphasises their imaginative freedom, particularly as they approach adolescence. As Almond himself describes, speaking about *My Dad's a Birdman*, '[t]hey're not trying to fly across the Tyne to reach heaven, they're trying to have a good time. They're not trying to transcend this world, they're trying to leap into the wonderful parts of this world. They're trying to leap into happiness in this world.'[15] In contrast with many of the children portrayed elsewhere in children's fiction of the North-East who yearn to leave the region behind, when Almond's characters acquire the ability to rise and soar above the landscape, the North-East is itself the site of flight.

In *Skellig*, Michael begins (as with the narrator of *Counting Stars*) by wondering about the purpose of shoulder blades:

> 'They say that shoulder blades are where your wings were, when you were an angel,' she said. 'They say they're where your wings will grow again one day.'
>
> 'It's just a story, though,' I said. 'A fairy tale for little kids. Isn't it?'
>
> 'Who knows? But maybe one day we all had wings and one day we'll all have wings again.'
>
> …
>
> Before she went away, I held the baby for a while. I touched her skin and her tiny soft bones. I felt the place where her wings had been. (*S*, pp. 36–7)

On two occasions later in the novel, Skellig affords both Michael and Mina the experience of having their own wings returned, and Michael describes how they 'turned and turned until the ghostly wings rose from Mina's back and mine, until we felt ourselves being raised, until we seemed to turn and dance in the empty air' (*S*, p. 158). A similar image occurs at the end of *My Dad's a Birdman*, when the young girl Lizzie and her family become so ebullient in their celebrations that they literally rise above the ground (pp. 118–19). Although the text here is ambiguous, leaving open the possibility that Lizzie is imagining their flight, the accompanying illustration by Polly Dunbar shows all four figures floating in the air, surrounded by magical-looking stars. Learning to fly is part of Joe's transformation in *Secret Heart*, too as, under the guidance of the appropriately named Corinna Finch, he leaps 'into the empty air, through memories and dreams' (*SH*, p. 188). Michael, Mina, Lizzie and Joe start out as ordinary north-east children, but David Almond's North-East is a place where ordinary children can learn to fly.

Even when Almond's characters cannot actually fly, they dream of doing so. In *My Dad's a Birdman*, the father dreams of becoming 'the first one to fly across the River Tyne' in 'The Great Human Bird Competition' (p. 10). Again, his flight will not take him outside the region; rather, what is significant is that the competition takes place in Tyneside. In *Heaven Eyes*, birds and flight do represent escape for Erin, who is visited in her bedroom by '[t]he bird of life'; its symbolic message, interpreted by her mum, shows the way to escape from her current situation, not through physically escaping from her place, but rather through altering her perception and heeding the recommendation that 'if we're brave enough, we flap our wings and fly' (p. 23). Erin remains in the urban North-East, but learns to see her world through different eyes.

... from the deepest darkness, from the depths of the earth ...

Often in Almond's fiction, the coterminous existence of the industrial within the natural landscape of the North-East is manifested in the relationship between what lies above and below ground. North-east children often move underground, frequently digging or burrowing into the landscape, or entering the sites of previous excavations. Key events for the children in Almond's fiction often occur in dens, caves or abandoned mines. Such images of exploration below the surface of the physical landscape function in various ways: the act of digging itself draws upon iconic images of the area's heritage, so associated with the coal-mining industry; often, the children recover formerly industrial sites, and make use of them in their exploration of both the physical and psychological landscape of their adolescence. Sometimes the imagery is inverted, and the act of digging exposes the natural world below to the urban landscape above. Always, entering into the earth leads children to reassess the landscape of the region, in the light of those newly uncovered depths it reveals. Almond's fictional North-East comprises what Rob Shields describes as the way 'landscapes … reflect different historical uses and projects "sedimented" in any given site or region'.[16]

In *Kit's Wilderness*, two underground locations feature significantly. In the first part of the novel, Kit is drawn to the underground den of John Askew, where the group of children play the game called Death. The place is cavelike, 'a deep hole dug into the earth with old doors slung across it as an entrance and a roof' (*KW*, p. 5). Askew has apparently carved the den out of the earth himself, and it is a terrifying place, redolent of ancient burial chambers and pre-historic dwellings:

> The floor was hard-packed clay. Candles burned in niches in the walls. There was a heap of bones in a corner. Askew told us they were human bones, discovered when he'd dug this place. … Askew had carved pictures of us all, of animals, of the dogs and cats we owned, of the wild dog, Jax, of imagined monsters and demons, of the gates of Heaven and the snapping jaws of Hell. He wrote into the walls the names of all of us who'd died in there. My friend Allie Keenan sat across the den from me. The blankness in her eyes said: You're on your own down here. (*KW*, pp. 5–6)

Despite the den's frightening appearance and atmosphere, Kit feels compelled to visit the place. He links this compulsion to the industrial background of the Stoneygate landscape, feeling 'driven to it like Grandpa had been driven to the darkness of the pit' (*KW*, p. 48). The suggestion is that the desire to explore beneath the surface of the landscape is an irresistible natural urge, felt particularly acutely by those people native to the region. Like Kit and his grandfather, John Askew comes from one of 'the old families', and he too is associated with the subterranean landscape; Kit describes the experience of holding Askew's gaze, presumably an insight through the windows of his soul (*KW*, p. 10):

> I looked into his eyes. It was like looking into a tunnel of endless dark. I felt myself staring deeper, deeper. I felt myself driven to the dark. (*KW*, p. 49)

Ultimately, this drive to explore underground leads Kit to join Askew in an old drift mine.

As the novel progresses, Kit becomes more and more aware of the relationship between the town of Stoneygate and its industrial past. His grandfather shows Kit that the legacy of the town's coal-mining past permeates the place, shaping the very physicality of the landscape:

> He took me walking and showed me that the evidence of the pit was everywhere – depressions in the gardens, jagged cracks in the roadways and in the house walls. Fragments of coal darkened the soil. … He showed me where the entrances to the shafts had been, told me about the dizzying drop in the cage to the tunnels far below. He pointed up to the hills past Stoneygate, told me they were filled with shafts, potholes, ancient drift mines.
>
> 'Look at the earth and you think it's solid,' he said. 'But look deeper and you'll see it's riddled with tunnels. A warren. A labyrinth.' (*KW*, p. 18)

Clearly, what lies beneath the surface is as worthy of exploration as what lies above.

This idea is central to *Kit's Wilderness*. Such explorations are metaphorical, and they enable both Kit and Askew to confront and overcome problems of some emotional depth and complexity, and to connect with the traditions of their forebears; as Geraldine Brennan notes, '[t]oday's Stoneygate children are not sent down the mine', but instead they descend into the earth to play the game called Death.[17] At one point, Kit dreams of following the figure of Silky, an apparition recalled by his grandfather from his days as a coal miner, into the drift mine. Silky leads Kit further and further 'into the endless deep dark … . Far into the earth', until he eventually discovers his grandfather lost and alone (*KW*, p. 96). The dream is symbolic of Kit's fears for the health of his Grandpa, who is suffering from some kind of degenerative dementia, unspecified but suggestive of Alzheimer's disease; just as Kit travels back into the underground physical landscape inhabited by generations of his ancestors, so too his grandfather turns to memories of his time below ground in order to reorient himself.

For Askew, the time he spends with Kit in the drift mine allows him to connect with a much more ancient, prehistoric past, and to recover his own tender humanity. Both boys excavate deep, dark fears from within their own psyches, and resurface with stronger psychological foundations. Such a metaphorical reading of the significance of the subterranean seems particularly apt in the light of Almond's own comments on such images. Referring specifically to the writing of *Kit's Wilderness*, Almond describes how he attempts to expand and develop images of mining in particular.

I remember writing all that stuff in 'Kit' and it was just such a huge thrill to realise what I was dealing with. ... I thought, 'Oh, it's coalmines, coalmines, coalmines,' and then I thought, 'Well, that's what people would say you would write about,' but actually it's such a bloody huge metaphor for all kinds of stuff that it just came as this huge gift. Because coal mining's usually just written about in terms of the industrial heritage but it's got all these other massive implications as well, and it was wonderful to be able to take it and use it in this way.[18]

Almond's comments here relate to his initial reluctance to find himself labelled as a north-east writer, and therefore his trepidation at employing such iconic imagery when writing about the place. He is attempting to steer readers away from clichéd expectations. Nevertheless, Almond is drawn repeatedly to images of digging and mining. Just as his landscapes seek to reconcile the industrial with the natural, so his imagery here seeks to reconcile the particular, northern industrial experience, with the transcendent.

In the following passage, John Askew explains to Kit the appeal that the drift mine holds for him:

'Down here,' he said. 'There's no day, no night. You're half-awake and half-asleep, half-dead and half-alive. You're in the earth with bones and ghosts and darkness stretching back a million million years into the past.' (*KW*, p. 187)

Such sentiments, which could as equally describe the experience of men working the coalface as this young boy seeking oblivion beneath the earth, have the effect of simultaneously evoking and transforming images from the North-East's industrial heritage. Almond here both affirms the young boy's affiliation with the region's industrial traditions, and also elevates such traditions by ascribing them a transcendent existence 'stretching back a million million years into the past'. It is clear from this image that travelling below the surface of the physical world also frequently initiates travelling back through time, down into the history of the landscape. In this way, derelict urban scenery, as found on the surface, is to be seen as linked, by such features as abandoned mining and quarrying works, with the much older world below ground.

Almond's fiction positions the ruined urban places of the North-East as *manifestations* of the region's history, both through the way in which the urban landscape is frequently presented as crumbling and decaying into the world that lies beneath (in, for instance, such places as the deep, dark holes explored by the children in *Heaven Eyes*), and also by virtue of its connection via the openings of spaces such as abandoned mines, quarries and the like, which sink into the ground like roots reaching down from the towns and cities above. As historian Simon Schama notes, '[t]o see the ghostly outline of an old landscape beneath the superficial covering of the contemporary is to be made vividly aware of the endurance of core myths'; in Almond's novels, such myths invest the present-day region with the immanent presence of its industrial tradition.[19]

Digging is also important in *Heaven Eyes*. On arrival at the Middens, the children realise that they and their raft are being 'slowly sucked down into the sodden earth' (*HE*, p. 47). Although such an image is frightening, it also holds a strange appeal for the character of Erin, who momentarily desires the oblivion it offers:

> I slithered forward. I felt how at any moment I could stop and be taken down The Black Middens. … I began to let myself be taken down. I felt the mud gathering around me. I felt the great contentment that might come if I just let go, if I sank here, if I just let myself go down to her, if my mouth was filled with mud, if my eyes and ears were filled with mud, if there was nothing but mud surrounding me, encasing me. (*HE*, pp. 48–9)

The landscape of The Black Middens exists in a constant state of flux, and life there for Heaven Eyes and her Grampa revolves around digging down into the mud. Grampa remembers how he 'dug out Heaven from the Middens one starry night', and Heaven Eyes tells the others of how Grampa has promised he will dig her 'treasures' out of the Middens, treasures which do turn up from below the surface of the mud, and hold the key to Heaven's origins and the tragic loss of her family in a boating accident (*HE*, pp. 69, 87). In *Heaven Eyes*, as in *Kit's Wilderness*, Almond's north-east children are able to recover their roots in the region's ancient traditions, by digging down into the muddy landscape. In this novel too, the world above ground is nourished by the subterranean world as the mud gives forth its treasures. In a key episode, Mouse discovers what he believes to be the body of a murder victim in the mud, which January and Erin then bring to the surface. In doing so, the children almost become at one with the mud of The Middens, as they sink into the landscape:

> We started to dig. We lifted great spadefuls of oily, silty, stinking mud and water. Our shovels slopped and sucked. Within seconds we were filthy. We slithered down into the holes we dug. … I looked across at Jan and he whooped and was like a crazed black creature made of the mud itself. …

> I dug and spat and wiped my face and dug deeper, deeper till I was sick
> of it all and was just about to tell Jan that I was giving up when I saw the
> tips of the fingers in the black black mud. (*HE*, p. 149)

The body, which is described by the characters as 'the saint', is
found with its hand outstretched, 'as if waiting for a gift, an offering',
which he ultimately receives, in the form of Grampa's spirit after
his death (*HE*, p. 151). In this way, as the saint from below ground
and from an earlier time takes Grampa away from the urban world,
the connection between the subterranean and the landscape above
ground is reaffirmed. This episode is yet another example of how
explorations beneath the surface of the north-east landscape are also
explorations of the region's history, particularly its spiritual tradition.

There is a clear difference between this saintly figure, who comes
out of and is also at one with the very matter that makes up the
mud of The Middens, and, say, Robert Westall's St Cuthbert in *The
Wind Eye* (1976), who, despite his affiliation with the natural world
through birds and animal life, nevertheless remains most closely allied
to what lies above ground, in particular the wind. Both are forces of
nature, but Almond's is much more *of* the earth. Also, there is a clear
difference between such underground forces in Almond's North-East,
such as the saint here, or Silky and the other ghost children in *Kit's
Wilderness*, and those spiritual forces which emanate from the landscape in novels such as Peter Dickinson's *Annerton Pit* (1977). Both are
manifestations of the enduring presence of the North-East's industrial
heritage just below the surface (both physically and metaphorically),
but whereas Dickinson's supernatural force attests to the way in
which such activities have wounded and enraged the landscape, in
Almond's work the forces of heavy industrial power and natural spirituality are reconciled and the effect is redemptive rather than injuri-
ous. Almond's is a North-East in which the landscape is much more
at one with its traditions, derelict though they may be.

Clay also features the subterranean landscape, in particular through
its use of caves and cavelike spaces. The novel's opening sees Davie and
Geordie heading 'into the cave' where there 'was writing on the wall
again', suggestive of prehistoric cave dwellings similar to those evoked
in *Kit's Wilderness* (*C*, p. 2). Such images are compounded when the
two boys meet at the cave entrance, and set about fortifying it against
attacks from the bully, Mouldy:

> We were at the cave. We both had knives. We were sharpening sticks. We
> were going to set them up at the quarry entrance, stick them in the mud,
> pointing upwards, like a trap. (*C*, p. 21)

When young people move underground in *Clay*, they do so in order to connect with a more primal way of life. Rather than suggesting savagery, such images are employed by Almond to gesture towards a deeply rooted sense of history as permeating the landscape of the region. Uniquely among children's books of the North-East, Almond's imagery of the underground landscape repeatedly evokes the prehistoric world, and indeed the origins of human society and culture. The effect of this is to iterate that ancient culture underlies the life of the North-East today. The sacred, mystical underground places found in Almond's fiction almost always feature writing and artwork on their walls. One such place is the cave at the conclusion of *The Savage*. Here the central character Blue ends up crawling 'through the stones towards the hidden cave beneath' where he finally encounters the savage (*TS*, p. 72). He describes how the 'pictures on the cave wall were works of wonder', and is amazed to discover that 'the savage had drawn me long before I ever started writing him' (*TS*, p. 75). This revelation awakens Blue to the miraculous, and it is here that he communicates with his dead father. The suggestion is that such magical places, hidden beneath the surface of the everyday world, have always been here in the North-East, even to the point that the savage's cave can exist independently and pre-date its own creation in Blue's story. This would be impossible in reality, but what Almond is exploring here is the idea that Blue's imagination does not simply create the savage, miraculous though this would be in itself; rather, the creative act is a kind of conduit through which the essential mysticism of the savage's world, a magical realm just below the surface of the everyday world, can flow into and permeate life above. In Almond's fiction, the North-East is the site at which such magical connections occur, as the region's children discover such realms lying below their feet.

Just as the saint in *Heaven Eyes* emerges from beneath the surface of the landscape, so the mystical figure of *Clay* originates underground. Davie describes how Stephen 'reached down deep ... and lifted out a dripping handful of pale clay' from Braddock's Garden, which provides the raw material for his creation, and he also chooses the cave as the location for the ritual which will bring Clay to life, commenting on how 'Saints used to live in caves like this' (*C*, pp. 35, 53). This again suggests that the landscape of the North-East is particularly well suited to the miraculous and spiritual, and although such qualities are especially potent in the underground landscape of the region, this is seen as permeating the landscape above ground as well. When Davie visits the cave with Maria, again emphasising the sacred nature of the place, he comments on how people from the area have plundered Braddock's and how 'all the gardens in Felling had bits of this garden in them' (*C*, p. 112). Ultimately, Clay himself ends up in Davie's father's garden, and along with bringing the natural landscape into the urban as I explored earlier, this also brings the substance gleaned from the earth of Braddock's Garden into the garden of Davie's home, where it once again sinks beneath the ground.

Links between underground spaces and the miraculous occur in *The Fire-Eaters* and *Secret Heart*, too. As *The Fire-Eaters* approaches its climax, the character of McNulty, himself associated with the mystical and miraculous and described by Almond as 'an old Catholic saint', camps out in one of the abandoned holiday shacks in the dunes at Keely Bay.[20] Bobby and Ailsa visit him there, to persuade him to join the others on the beach in facing what they believe to be their imminent oblivion.

> I saw there was another window in the back wall of the room, but the dune had grown over it. Behind the glass were sand and soil and roots. There were seashells and stones and bones. He saw me looking.
> 'It's deep as the grave in here, bonny,' he said. 'We're down where the dead live. You want to see the needles and the skewer stuck in?' (*FE*, pp. 185–6)

This place, sinking below the surface of the landscape, connects with the underground land of the dead – an idea reprised in the *Skellig* prequel, *My Name is Mina* (2010). Here, 9-year-old Mina enters an abandoned mineshaft in order to travel to the Underworld, 'there, behind the rhododendron bushes, in Heston Park', in the hope of persuading Pluto and Persephone to 'let her bring her dad back into the world'.[21] As with the children in *Kit's Wilderness*, *Heaven Eyes*, *The Fire-Eaters*, *Clay* and *The Savage*, Mina too experiences the transformative nature of the north-east landscape; following her journey into the depths of the earth, she too will have her outlook radically realigned as wilderness, wild animals, and ultimately, birdmen, reveal their presence at the heart of her north-east world.

Notes

1. David Almond, 'Personal Interview with Nolan Dalrymple', in Nolan Dalrymple, 'North-East Childhoods: Regional Identity in Children's Novels of the North East of England' (doctoral thesis, University of Newcastle, 2008), 10443/890/1/Dalrymple09.pdf (accessed 13 May 2014).

2. For an extensive discussion of such images across a wide range of children's fiction set in the region, see Dalrymple, 'North-East Childhoods'.
3. *Wild Girl, Wild Boy: A Play* (London: Hodder, 2002), 'Afterword', p. 83.
4. *Wild Girl, Wild Boy: A Play*, p. 87.
5. 'Any good story … is not a tame, trapped thing. It still has wildness in it '; *Wild Girl, Wild Boy: A Play*, p. 88; also, 'All children have a wildness about them'; quoted in Kit Spring, 'A Hit from a Myth', *Observer* (23 November 2003), http://www.guardian.co.uk/books/2003/nov/23/booksforchildrenandteenagers.features (accessed 3 June 2011).
6. 'Personal Interview with Nolan Dalrymple'.
7. Robert Westall, *Falling into Glory* (London: Methuen, 1993; reissued Mammoth, 2000).
8. Geraldine Brennan, 'The Game Called Death: Frightening Fictions by David Almond, Philip Gross and Lesley Howarth', in Kimberley Reynolds, Geraldine Brennan and Kevin McCarron, *Frightening Fiction* (London and New York: Continuum, 2001), pp. 92–127, p. 95.
9. Cultural critic Marina Warner, writing of Philip Pullman, notes how he 'is not the only children's writer who is generating new metamorphoses for our time; and … many of the most successful fiction writers for adults also operate in this metamorphic and supernatural territory'. See Marina Warner, *Fantastic Metamorphoses, Other Worlds: Ways of Telling the Self* (Oxford: Oxford University Press, 2002), p. 208.
10. Rachel Falconer, *The Crossover Novel: Contemporary Children's Literature and its Adult Readership* (New York and London: Routledge, 2009), p. 255.
11. In interview, Almond describes the location as follows: 'It's unspoken. It is the North-East, but it's not a named place. It's a bit more rural than a lot of the stuff, a bit more like here I suppose.' Almond currently lives in rural Northumberland (see 'Personal Interview with Nolan Dalrymple').
12. *Secret Heart*, pp. 73, 77–9, 91, 201.
13. This tradition of writing about the region in children's fiction is explored in Dalrymple, 'North-East Childhoods'.
14. For example, E. Nesbit, *The Phoenix and the Carpet* (1904); J.M. Barrie, *Peter and Wendy* (London: Hodder & Stoughton, 1911); Raymond Briggs, *The Snowman* (London: Hamish Hamilton, 1978).
15. Madelyn Travis, 'Flying Across the Tyne: Madelyn Travis talks to David Almond about the inspiration behind My Dad's a Birdman', http://www.booktrustchildrensbooks.org.uk/show/feature/Features%20Interviews/Interview-with-David-Almond-07 (accessed 3 June 2011).
16. Rob Shields, *Places on the Margin: Alternative Geographies of Modernity* (London: Routledge, 1991), p. 24.
17. Brennan, 'The Game Called Death', p. 103.
18. 'Personal interview with Nolan Dalrymple'.
19. Simon Schama, *Landscape and Memory* (New York: Alfred A. Knopf, 1995; Vintage, 1996), p. 16.

20. 'Personal interview with Nolan Dalrymple'.
21. David Almond, *My Name is Mina* (London: Hodder Children's Books, 2010), p. 47; the young girl's point of departure, coupled with her use of traditional pitmen's songs to soothe a creature she believes to be Cerberus, underscores the affinity between her name and the role she performs (i.e. Mina/miner).

7

'They thought we had disappeared, and they were wrong': The Depiction of the Working Class in David Almond's Novels

Carole Dunbar

In an interview with Peter Hollindale in 2003, David Almond relates how, with his success as a children's novelist, came widespread disbelief that he still chose to live in his native Tyneside, close to the working-class districts in which he spent his childhood.[1] Implicit in the consistency of this reaction is a disbelief that anyone, given the choice, should opt to remain in the north of England. Almond's birthplace, however, dominated by strong working-class mores, as demonstrated in both his fiction and his fictionalised autobiographical work, *Counting Stars*, is fundamental to his art. It is his identification with the working-class life he portrays which gives his writing the vibrancy, depth and individuality which is indivisible from his own social roots. The poet Seamus Heaney, writing of his attachment to his home place through the eponymous mythological character of Antaeus, who gained strength from contrast with the ground, insists:

> I cannot be, weaned
> Off the earth's long contour, her river-veins.
> Down here in my cave
>
> Girdered with root and rock
> I am cradled in the dark that wombed me.[2]

For Heaney this deep-rootedness has as much to do with class as with geographical location. While his poetry cites a litany of South Derry locales – Lough Neagh, Ardboe, Anahorish, Toome, for instance – their landscapes give rise to 'the diviner', 'the last mummer', 'the thatcher' and the 'navvy'. Almond's writing, too, is intimately concerned with his native sod, but even more prominent are the poor who found a home and expression in such a landscape. With good reason, Almond's fiction for the young has been described as a form of magical realism, but in order for the element of the unworldly to be effective, the realism must have both depth and clarity. It is this realism, this authenticity, especially in relation to the north of England poor, that this chapter will address.

In the 1950s the phrase 'new wave' was coined to describe the upsurge in writing which was dominated by working-class writers from the provinces, many of whom emanated from the north of England. In an article which pays tribute to the Salford-born playwright Shelagh Delaney, the novelist Jeanette Winterson, from neighbouring Accrington, asserts that within the movement 'the (male) northern working classes stripped life down to the raw'.[3] This new frankness, suggested by Winterson's phraseology, is seen in the portrayal of the poor, in the depiction of their domestic and working lives, their sexual expression and the exuberant and colourful use of language, employing both the vernacular and frequent expletives, all apparent in the early works of northern writers such John Braine, David Storey and Alan Sillitoe, in addition to Delaney herself. It is a movement which was instrumental in 'the growing acceptance of the importance of hitherto neglected geographical and social sections of British society'.[4]

Things were changing in the realms of British children's literature also, although arguably more tentatively – not surprisingly, perhaps, given the target audience. John Rowe Townsend, from Leeds in Yorkshire and writing for the then *Manchester Guardian*, published his novel *Gumbler's Yard* in 1961, a year after the iconic British soap opera, *Coronation Street*, set in working-class Salford, made its first appearance. It was 'acclaimed for its depiction of life in deprived inner cities' which, according to Gamble, ushered in a new era in children's literature in which 'the middle-class family was no longer the dominant representation'.[5]

Other authors followed where Townsend had led and pushed the boundaries ever further. Barry Hines, in his highly prestigious novel *Kes* or *A Kestrel for a Knave*, savagely denounces contemporary society for what he sees as its criminal neglect and disregard for both the welfare and future of the young urban poor. As I shall argue, there are parallels to be drawn between the work of Almond and that of one of Britain's most respected fantasy writers for the young, Alan Garner. He, like Almond, published a fictional work drawing on his own family history, *The Stone Book Quartet*, which features the proud working traditions of generations of his family, all of whom lived in the area he still inhabits.

Education and class

It is no accident that the late 1950s/early 1960s brought a burgeoning of literature featuring prominent and realistic portrayals of working-class life from those who had experience of it. Most of the writers discussed had benefited from a grammar-school education under the relatively recent 1944 Education Act, an Act which significantly increased the opportunities of children from poor families. As a result of this, for the first time in any numbers, the erstwhile poor were writing about their own communities, for their own communities, in addition to a wider audience – a step which transformed literature for both adults and children. David Almond carries on this tradition.

This relatively new phenomenon of educating a larger proportion of the working-class young in a system dominated by middle-class children, from its inception and the social consequences of such an Act, is a major theme of Almond's novel, *The Fire-Eaters*; indeed, the young working-class protagonist's name, Bobby Burns, alludes to it. The poet Robert Burns, born into a poor Scottish farming family in 1759, escaped his background as a result of a literary education. His championing of the class into which he was born and his belief in equality, both of which led him to support the French Revolution, are captured in such poems as 'For A' That and A' That', and are issues akin to those facing Almond's character.

The notion of class revolution, in several senses, is at the forefront of Almond's novel. Education is what broadcaster Melvyn Bragg (who, like Almond, originates from a working-class region, Cumbria) calls 'a route out of poverty',[6] as seen in the case of Robert Burns, a way of elevating the impoverished young and, through them, their community. In *Kit's Wilderness*, for instance, Kit's granddad's assertion that through schooling his grandson will 'go a long way' (*KW*, p. 43) is contrasted with his own experience, in which 'as a lad I'd wake up trembling, knowing that as a Watson born in Stoneygate I'd soon be following my ancestors into the pit' (*KW*, p. 19). The old man is defined by family, and therefore by class, and consequently was heir to the constraints and terrors of work underground. The word 'pit' suggests not only physical claustrophobia, but its inherent darkness symbolises mental and educational deprivation. It also has notions of 'trap', from which poor children could not escape. Conversely, Kit's destiny will be controlled by no such constraints. The phrase, 'go a long way', embraces ideas not only of eminence, but suggests his future will be far removed from that of previous generations. In *The Fire-Eaters*, Bobby's dad tells his son, the first member of the family to attend grammar school, 'you can do anything ... you're privileged and free' (*FE*, p. 60), a sentiment which echoes that of Almond's father's belief that his grammar-school son 'had the world in the palm of [his] hand' (*CS*, p. 47).

This privilege and freedom is not a gift to the poor from their social superiors, however. Bobby's dad, echoing the politics of Robert Burns, asserts that 'everything that's been won by folks like us has been won by fighters. ... Fighters that wouldn't kowtow and cringe, but looked the oppressor in the eye and said things had to change' (*FE*, p. 194). He stresses that the fight is not over. As Almond's teacher has it, there is a 'duty' to 'keep history moving forward' (*CS*, p. 75).

This demand for an egalitarian society on the part of the lower class, implicit in the image of meeting authority 'eye to eye', is seen elsewhere in the novel. The humorous scene in which Bobby revels in the apology of his friend Joseph is telling. Having insisted that Joseph's repentance is more elaborately phrased, Bobby demands:

'Say, I'm dead dead sorry, Bobby, sir.'
He grinned. We looked at each other.
'Hadaway and shite,' he said.
'Aye,' I said, 'OK.' (*FE*, p. 154)

Joseph balks at the word 'sir', and the social superiority it connotes. He refuses to recognise a system that sees him as inferior, and his use of the vernacular allies him with the wider Cumbrian working class. Bobby's good natured and approving reply re-establishes equality between them.

This aggressive confrontation between authority and the northern poor, which is alluded to in Joseph's reaction, is historical in nature and exercised those in the highest political echelons during the Victorian era, as is evident from a letter addressed to the monarch in 1842:

Lord Melbourne hopes that these tumults in the manufacturing districts are subsiding, but he cannot conceal from your majesty that he views them with great alarm – much greater than he generally thinks it proper to express.[7]

There are distinct echoes of the social tension Lord Melbourne refers to in the grammar school that Bobby Burns attends in *The*

Fire-Eaters. The book is set in 1962, the same year as a survey of 88 adults who, as working-class children, had been educated in Huddersfield's grammar schools, the authors, Brian Jackson and Denis Marsden, sharing a similar geographical, familial and educational background to the people they interviewed. They quote one head-master as saying, 'I see grammar school education very strongly as a matter of communicating middle-class values to a "new" population.'[8] It is a task that Mr Todd embraces with sadistic enthusiasm. Addressing the new consignment of eleven-plus successes, which included young people from poor homes, he asserts:

> 'You may have proved that you have something like a brain. But you have not yet proved that you are suitable to be with us. … You are half civilised. You are wild things. And you must be taught to conform.' (*FE*, p. 92)

Daniel's use of phrases such as 'half-human', 'stupid' and 'throwback' (*FE*, pp. 115–16) to describe his neighbours, depictions which imply degeneracy and primitive and debased qualities and hark back to Malthusian concepts of the poor, allies him, in the early stages of the book, to the perceptions of class held by the teacher. Todd's phrase 'wild things' shares notions with the word 'savages', a common sobriquet for the poor in the nineteenth century and beyond. Frances Hodgson Burnett uses it to describe the street-child Anne in *A Little Princess*, for example. These are labels designed to exalt those who use them and to belittle those so described. As we see from Almond's book *The Savage* there clings to the description notions of the subhuman, won-derfully captured by Dave McKean's illustrations. Almond's eponym-ous character lives outside the town, a reference to living beyond the pale, perhaps. Superficially, he is seen to engender fear because he is associated with the threat of violence and the overthrow of societal norms. There are strong overtones here of the nineteenth-century middle-class fear of 'the mob', it being composed, as it were, of a multitude of 'savages'. Mr Todd's language also denotes colonialism: his wish to replace what he deems is the barbarism of working-class culture with a civilising middle-class mores. The conformity he cites is not academic in nature, but amounts to the relinquishing of family and class values, elements which render the pupils 'unsuitable'. These social prejudices are shared by the school's principal, who muses, 'The lower orders. Perhaps it is a fantasy that they are ready for true education' (*FE*, p. 198). The use of the word 'true' again underlines the teachers' belief that they are the sole repositories of discernment and wisdom. It was an attitude shared by so many grammar-school heads interviewed by Jackson and Marsden that the authors question its validity:

> And is it so impossible; is it at all true, as the head-teachers say, that the working class (three-quarters of the 'nation') bring nothing of their own to meet the cultural inheritance? Are they so 'new,' so raw, so blank?[9]

As Bobby's dad declares, "'there's more to education than reading books ... There's ancient battles to be fought. We didn't fight a war so that berks like your Mr Todd could hold sway'" (FE, p. 218).

But as the arrival at the end of the novel of Miss Bute, the symbol of universal respectfulness, suggests, her more humane approach to her pupils will prevail over the intolerant brutality of her more senior colleagues. Therefore, the two young dissidents, middle-class Daniel and working-class Bobby, along with Ailsa Spinks, 'the brightest and boldest of us all' (FE, p. 248), are re-embraced by the school body. For, ultimately, one of the book's major themes is social realignment, as seen in the scene on the beach where Daniel and his parents approach their fellow villagers. Significantly, as Bobby's mother remarks, they leave their camera at home and with it ideas that their neighbours are merely objects to photograph. Instead they bring wine, a symbol of their class, certainly, but also a Eucharistic statement of a belief in a common humanity. The wine is received and the bargain of mutual acceptance is struck. Significantly, one of its major planks is the recognition by Daniel's father that his son and Bobby are 'a pair of fighters', brought up sharing a similar philosophy which underpinned their battle for justice (FE, pp. 229–30).

First-generation educated

This positive relationship between a working-class father and his grammar-school son portrayed in *The Fire-Eaters* differs from depictions of similar associations in earlier books for the young. Aidan Chambers's teenage novels of the 1970s and 1980s, for example, often contain adolescent protagonists alienated from their dads, due partly to the complexities of growing up, but also because the young central character is torn between a non-literary working-class home life and the intellectual challenge and excitement offered at school. In *Breaktime* Ditto remembers his father's pride at his son's success in his new secondary school. By the end of the novel, when Ditto is approaching the end of his school career, their intercourse is characterised by mutual antagonism and incomprehension. The poet

Tony Harrison, speaking of a very similar experience with his father, explains in his poem 'Book Ends', 'What's still between is / Not the thirty or so years, but books, books, books'.[10]

This gulf between an educated child and his sparsely schooled parents forms one of the aspects of an interview given by Alan Garner, a contemporary of Chambers. He maintains that 'the fact is that the parent cannot encompass the effect of his child ... being educated'. This resulted for Garner in a 'traumatisation within the family resulting in a total failure of communication, absolute social breakdown, collapse'.[11] Even as an adult living in the same area, Garner chooses not to meet his parents.

Jackson and Marsden maintain that adults who were first-generation educated and who still live in the area in which they grew up can often 'move into a distorted adulthood'.[12] Garner describes himself as a young man as being 'unbalanced'. He was, he says most poignantly, 'educated to understand what it was I had lost',[13] a notion present in Almond's writing, although the poignancy is often offset by the familial and cultural past being seen as a continuum of the working-class experience. In *Kit's Wilderness* we see the pride with which Kit's grandfather shows his grandson his working-class inheritance. The children in their modern classrooms are allied to their counterparts in the nineteenth-century mines, who are seen to inform the experiences of the young generations later.

Tradition and change

Almond's novels are generally aimed at a younger age group than those written by Garner and Chambers, the age of the protagonist reflecting this. The books do not go much beyond the first tentative forays away from the family: any notion of a generation gap is yet to emerge. In a body of work that reflects so much of Almond's childhood – religion and topography, for instance – perhaps one reason he chooses not to feature his later adolescence is in the premature death of his father, when the author was only 14. It is possible that in some sense this catastrophic event marked for him the end of his adolescence, just as it marked the end of his relationship with his father.

Almond's target audience, however, does not mean that education is not treated as divisive. In the north of England reluctance to allow children to remain in school after the law allows them to leave has a history as long as compulsory education itself. It was the only region to vote against the abolition of the so-called half-time system, whereby children could divide their time equally between school and work, thereby contributing to the family's budget. J.S. Hurt tells us that 'children worked in the mills because "it was the proper thing to be done," not because of poverty'.[14] This demand for the young to work often dominated even as late as the 1950s and 1960s, over the perception that education was a positive force. While Bragg assures his readers that, amongst the working classes, by 1960 education was more highly prized than previously, he also relates that, as a student at that time, he was often confronted by questions about 'when are you going to get a job'.[15]

Such a negative attitude is not restricted to adults. In 1982, the award-winning children's author, Berlie Doherty, brought up in working-class Liverpool, published a collection of short stories entitled *How Green You Are*. The title alludes to the colour of the protagonist, Julie's school uniform and the phrase is used as a taunt in a bullying campaign instigated by her erstwhile friends, who, like Julie, have just begun secondary school. Although not stated, the ethos of Julie's school, its extra-curricular activities and the nature of the uniform itself suggest that she is attending a grammar school, while her persecutors are not. The denunciation of her as a 'snob'[16] reinforces this notion.

In *The Fire-Eaters*, Joseph's reaction to what he perceives as Bobby's elevation through his eleven-plus success is ambiguous. While there is a begrudging pride at the younger boy's achievement, he is poignantly aware that it inevitably heralds the death of their friendship and, in a similar fashion to Doherty's bullies, Joseph ridicules Bobby's new status, which, he considers, renders him a 'nancy boy' (*FE*, p. 24). Similarly, shortly afterwards he condemns middle-class Daniel with the term 'jessie'. Both sobriquets carry with them connotations of weakness and effeminacy; indeed both challenge the addressees' sexuality. The inference is that Bobby's grammar-school education and Daniel's social class and education remove them from the manifestation of maleness, manual labour, and therefore from maleness itself. Joseph's jocular ideas of their curriculum containing such apparent female disciplines as 'flower-sniffing', 'dancing' and elocution give weight to this argument (*FE*, p. 84).

Such narrow definitions of masculinity are seen in other novels by Almond, such as *Secret Heart*, for instance, and in Joff's philosophy of 'survival of the fittest. Kill or be killed' (*SH*, p. 21). His regular forays back to nature, which facilitate the indoctrination of the young and produce 'men', ally him to the Hitler Youth movement. The culmination of Joff's vision, the destruction of the beautiful and majestic panther, is a metaphor for the negation of the sensitive, aesthetic and

imaginative sensibility that Joe embodies. In the same novel Almond
seemingly denounces right-wing political ideology such as that
espoused by organisations like the National Front. The depiction of
the condemnation and belittling of those perceived as different, in the
guise of the circus people, by those characterised as thugs, reaches its
height with the bringing down of the mighty Hackenschmidt, whose
qualities of gentleness, bravery and humanity speak of an earlier time
which espoused a more noble form of manliness.

In *The Fire-Eaters* Joseph is the mouthpiece for the non-aspiring
working-class boy. Significantly, he sees his adult future spent 'in the
building trade, like me dad'. Unlike Bobby who, the perception is, is
destined for university, Joseph is proud to be replicating a career traditional to his class, as represented by the reference to his father. Despite
Joseph's clinging to conventional options, what he envisages building –
'offices and restaurants and hotels and the motorway' – suggests that
contemporary society, if not the young man himself, is reflecting
Bob Dylan's observation, encapsulated in the title of one of his most
famous songs and recorded two years after Almond's book was set,
that 'the times they are a-changin''. Joseph's anticipation of 'money in
me pocket, pints of beer, lasses' (*FE*, p. 35) mirrors the thrill of Tony
Harrison's companions in the poem 'Me Tarzan' in which he purport-
edly remembers, as a teenager, his non-academic friends inviting him
out. They were 'off laikin, then to t'fish 'oil all the boys, / off tartin',
off t'flicks'. Young Tony, shackled to his education, declines their offer,
'A bloody can't ah've gorra Latin Prose'.[17] The tension between the
academic and working-class cultures is wonderfully captured in this
line. The dialect representing his background is involved in a tug-
of-war for this first-generation, classically educated boy, suggested by
the phrase 'Latin prose', its place at the end of the line suggesting its
dominance. The word 'bloody' embodies the struggle between these
two seemingly opposing forces within the youth, and his use of the
vernacular implies that, while education imposes on him a different
ethos than that of his community, Harrison wishes to embrace its
values without relinquishing his working-class identity.

Just as Harrison's poetry contains images of change in previously
established norms of working-class culture, so in Almond's fiction
there are recurring images of a society on the edge, totally applicable,
it can be argued, in works for children on the verge of adolescence.
Significantly, *The Fire-Eaters'* location is in the margin between sea and
land, while the narrative concerns itself with dualities such as childhood and puberty, peace and war, and, as symbolised by the Spinks,
tradition and modernity. As seen in their attitude to educating girls,

the Spinks family embrace a philosophy from another age. When Daniel asks how long they have been sea-coalers, Bobby replies 'forever' (*FE*, p. 116), an answer which allies them and their occupation to a significantly earlier period. In Henry Mayhew's work *London Labour and the London Poor*, initially published in serial form from 1849 in the *Morning Chronicle*, there is reference to so-called mudlarks, working in the rivers, scavenging for 'coals, bits of old-iron, bones and copper nails',[18] an apt description of the family's trade. The name of the Spinks's horse, Wilberforce, further links the family to a past age, to stability, conservatism, but also to an outmoded way of life.

Images of the death of one culture and the emergence of another abound in Almond's writing. As Hollindale has it, the 'stories repeatedly evoke ghosts of the past as modern life takes over'.[19] He cites a derelict garage in *Skellig*, the ruined warehouses in *Heaven Eyes* and the abandoned mines in *Kit's Wilderness* and, one may add, *My Name is Mina* and the caves in *Clay* – notions here of Heaney's 'root and rock' and 'dark places'. The images of the earth being less than solid, inherent in the notion of caves and mines, feed into impressions of uncertainty, of there being a lack of firm foothold in these periods of transition, both on a societal and a personal level, for in Almond's work these are often intertwined. Vitally, however, the porous nature of the ground often allows influences of the past to emerge, and it is only through embracing what went before that communities and individuals can mature and progress.

Almond and Garner

In Alan Garner's elegiac autobiographical work, *The Stone Book Quartet*, already mentioned, the first story features young Mary, who as the eldest child and on the verge of her teens, is taken by her father through a cave and tunnel to a narrow opening which only a child can crawl through. From the passageway Mary emerges into an area whose walls are decorated by her father's mason mark, the symbol of his trade, and a handprint exactly the same size as her own. The floor was covered with 'footprints of people, bare and shod … hundreds pressed where only a dozen could stand. Mary was in a crowd that could never have been.'[20] She finds herself as part of a continuum; the drawing of a bull she sees harks back to primitive cave painting. She is travelling the same path as generations before her, experiencing, like them, the materialising transition from a child to an adult. At the heart of Mary's experience, as with many of Almond's protagonists, is mystery, suggested by the handprint and the myriad footprints. But

her rite of passage, in both a literal and metaphorical sense, is fundamentally bound up with her class, as symbolised by her father's craft
mark which was already there when he in turn made his pilgrimage
to this shrine to working-class roots. In the penultimate story of the
collection, his mark is seen by his antecedent at the top of a steeple
he built, the same steeple whose weathercock Mary rode before she
descended into the bowels of the earth. Garner sees the stamp of
craftsmen on civilisation as being ancient, ubiquitous, profound and
spiritual.

Many of Garner's images are echoed in Almond's writing. Although
in *My Name is Mina* the eponymous figure allies her search for her
father underground to mythological sources, yet her journey closely
mirrors that of Mary as she seeks her past, albeit her immediate past,
like Garner's character, beneath the earth, a decision sparked off, interestingly, by a teacher whose grandfather was a miner and sang him a
lullaby as a child which he in turn sang to his class:

> Your daddy's doon the mine, my darling,
> Doon in the Curbly Main,
> Your daddy's howkin coal, my darling,
> For his own wean (*MNIM*, pp. 52–3)

History and modernity

This rootedness in working-class culture, this underpinning of
modernity with an appreciation of history and related ideas, is at the
heart of Almond's preoccupation and is often beautifully captured
by the use of folk songs. Tellingly, A.L. Lloyd, the renowned singer
and folklorist, claims that 'the mother of folklore is poverty',[21] and
Almond's choice of ballads suggests the poor through theme and the
use of dialect. For Mina (her name, seemingly, linking her intimately
with the song), the voice of the singing teacher became that of her
recently dead father, and the sentiments of paternal love, sacrifice and
devotion of which he sang, seen through generations of labouring
men, remind her acutely of the enormity of her loss.

In *Kit's Wilderness*, Kit's grandfather repeatedly captured his youth-
ful physical prowess, and by extension, that of the then mining community in song. 'When I was young and in me prime / eh, aye, I
could hew' (*KW*, p. 18). It was a vehicle which allows 'things passing
down generation to generation' (*KW*, p. 26). This interconnectedness
of past and present is impressively contained in the construct of the

memorial to trapped child miners, who, in a sense, are reincarnated in the contemporary young villagers. Their ghosts haunt the narrative, but are seen in the modern generation only by Kit and John Askew. It is no surprise that when John seeks a sanctuary from the pain of modern life and the brutality of his father it is to the now derelict pit that he flees. He is accompanied by Kit and the familiar spectres, 'the others that walk beside us in the world' (*KW*, p. 11). It is through the power of story and the comforting figures of erstwhile victims of adult exploitation and through his growing friendship with Kit that John finds the strength to leave. The mine is then rebuilt and used by local schools to explore working-class life.

Perhaps the antithesis of Almond's use of underground settings is his employment of images of flight, used so effectively by Hines in *Kes*, which connote ideas of freedom, escape and elevation, all of these utilised in Almond's first novel for children, *Skellig*. Interestingly in a work which continually evokes William Blake, Skellig's progression can be seen to be closely in keeping with that described in *Heaven and Hell* written by the eighteenth-century philosopher, Emmanuel Swedenborg. Peter Ackroyd, Blake's biographer, attests to Swedenborg's influence on the poet.[22] One of the philosopher's beliefs contained in his work is discussed under the subtitle 'Changes of State with the Angels in Heaven'.[23] He argues that, just like men, angels differ in spiritual strength depending on the degree to which they espouse love and wisdom. Those with the least perfection 'are in shade and cold and in their obscurity and undelight'. This lack of ecstasy is due to an obsession with the self. They are unenlightened, an impression suggested by images of darkness and cold. When their love of God becomes profound they are exposed to 'the light and heat of their lives', being 'withheld from the love of self, their perception, and sense of good rendered more exquisite'.[24]

Michael's first view of the angel is through the beam of a torch in the dimness of the collapsing garage. He is irascible, anti-social and obsessed by his own physical discomforts. When removed to the relative light of the attic, and significantly when selflessly and lovingly he visits Michael's sick sister, his recovery, and especially his spiritual growth, blossom. 'It was her that gave the strength to me' (*S*, p. 157). That same strength, the manifestation of Skellig's new lack of egotism, allows two epiphanies to take place in which Michael, Mina and Skellig, forming a ring, are lifted from the suffering and the prosaic into what Swedenborg calls the 'exquisite', emphasised by the light of the moon illuminating their faces, dispelling the gloom, the negative and the unenlightened and allowing the unity of the human and the divine.

Skellig's grammar and phraseology, his identification with brown ale and Chinese takeaways, allies him to the north of England working class. His escape from the decay and obsolescence of the garage and his eventual elevation on to a higher plane can be seen as a metaphor for the changing fortunes of a section of the poor by such profound changes as improved educational opportunities and England's transformation into a post-industrial country, but also as an intimate and loving re-evaluation of what in previous generations had been dismissed as 'the lower orders', all elements, as I have argued, charted in Almond's fiction. Perhaps the rise depicted in *The Boy Who Climbed into the Moon* can be seen as reflecting the journey the author took, away from home and back again. Inherent in the title is an image suggesting ambition – reaching for the moon, and the means by which Paul reached his destination – climbing a ladder – also feeds into ideas of social aspiration. Significantly, Paul renounces the attractions of the lunar world in favour of the familial and the familiar, and, like Almond's return to his native place, Paul brings with him from his travels elements of the other in the form of the young circus performer, Fortuna. She embraces similar characteristics to Corinna in *Secret Heart*, which in turn borrows much from Dickens's *Hard Times*, elements of the exotic, the creative, and all embracing notions of freedom and self-expression, providing an antithesis to a narrow, sometimes hostile and utilitarian society seen in Almond's writing and perhaps gently referred to in Paul's restriction to the basement flat at the beginning of the book. Almond, from his sojourn away from the working-class area of his birth, returned enabled by education, experience and maturity, rich souvenirs indeed, to re-create his place and his people through the medium of his creative imagination, out of which comes his humane and affectionate homage to his class.

Notes

1. Peter Hollindale, 'Autograph No. 142: David Almond', *Books for Keeps* 142, http://booksforkeeps.co.uk/issue/142/childrens-books/articles/authorgraph/authorgraph-no142–david-almond (accessed 1 September 2003): 8–9.
2. Seamus Heaney, *North* (London: Faber & Faber, 1976), p. 12.
3. Jeanette Winterson, 'My Hero: Shelagh Delaney', *Guardian* Review (18 September 2010), http://www.theguardian.com/books/2010/sep/18/jeanette-winterson-my-hero-shelagh-delaney (accessed 20 January 2014).
4. Arthur Marwick, *The Sixties* (Oxford: Oxford University Press, 1998), p. 129.

5. Nicholas Tucker and Nikki Gamble (eds), *Family Fictions* (London: Continuum, 2001), pp. 23–6.
6. Melvyn Bragg, 'At First, Oxford to Me was Unreal, like Camelot', *Daily Telegraph* Weekend (31 May 2003).
7. David Newsome, *The Victorian World Picture* (London: Fontana, 1998), p. 44.
8. Brian Jackson and Dennis Marsden, *Education and the Working Class* (Harmondsworth: Pelican, 1961), p. 238.
9. Jackson and Marsden, *Education and the Working Class*, p. 244.
10. Tony Harrison, *Selected Poems* (Harmondsworth: Penguin, 1985), p. 126.
11. Justin Wintle and Emma Fisher, *The Pied Pipers: Interviews with the Influential Creators of Children's Literature* (New York: Paddington Press, 1974), p. 225.
12. Jackson and Marsden, *Education and the Working Class*, p. 241.
13. Wintle and Fisher, *Pied Pipers*, p. 225.
14. J.S. Hurt, *Elementary Schooling and the Working Classes 1860–1918* (London: Routledge & Kegan Paul, 1979), pp. 190–2.
15. Bragg, 'At First'.
16. Berlie Doherty, *How Green You Are* (London: Mammoth, 1996), p. 9.
17. Harrison, *Selected Poems*, p. 116.
18. Henry Mayhew, *London Labour and the London Poor* (London: Penguin, 1985), p. 210.
19. Hollindale, 'Autograph No. 142'.
20. Alan Garner, *The Stone Book Quartet* (London: Collins, 1983), p. 45.
21. A.L. Lloyd, *Folk Song in England* (London: Panther, 1969), p. 9.
22. Peter Ackroyd, *Blake* (London: Sinclair-Stevenson, 1995; Minerva, 1996), p. 102.
23. Emmanuel Swedenborg, *Heaven and Hell* (London: Swedenborg Society, 1937), p. 99.
24. Swedenborg, *Heaven and Hell*, pp. 199–202.

8

David Almond's *Heaven Eyes* as a Complex Variation

Perry Nodelman

Coming to my first reading of *Heaven Eyes* after having already experienced a number of other Almond novels, I found it both familiar and strange – familiar in part because it was strange, but also strange in ways less familiar. As Michael Levy says, 'The amazing thing about Almond's work, of course, is that everything ties together.'[1] *Heaven Eyes* clearly occupies the same imaginative territory as the rest of Almond's books, and similarly evokes a characteristic concrete and naturalistic yet decidedly magical atmosphere. But it stands apart from the novels for older child readers I discussed in an earlier chapter in this book by having a female protagonist. That makes a sizeable difference. It seems to lead the novel into intriguingly ambivalent combinations of features – types of characters and images – that are separate and even opposite in the novels about boys. As a result, *Heaven Eyes* seems even more assertive than Almond's other novels in its claims to a meaningfulness beyond its surface events, and in its invitation for readers to attempt to interpret those events in order to discover that meaning – and even more resistant to a satisfyingly complete interpretation. After spending some time with the novel and comparing it with Almond's other books, I think I understand a lot about it. But for all that, I also have the sense that I do not really understand it at all, that whatever interpretations I have come up with seem to describe a text much less resonant and evocative than the satisfyingly mysterious one Almond actually wrote.

Like almost all of Almond's writing for young people, *Heaven Eyes* centrally features its protagonist's meeting with and connection to a wild and exotic 'other' in a dark, decaying place redolent of the Tyneside past and in a transition to a new world to come; in this case, the site of the industrial wasteland Erin enters displays billboards depicting the new development planned for it and 'showing how the world would be' (*HE*, p. 184). There is the usual voyage away from home and into the dark and the wild, into what the novel itself announces as a borderland: 'the edge of the Black Middens, where mud and water mingled; where the most mysterious of creatures – Heaven Eyes, the saint – could be discovered' (*HE*, p. 212). The Black Middens are a somewhat more liquid version of the various deathly caves, graves and holes in the ground that characters descend into and arise from in the other novels, and the deserted printing plant where Erin finds Heaven Eyes also contains other gravelike holes similar to ones found throughout Almond's work: 'places to tumble out the world and not get found again' (*HE*, p. 94), where, Erin says as she gets lost in one, 'Death grew all around and drew me in' (*HE*, p. 104). In these dark places, Erin meets her own version of a wild being, the 'fishy froggy thing' (*HE*, p. 155) named Heaven Eyes whose webbed fingers are reminiscent of Skellig's wings, and who must, like Askew, Clay, Oliver, Mole and other only partially wild youngsters in other Almond novels, be brought out of the wild.

As in those other novels, furthermore, 'damaged children' (*HE*, p. 4) play central parts, especially those missing parents. Like Joe in *The Fire-Eaters*, Erin is the product of a one-night stand and never met her father, and like Oliver and Crystal in *Raven Summer* and Stephen in *Clay*, all the children in *Heaven Eyes* seem to have lost both their parents (Erin's friend January becomes an exception only at the end). Like Almond's other central characters, Erin is torn between two friends – a boy and a girl who appear to represent opposite choices for her future – and there is a declaration of love between the central girl (herself) and the central boy. Erin feels the same need to protect those she understands to be her siblings as did Michael in *Skellig* and Askew in *Kit's Wilderness*, and Heaven Eyes's 'Grampa' represents and tries to maintain the same ties to the past as does Kit's grandfather. Furthermore, as happens throughout Almond's work, the characters significantly engage in forms of art – writing and storytelling in *Kit's Wilderness*, modelling figures out of clay as in *Clay* – and connect to the past by means of old photographs. Also, birds figure significantly, and the birds that twice fly into rooms here imply symbolic resonances much as do the owls in *Skellig* and the raven in *Raven Summer*; Erin explicitly identifies one of them as 'the bird of life' (*HE*, p. 211).

Heaven Eyes maintains these connections to Almond's other work in the context of a plot that explicitly follows what Mavis Reimer and I identify in *The Pleasures of Children's Literature* as the most typical pattern of children's fiction, the home/away/home story of an escape into dangerous freedom and a return to restrictive safety.[2] The novel is divided into three sections whose titles refer to either the home place or the away one: Whitegates/the Black Middens/Whitegates. That the novel conventionally proposes these as representations of opposite values central to its meanings becomes clear in the distinction in their names between black and white, and in the repetition of the same pattern of home values on either side of the away ones in the words painted on the doors that form the raft Erin and her friends travel away on: '**ENTRANCE DANGER EXIT**' (*HE*, p. 37).

But what seems so clear at first glance is less so upon further consideration. While the home here is certainly meant to be a safe place, Erin experiences it as dangerous, and not just because it has a prisonlike garden paved in concrete and a metal fence and 'they're always telling you it's not a prison here' (*HE*, p. 11). In fact Whitegates is not very imprisoning, and as Erin describes it, the children who live there seem remarkably free to do what they wish (including a long history of escapes to and willing returns from 'freedom'), and remarkably lucky in their affection and concern for each other. In contrast to most real experiences and fictional depictions of orphanage life, Whitegates is surprisingly utopian. Indeed, its real danger as Erin sees it is the threat, not of too much cruelty but of too much love. Erin perceives Maureen, the woman who runs the home and yearns to love her, as trying to replace her real mother, so that even the love offered by this safe home is viewed as imprisoning, and its safety as threatening; as Erin escapes, she says, 'I wanted to see Maureen watching us. I wanted to see her weeping as we left' (*HE*, p. 33).

While Erin seems to be right to think of Maureen's urgent need for love as dangerous and escape from Whitegates as necessary, it is not exactly clear why – especially when the escape clearly depends on the assumption that return is not only possible but inevitable. Indeed, as the ruling spirit of Whitegates, Maureen is as ambiguous as the mixture of love and bitterness Erin sees in her eyes. Maureen is as damaged as the 'damaged children' (*HE*, p. 4) she has in her care, and, as a vulnerable female herself in need of care, she might be viewed as this novel's equivalent of the younger sisters and infants who need care from a stronger sibling in Almond's other books; at the end, Heaven Eyes says, 'Maureen is the little girl. So where is the Mummy of Maureen?' (*HE*, p. 221). Then Heaven Eyes and the others become something like mothers for her. Erin and Heaven Eyes allow Maureen into their family-like circle not in the role of a parent but as someone equally vulnerable and so, equally childlike, and so confirm Erin's own need to nurture as well as be free. The child becomes the parent as the parent becomes the child.

Before that, Erin understands Maureen as an enemy not just because she sees Erin as a threat to her own memories of her mother, but because she enforces theoretically therapeutic activities as a way of dealing with the children's damage; i.e. making the children something other and supposedly better than they understand themselves to be. But again ambivalently, the therapy Maureen enforces merely duplicates what the children already do on their own (perhaps because she taught them how to?). When Maureen asks the children to tell the stories of their lives 'even if it was a mixture of fact and memory and imagination' (*HE*, p. 6), Erin insists that 'I don't need to build a stupid Life Story Book' (*HE*, p. 9). But then she goes on to describe her own version of the impossibly utopian time before her mother's death – a 'Paradise' (*HE*, p. 22) that is surely her own mixture of fact, memory and imagination. Maureen also leaves her charge Wilson Cairns free to 'dream, work with clay, and imagine his own astounding world' (*HE*, p. 15), so that 'behind his glasses, beneath his fat, Wilson roamed the limits of his imagination' (*HE*, p. 15). In encouraging such activities, in allowing frequent escapes and returns both mental and physical, Whitegates under Maureen's management is less an imprisoning place of limits than a borderland – already in part an 'away' place.

This is not to say that, despite her claim that Whitegates is 'a safe place' (*HE*, p. 14), Maureen does not legitimately represent the danger Erin sees in it – just as we might expect an 'away' place to do. Erin rightly resists the idea that she is essentially and primarily what Maureen sees in her – 'Damaged child, wild mind, thinks we can do anything but she'll come to nothing' (*HE*, p. 18) – and insists, instead, 'There's nothing wrong with us. We can do anything we want to do. Anything' (*HE*, p. 18). In this surprisingly utopian novel about children in need, Erin seems to be right about that, and Maureen's more cynical and much more realistic view of how early damage actually does affect vulnerable youngsters in real life seems merely limiting of larger potential, a trap to avoid. Caught up in her realistic pessimism, Maureen cannot understand how Heaven Eyes can be happy despite the awful things that have happened to her (*HE*, p. 207), and so her attempts to impose her view of who Heaven Eyes is on Heaven Eyes are bound to be counterproductive. As Erin says, 'you wouldn't know how to just love her, leave her alone and let her be Heaven Eyes, and let her story come out slow as slow' (*HE*, p. 208).

The major problem with Maureen's regime is simply that she privileges what she considers to be normal and then tries to impose her version of and dismay at their inevitable abnormality on the children in her care, and their consequent need of her parental protection. In opposition to this limiting view, Erin and her friends have imagined and created a quite different kind of family, one in which the children are equal partners in caring for and getting care from each other, and in parenting not only each other but themselves. Erin's acts of putting on her mother's make-up to become something like her mother herself and then sharing this form of motherhood with the equally motherless Heaven Eyes resonates as an image of the novel's way of understanding how children without parents can in fact be successfully parented.

As in most home/away/home stories, the Whitegates at the end of the novel is a different place than it was at the beginning, at least for Maureen, who now shares the children's vision of what parenting and home actually are and can be. It is now a safely loving home – and yet still, ambivalently, something of a prison, something the children will still need to escape from, from time to time.

If this home is ambivalently both prison and refuge, and also both home and, as an inadequate replacement for supposedly normal homes, a place away from home, the Black Middens are an equally ambivalent place away from home – and also, for their inhabitant Heaven Eyes, both a prison and a refuge. For Erin and her friends January and Mouse, however, their journey there represents freedom beyond the border, out in the wilds where they can be 'free as the beasts and birds' (*HE*, p. 12). But the wildness of this freedom is something of a deception. To indulge in it, the children don garments already established as being their running-away clothes, and know for certain they will return, for they always do. Much as Whitegates is an incompletely imagined home, then, the journeys away from it represent a temporary, imagined, and therefore surprisingly incomplete freedom. But while the children do once more return from the particular journey reported in the novel, and do plan at the end to keep on repeating their escapes, this trip does have its consequences. Something different and important does happen, something that transcends play and both confirms and undermines the need for freedom – something that adds to the novel's ambivalent rendering of what is home and what is away from home.

The beginning of the journey sounds like the introduction to a horror story. As Erin climbs onto the raft, she says, 'I thought I was climbing down to my death' (*HE*, p. 42). As the raft moves away from the lights into the darkness, the children are 'in terror that we'd be lost, in terror that this journey was nothing but a journey into death' (*HE*, p. 46). They then experience the Middens as 'wet black lethal mud' (*HE*, p. 50) that is slowly sucking them down into what sounds like a living death in a grave, Erin imagining she is joining her dead mother as her eyes and ears fill with mud. In the midst of this gravelike underworld, Erin feels a hand on her shoulder and turns in terror to see her first glimpse of Heaven Eyes, a mysterious creature with webs stretched between her fingers who introduces them to a looming figure, 'black as the night and mud' (*HE*, p. 54), who wants to 'dig them back into the mud' (*HE*, p. 55). Heaven Eyes then leads them to a place ominously labelled **'KEEP OUT, KEEP OUT, KEEP OUT!'** (*HE*, p. 58), and then offers Erin chocolates in what comes across as a dangerously satanic temptation: 'Take more. ... Take more. Be not feared. Take the thing that looks nicest of all' (*HE*, p. 64).

January appropriately responds to all these signs of doom by saying that Heaven Eyes and her Grampa are 'bloody freaks. ... like something from a bloody nightmare' (*HE*, p. 67) that has Erin under its spell. Later, he adds that the printing plant feels 'like a mad place, an evil place. ... It feels like death, Erin' (*HE*, pp. 96, 97). What started as play seems to have turned into some sort of genuinely terrifying vampire story in a deathly house of horrors.

Anyone familiar with the conventions of children's literature might make a pretty safe guess about what is likely to happen next: the children will barely escape this horrific nightmare and then rush back from whence they came, now absolutely certain that home is best and that they are too fragile to cope with the dangers of the world beyond its walls. But of course, that does not happen here. Heaven Eyes is not a dangerous temptress, but a vulnerable creature in need of help. Even more interesting (and confusing), Grampa, the adult 'caretaker' of the Black Middens, is not so much the demonic antithesis of Maureen, the adult caretaker of Whitegates, as he is a somewhat exaggerated version of her. Away is merely home writ large.

Like Maureen, Grampa is a surrogate parent, a pretender to a family relationship with a 'damaged' child he devotes his life to protecting. In order to create a safe home for Heaven Eyes, whose family died in a boating accident, he has kept her cut off from the rest of the world and in ignorance of it, much as Maureen hopes the walls of Whitegates will protect her charges from the past that has damaged them and the present that she is convinced will do nothing but more damage. Grampa has protected Heaven Eyes by persuading her that the other people she can see on and across the river – and also, the family she still dreams of – are 'ghosts' and dangerous to her. His conviction that the story about Heaven Eyes that he weaves around her is safer than the real truth, and his endless writing about events that is part accurate record and part imagined strangeness is an image of the work of a caretaking historian that echoes Maureen's belief in the children's need for at least partially imagined stories about themselves that she elicits and sanctions. It also echoes the children's own stories about themselves: "'It's our story," said Jan. ..."Truth and dreams and bits made up'" (*HE*, p. 179).

When Erin and her friends discover evidence of what actually happened to Heaven Eyes's family, Grampa admits his lies and asks, 'Is there great wrongness in this hiding things?' (*HE*, p. 168). Heaven Eyes assures him there isn't: 'There is no wrongness, Grampa. You is Caretaker. You is been only trying to take care' (*HE*, p. 169). And that seems to be true: while the homes and the stories about themselves that both Grampa and Maureen offer the children in their care are imprisoningly overprotective, they are also, nevertheless, usefully protective – as are the children's own stories about themselves.

The place Grampa takes care of, separated from the ghosts of living beings, is actually a sort of death – as Erin imagines Whitegates is. Entering Grampa's territory is like a descent into the earth, a kind of dying, even, as Erin's use of the phrase 'Hell's Teeth' (*HE*, pp. 38, 50) as she enters it might imply, an entry into Hell. Its gloomy blackness is filled with the remnants of the dead past – with unused machines and scattered type and boxes full of old things, many of them buried in and dug out of the muck. Grampa himself is a remnant of the past, a worker from the days when the printing plant operated, a sort of ghost of what once was. When he dies, he has told Heaven Eyes, she will have to 'cross the river to the world of ghosts' (*HE,* p. 79), a journey that, as Levy suggests, evokes the crossing of the Styx in Greek mythology to arrive in the underworld of death. Ironically, however, it is life across the river, not death, and the underworld of the Black Middens is the place inhabited by ghosts, including, as Erin says, 'the ghosts of those who had worked here' (*HE*, p. 102). Grampa is one of those ghosts, albeit a living one.

Even so, this deathlike place is a place where life – the life of Heaven Eyes – has been protected. Heaven Eyes, a 'froggy fishy thing', sees herself in Erin's treasured photo of herself as a similarly froggy fishy thing inside her mother before birth: 'the black Black Middens was the mum' (*HE*, p. 93), she says, and she 'the fishy or froggy thing swimming in the water' (*HE*, p. 93). Now out of the muck, she nevertheless remains froggy and fishy and still inhabits a dark place that keeps her safe as she grows. The Black Middens are, then, a protective womb as well as an apparently deathlike tomb – an away place exactly as safe and as stultifying as the home of Whitegates is. The end of the journey confirms the parallels as Grampa transfers his care of Heaven Eyes to the group of children, just as Maureen will do once they all return to Whitegates – a way of allowing the children's need to be away from adult control to become available at home. In *Heaven Eyes*, then, away is less an opposite than it is another version of home. Away is home, just as home is to some extent away.

The return home in Heaven Eyes varies from convention in terms of its length. Rather than a perfunctory 'they all lived happily ever after', Almond offers almost 44 further pages after the return, describing not only how Heaven Eyes enters the life of Whitegates and how the children change Maureen's relationship to them, but also how January's mother returns for him. The bulk of this final section emphasises the significance of returns – as does the entire novel in various ways. As Wilson Cairns tells Erin before her journey begins, 'It's easy to go away. The magic thing is to come back again' (*HE*, p. 31).

Magic or not, the children have always returned from their adventures, and do so once more, as does the sailor in the old song Erin remembers her mother singing: 'Bobby Shaftoe's gone to sea ... He'll come back and marry me'. The seaman who fathered Erin went to sea and never did come back to marry this singer – perhaps like the sailor in the song Grampa sings 'about the sea, about someone who had gone too far out and couldn't find his way home again' (*HE*, p. 71). But some girls on the bank shout 'Bobby Shaftoe' as the children pass by on their raft (*HE*, p. 45) and they do come back – as Erin says at the beginning of Part 3, 'Back to where we started from' (*HE*, p. 189). Unlike Bobby Shaftoe, Erin doesn't marry – but she does experience a sort of marriage in her new familial relationships with both Heaven Eyes and Maureen.

Nor is that the only return. Knowledge of Heaven Eyes's past returns, unearthed from boxes full of old papers and photographs. January's mother returns, as he has wished; and as might happen in a fairy tale, they immediately recognise each other. The 'saint', the corpse of a dead workman perfectly preserved by the muck, returns from below the surface, and then what appears to be his spirit guides Grampa's spirit after his death towards what might be a new life away from the dead place he watched over.

That sounds something like a resurrection, and there is a sense in which the central arc of the plot of *Heaven Eyes* is a move out of life down through the earthy muck into a place of death and then out again into a better place. Indeed, all the returns I have mentioned

result in coming back to the same place made better by the journey
away. As part of new families, both Heaven Eyes and January develop
a new relationship to their resurrected pasts; like the saint, they have
been held in a state of protective stasis that has readied them for a
better, changed life after the stasis. According to Erin, she and her
friends also return home different: the river 'carried our stories home
with us. It carried our sister home with us' (*HE*, p. 189). Those stories
are about how a dead place preserved old life – made a tomb a womb.
Those stories, then, enter into the life and meaning of the place they
are brought back to. They thus change the meaning of both the Black
Middens and Whitegates, for they describe, first, how a place away
from home is also a nurturing home, and second, how those nurtured there then enter the original home as a form of alien awayness
that paradoxically results in it becoming more homelike. The return
represents a healthy invasion of home by away, an away already itself
invaded by home values.

As *Heaven Eyes* offers these intriguing variations on and compli-
cations of conventions central to writing for children, it also varies
and complicates the specific tropes and patterns that make Almond's
work so immediately recognisable as distinctly his. Apparently because
she is a girl, Erin experiences none of the temptations of aggression,
as do the male protagonists of the other novels; her attraction to the
freedom of the wild does not engage her in a consideration of the
machismo of savagery. Instead of being pulled by male friends like
Askew or Stanny Mole or Stephen Rose *towards* expressions of violence, Erin is pulled by her male friend January *away* from something
she perceives as threatening violence to herself: Maureen's need for
her. She seeks freedom from being nurtured, and seems to define
'freedom' as being self-reliant.

Nevertheless, both she and January require each other in order to
experience this form of self-reliance, and Erin cannot resist allowing
her other friend Mouse to join them on the raft. Her journey into this
form of wildness is already significantly qualified by evidence of her
concern for and need for contact with others, and more a symbolic
gesture than an actual urge. It is not surprising, then, that the wild
being she confronts away from home should be an orphaned child
much like herself, or that, despite her initial insistence in response to
Heaven Eyes's invitation to be her sister, they are not connected and
that 'each of us is all alone' (*HE*, p. 62), she then quickly gives in to
it. In what presents itself as a wild place of death, she merely recon-
firms the vital ability to care for others she had already expressed
back home.

Furthermore, the wild creature who allows that to happen is at the same time, and for all her fishy froggishness, a girl much like herself. As Heaven Eyes says, 'Erin is like Heaven Eyes and Heaven Eyes is like Erin' (*HE*, p. 93). Not only are both orphans cared for by adults not their parents, but both have a gift of hope. Erin can persuade herself and the other children that, far from being damaged, 'We can do anything we want to do' (*HE*, p. 18); and according to Grampa, Heaven Eyes 'does see through all the grief and trouble in the world to the heaven that does lie beneath' (*HE*, p. 72). On her trip into the wild, then, Erin meets a version of herself. I might argue that Askew in *Kit's Wilderness* or Clay in *Clay* or the tiger in *Secret Heart* are symbolic representations of wild aspects or desires of the boys they interact with; but Heaven Eyes is not so much what Erin wants as what she already is, presented in a form different enough to allow her to the clarity of self-perception at one remove. The act of bringing Heaven Eyes out of the wild and home again, then, becomes a form of self-acceptance – and acceptance of her own need to be home and cared for also.

Erin's acceptance of Heaven Eyes as a sister puts Heaven Eyes in the role occupied by baby sisters in the other novels; or, I might argue, Heaven Eye's acceptance of Erin put Erin in the role of that needy infant. In fact, both girls can be viewed as filling the roles of both nurturer and nurturee. Heaven Eyes is, then, this novel's equivalent of three central roles present in and represented by different characters in Almond's other work: the wild creature, the needy youngster, and the girl of the same age as the protagonist who represents love in opposition to the urge to wildness, the last signalled here by January's desire for freedom and consequent effort to separate Erin from Heaven Eyes.

In an equally complicated way, Grampa is both another manifestation of wildness – an older man like McNulty in *The Fire-Eaters*, damaged and made apparently savage and demonic by his long experience of separation and pain – and also a representative and preserver of a past on the verge of being forgotten, an older man like Kit's grandfather who knows what once was and keeps it intact enough to be passed on before he dies. While both Heaven Eyes's Grampa and Kit's Grandpa represent a connection between the industrial past and the developing future, Kit's relatively harmless and certainly saner Grandpa lacks the potential for exploring the more dangerous and restrictive aspects of cleavage to the past. As an ambivalent combination of Kit's kind Grandpa and the damaged McNulty, Heaven Eyes's Grampa is more unsettled and unsettling.

The ambivalence of Erin's closest male friend January becomes clear in terms of his antipathy to Grampa; the young male encourager of wildness has no interest in the wildest male in the novel, and pulls Erin away from the ruined wild place Grampa reigns over – but towards the wildness of freedom, as the male friends of Almond's male protagonists do. Erin herself declares her love for January as many other girls declare their love for Almond's other boys, in a way that both supports and conflicts with her own wild desires. She is both the wild-seeking protagonist and the girl who loves a boy and pulls him away from too much wildness – as paradoxical as the combination of her first name Erin (Erring? Errant?) and her last name Law.

As the boy who tempts the protagonists to wildness, January carries the expected knife and expresses the expected celebration of the exhilarations of danger. After Erin looks at what she first sees as a 'churning filthy river' (*HE*, p. 38), January joyously shouts 'Freedom!' (*HE*, p. 43). But his wildness is qualified by his need for nurturing and particularly, his need for Erin; he finally admits, 'I can't leave you, Erin' *(HE*, p. 150). In moments like these, as the would-be free man pulled back from the wild by his feelings for a girl, January is more like the male protagonists of the other novels than Erin is. Indeed, I can easily imagine a less interesting novel about these events much more like Almond's other books, in which January would be the central focalising character.

As a second and less central boy, Mouse seems to fill the position occupied by more savage and more macho boys in the other novels. But despite his animal name, he is anything but wild. He has a tattoo as the wild boys often do, but his says, 'Please look after me' (*HE*, p. 40). He is yet one more version of a younger child in need of care – while at the same time being himself a nurturer of a weaker creature, the pet mouse that gives him his name. Furthermore, Mouse is also connected with Grampa, the caretaker of the Black Middens, by means of his similar obsession with digging up remnants of the past. As Grampa's 'Little Helper', Mouse represents not the dangerous appeal of moving into the wild but the opposite dangers of not going anywhere – being so caught up in recovering the past that one neglects to move forward in the present and into the future. Once more, *Heaven Eyes* replicates in Mouse the same role as that represented by characters in each of Almond's other novels, but invests that role with meanings quite different from those the similar characters in the other novels all share.

As I suggested earlier, the plot of *Heaven Eyes* both follows and significantly varies from the conventions of children's literature and the events of Almond's other novels. It does so specifically in terms of a connected set of concerns about the past, and by establishing a parallel between Grampa's and Mouse's activities in digging up the relics of the past and the children's preservation and recovery of their own pasts. Like all of Almond's work, the novel offers a sense of life in the Tyneside area as a matter of living amongst ruins, surrounded by the decayed detritus of a once glorious industrial era now over. The children of Whitegates equivalently live among the ruins of their parents' absence; as 'damaged', perhaps they even *are* those ruins. As the civic officials work to move past desolation and remove and replace the physical ruins with the gleaming new structures depicted on the billboards, Maureen works to replace the ruins left by the children's past with a utopian version of normalcy. The issue both civically and personally is the relevance of memories and artefacts of the past in the building of the future. Should what once was and is now gone merely be wiped out and forgotten in the new life replacing it? Should one assume, alternately, that life in the ruins is the only possibility, hide oneself in the past, and refuse to move beyond them? Or is there some way of moving forward while still maintaining a connection with the past?

Seen from this angle, Maureen and Grampa seem less similar than opposite. While Maureen's efforts to shape the children's stories echo the billboard's replacement of what once was with a new vision, Grampa's acts of recovery and preservation represent resistance to moving forward. He keeps the ruins of what once was as intact as he can, and resists any attempt to connect with life outside. Even the food he and Heaven Eyes live on consists of leftover remnants, canned and boxed in days gone by. But after Erin and the others enter into the space filled with the things (and the person) Grampa has preserved, a new dimension of his care-taking becomes evident. What he has cared for has survived intact enough to be carried forward out of the past and into the future. His digging activities, like those of Mouse, reveal a conviction that not everything from the past is merely discardable garbage, that, as Mouse claims, 'the earth was filled with objects from the past and that one day he'd find real treasure, something really precious in the cold dark earth' (*HE*, p. 35). And after Grampa has preserved the past, the children can bring it with them out of the dark place that held it. As children now connected to and aware of the past that Grampa has preserved, Erin and January can bring Heaven Eyes out of the Black Middens, much as Kit brings Askew out of the mines and beyond the ghosts of the past he connected with there in *Kit's Wilderness*.

Among the things Grampa has found and preserved is the treasure of Heaven Eyes's past, including photographs of her family and
of herself as a child; so not only Heaven Eyes herself, but also her
knowledge of her past, can be salvaged and carried forward. Nor are
these the only photographs that figure significantly in the novel, and
that reveal connections between Almond's treatment of the Tyneside
past and the children's pasts. There is Erin's creased photograph of
herself and her mother and also, 'the photograph from the hospital
that showed me growing inside her' (*HE*, p. 21). And there is Mouse's
photograph of a number of men playing football: 'Sometimes he
pointed to one of the men and said this one was his father. Sometimes
it was another man' (*HE*, p. 8). Mouse's uncertainty reveals the ways
in which the past enters the present – part true history, part imagined,
but nevertheless sustaining.

The printing works also contains photographs of Tyneside's past
industrial glory, of many ships and many workers and of the printing
works in its prime. Among them is an image of a young man in a uniform like Grampa's: 'Was this the same man, years and years ago?' (*HE*,
p. 73). It seems it is, and that one of the treasures Grampa has taken
care of is himself. But this one must be let go of, just as Kit's Grandpa
must be let go of in *Kit's Wilderness* after he, too, has preserved and
passes on what remains of the past. Having passed on the past, the old
must, inevitably, pass on themselves.

Grampa passes on with the assistance of what he calls a 'saint' – the
preserved corpse the children have found in the muck of the Black
Middens. Erin asks, 'What did he mean by saying it was a saint?'
(*HE*, p. 162) – a surprisingly direct invitation to readers to think
about the significance of that. The answer might be found in Seamus
Heaney's poem 'The Tollund Man', about the corpse of an ancient
man similarly preserved in the muck of a peat bog in Denmark and
dug up centuries after his death, in 1950; in the poem, Heaney speaks
of 'Those dark juices [of the fen] working / Him to a saint's kept
body'.[3] Heaney identifies the Tollund man as a saintly relic because
the noose around his neck suggests he might have been a sacrifice
to a divinity of the bog, and parallels his sacrifice to that of labourers
killed in the much more recent Ulster Troubles, equally unwilling
sacrifices to more powerful forces in equal need of a resurrection
from anonymity. In a discussion of a number of Heaney's poems
about bog men, Anthony Purdy identifies each of them as a '*mnemotope* ... a chronotopic motif manifesting the presence of the past, the
conscious or unconscious memory traces of a more or less distant
period in the life of a culture or, metaphorically, an individual'.[4]

Almond's 'saint' is similarly mnemotopic. While January speculates that he might not be all that old, that the preserved corpse is that of a working man who died only a hundred years ago, he is nevertheless 'the man from the age that had been wiped away' (*HE*, p. 165); and as Heaven Eyes says, 'These saints is them from way back, way way back in the past, afore Grampa, afore Heaven Eyes, afore us all' (*HE*, p. 167). In being dug out of the Middens, the saint is similarly representative of the ongoing presence of the past – in this case, the past industrial glory he was once part of and, presumably, died during, and the ongoing remembering of which he now represents. His emergence from the muck that preserved him represents a potential for continuity and moving forward that ties together a number of the novel's threads.

As well as representing the preservation of memories of the industrial past the saint was martyred to, his journey into the muck and out again also parallels the journey of Erin and her friends into the muck and out again: emerging from the river, 'We were black glistening trembling things, like creatures formed from water, earth and blackness a million million years ago' (*HE*, p. 52), and later, Erin says, 'I felt the Middens mud drying on me, encasing me' (*HE*, p. 67) as she becomes something like a clay figure herself. Grampa, too, has parallels to the saint: digging in the Middens, 'he was like some ancient creature struggling there, like something made of the Midden mud himself' (*HE*, p. 116). And Heaven Eyes also has a parallel trajectory: Grampa found her in the same mud.

Heaven Eyes speaks of that moment in her past as she looks at the creature Wilson Cairns makes of clay: 'These is like me' (*HE*, p. 201), she concludes. Like the statues (and like the saint), she can be found in and raised from the mud. Apparently like the statues (and apparently like the saint), she has the potential to be restored to life again. In a much less ominous foreshadowing of Almond's *Clay*, Wilson suggests that the figures his imagination finds in the clay might actually come to life when he asks Erin if she can see one of them move. Similarly, when Erin first sees the saint, it seems so alive that she wonders if at any moments its eyes might open.

Later, in fact, the eyes do open. The saint's spirit emerges and awakens something of Grampa's exact shape out of his body, and then the two enter the river: 'Heaven said it was Grampa's goodness, Grampa's heart' (*HE*, p. 180) that has emerged and moves onward – just as the past he dug up and preserved can move onwards in the care of children. At this point, then, the saint's journey through muck into a new life beyond it comes to seem symbolic of what happens to Erin and

January on their journey to freedom, what happens to Heaven Eyes in her life with Grampa, and what happens when an artist like Wilson Cairns finds life in muck. Old ruins, dead pasts, damaged childhoods, memory, history, art – all become interconnected through the same central set of tropes, and through a saint who echoes the actions of the Tollund Man, who, in a later poem by Heaney, 'reawoke to revel in the spirit / They strengthened when they chose to put me down'.[5]

In the light of all this, and in the context of Almond's own Catholic upbringing, it is easy to conclude that the thrust of *Heaven Eyes* is in the direction of Christian understandings of rebirth and resurrection. Don Latham suggests something of that sort but normalises the novel into a standard young adult book about developing identity as he argues that 'the children themselves are reborn here in the sense that their experience changes them in profound ways and helps in the formation of their adult identities'.[6]

Even without reference to discourses like Catholicism or developmental psychology that might seem to account for its oddities, the novel's own language continually suggests a symbolic meaningfulness beyond its descriptions of what happened, and includes many statements that seem to insist on explicit explanations of what it is all about, from Erin's description of how life is like a bird in a room to her later assertions that miracles are available to those who know how to look for them: 'No need to go far. The most miraculous of things could be found a few yards away, a river's width away' (*HE*, p. 194). While neither particularly Catholic or developmental, statements like these and many others throughout the novel seem to demand a reader's attention as being explicitly thematic, and as satisfactorily explanatory of its oddities.

But for all that, and as the variety of different and unconnected means for explaining it imply, the novel still exceeds and transcends its apparent meanings. The saint may seem saintly in a traditionally Catholic way, but as Almond reveals later in *Clay*, figures who awaken out of earthy muck are not necessarily or purely good, and the descriptions of this one's beauty are surely too immediately and sensuously physical to represent merely transcendence of physical decay. In any case, none of the explanations of the saint I have come up with myself account adequately for the audacity of this reimagining of a river as a form of bog, of a bog man as a representative figure of the Tyneside past – or for its abiding and magical strangeness. Or in other words – Erin's words, this time – in reading *Heaven Eyes*, 'The most astounding things lie waiting … as each page turns' (*HE*, p. 232). As I hope I have shown here, the novel remains too

astounding to be accounted for by its own apparently thematic statements, or by Catholicism, or by developmental psychology. Nor is it
adequately explained by the many allusions and parallels to earlier
texts like Shakespeare's *The Tempest*, Dante's *Inferno* and T.S. Eliot's *The
Waste Land* that Levy convincingly describes. It is also too astonishing
to be accounted for by its apparent cleavage to conventions of writing
for young people or even by means of its astonishingly ambivalent and
therefore unsettling use of the patterns I have outlined as being typical
of Almond's writing as a whole. After all those aspects of it have been
acknowledged and taken into account, the novel itself, finally, is much
like Erin's final description of what Grampa wrote in his ongoing
journals: 'Like all stories, it has no true end. It goes on and on and
mingles with all the stories of the world' (*HE*, p. 232).

Notes

1. Michael Levy, '"They Thought We Were Dead, and They Were Wrong":
   Children and Salvation in *Kit's Wilderness* and *Heaven Eyes* by David
   Almond', *Foundation: The International Review of Science Fiction* 32(88)
   (Summer 2003): 29.
2. Perry Nodelman and Mavis Reimer, *The Pleasures of Children's Literature*
   (3rd ed., Boston, MA: Allyn & Bacon, 2003).
3. Seamus Heaney, 'The Tollund Man', Internet Poetry Archive, http://
   www.ibiblio.org/ipa/poems/heaney/the_tollund_man.php (accessed 27
   March 2014).
4. Anthony Purdy, 'The Bog Body as Mnemotope: Nationalist Archaeologies
   in Heaney and Tournier', *Style* 36(1) (Spring 2002): 96.
5. Seamus Heaney, 'The Tollund Man in Springtime', The Saturday Poem,
   Guardian, http://www.guardian.co.uk/books/2005/apr/16/poetry.
   seamusheaney (accessed 27 March 2014).
6. Don Latham, *David Almond: Memory and Magic* (Lanham, MD, Toronto
   and Oxford: Scarecrow Press, 2006), p. 70.

9

The Transcendent in David Almond's Play *Wild Girl, Wild Boy*

Michael Levy

David Almond apparently believes in the supernatural. His collection of autobiographical short stories, *Counting Stars* (2000), records instances of regular folk, the people he grew up with in and around Newcastle in northern England, meeting angels and talking with the dead. His novels, from *Skellig* (1998) to *Heaven Eyes* (2000) to *Secret Heart* (2001) on up to the most recent work, *The True Tale of the Monster Billy Dean telt by hisself* (2011) and *The Boy Who Swam with Piranhas* (2013), describe transcendental moments in the lives of their protagonists, moments when children discover that they have heretofore invisible angel's wings jutting from their shoulders, moments when a miraculously preserved body recovered from the industrial slime of the polluted River Tyne in Newcastle, England comes back to life, moments when William Blake's Tyger manifests itself in a northern woodland or an abused boy discovers he can heal the dead. David Almond also believes that the sublime is a part of ordinary life, that the most everyday matters can become extraordinary, can turn into moments of transcendence. Take the simple pleasures of gardening for example, particularly when mixed with the imagination and the sad fact of death.

Something to do with the way I see

In his poetic play *Wild Girl, Wild Boy*, which was first performed in 2001, Almond introduces us to Elaine Grew, a girl of indeterminate age, who can neither read nor write, but who has a highly developed imagination. Her father is similarly imaginative and their greatest joy in life is to go out to their allotment garden, which Don Latham has aptly described as 'a metaphor for the creative imagination – a literal "field of dreams"',[1] and enjoy the wildness and fecundity of nature together. Sometimes they fantasise about growing fairies, but Elaine's father, similar to Mina in Almond's first novel, *Skellig*, can also find wonder in a lark's egg shell or a sweet raspberry. Elaine's mother tolerates their behaviour, but doesn't take part in it; her chosen role is to be the anchor pulling them both back to reality. Less tolerant is their neighbour, Mr McNamara, who looks on from the next allotment garden with deep-seated disapproval and bears a secret interest (the word 'passion' seems too extreme, too imaginative) in Elaine's mother.

Elaine Grew is an oddball; like Joe Maloney in Almond's *Secret Heart* or Billy Dean of *The True Tale of the Monster Billy Dean telt by hisself*, she is someone barely of this world, a frequent truant from school, disabled, and the subject of much disapproval by her neighbours, but she is greatly loved both by her long-suffering mother and her eccentric father. Their life is a constant balancing act, but they get on – or, rather, got on, because as the play opens Elaine's father is recently dead and Elaine, half-mad in her grief, is attempting to write a story about her life called *Wild Girl, Wild Boy*, an impossible thing to achieve considering that she cannot in fact write.

> Look at it! Look at it! I'm not stupid. No,
> I'm not! I have problems ... writing.
> Something to do with the way I ... see
> or something. (*WGWB*, p. 11)

We're never told exactly what Elaine's problem is, but it seems likely to be an extreme form of dyslexia known as dysgraphia, perhaps with a touch of autism. When she sees words on a page they seem to 'slither and crawl and slide and stagger like wounded things' (*WGWB*, p. 12), although verbally she can be quite eloquent.

Larks appear repeatedly in *Wild Girl, Wild Boy*, where, as in any number of classic English literary and musical works, from Blake to Shelley to George Meredith to Ralph Vaughan Williams to the progressive rock band King Crimson, birds have the ability to both sing beautifully and fly extremely high.

> A song of light ...
> To reach the shining tops of day,
> And drink in everything discerned,
> An ecstasy to music turned[2]

as Meredith put it, stands as a symbol for transcendent beauty. When Elaine draws a picture of her father or just remembers him she invariably does so with him at work in her family's allotment garden and the larks soaring overhead (*WGWB*, p. 18). Though she spends much of the play locked in her bedroom, in memory and fantasy she often flees to the garden at a time before her father's death. There he had shown her a lark's egg.

> Speckled white outside.
> And brilliant white inside. A chick came
> out from this. Can you believe it?
> ....
> A miracle! Look! Larks, larks, larks ....
> ...They fly that high you
> think they fly right out of the world. (*WGWB*, pp. 18–19)

Elaine's dad never gave up on her, insisting that despite her problems at school, 'One day soon, we'll have your writing clear as your drawing, eh?' (*WGWB*, p. 19). He taught her a variety of fantastic games, one involving catching a (presumably nonexistent) spider out of the air, saying a magic spell, and wishing for a five-pound note; another involving growing a fairy using a 'fairy seed' (also snatched from the air), plus spit and horse dung. Of course no fairy ever actually appeared, but that, her father insisted, was because 'Some fairies take ninety-nine years to grow' (*WGWB*, p. 24). Later in the play, Elaine will use these two magic spells, the first in an attempt to ward off Mr. McNamara, who is showing interest in both her newly widowed mother and in reforming Elaine, the second to create the Wild Boy who becomes, in part, a childlike reincarnation of her dead father, and in part, perhaps, the spirit of wild nature itself, something that has been gone from the allotment garden since her father's death.

For Elaine, the allotment garden and the time spent there with her father were the central facts of her existence, the great joy of her life. It was a place where the prosaic and the imaginative met, where 'dreams and magic mixed with leeks and spuds and raspberries' (*WGWB*, p. 21), where, with her dad's blessing, she could indulge her dreams and fantasies, crawling deeper and deeper into the wild, overgrown garden (*WGWB*, p. 21) until her dad would call her back to reality. This, for Almond, is transcendence, finding that great sense of joy and the miraculous in picking and then tasting a raspberry. In opposition to these everyday miracles stands Mr McNamara, their disapproving neighbour who, even when Elaine's father was still alive, was given to making disparaging comments about their allotment, which he sees as a 'damn jungle' (*WGWB*, p. 22), and about Elaine, who, he warns her father, will 'turn out daft as you are. Poor girl' (*WGWB*, p. 22). McNamara, of course, represents society, the voice of propriety and tradition. Through most of *Wild Girl, Wild Boy* (albeit with a hint of a change of heart at the very end), he plays a role comparable to that of the aptly named Bleak Winters in Almond's *Secret Heart* or Mr Todd in Almond's *The Fire-Eaters*, that of killjoy and censor of the imagination. Working in a dramatic medium, Almond also introduces a veritable Greek chorus of disembodied voices to demonstrate society's general disapproval of Elaine's actions:

> –Did you see?
> –Eh?
> –That lass. That Elaine.
> –Her again.
> –Aye. Did you see her coming down from the allotments?
> –Talking to thin air.
> –Laughing at thin air.
> –Singing at thin air.
> –Babbling and laughing like a daft thing, she was.
> –Babbling and laughing and pointing at the larks in the sky.
> ....
> –They put you away for that, you know.
> –They don't.
> –They do.
> ....
> –Aye, a big white van and big strong nurses.
> ....
> –Lock her up, that's what I say.
> –Aye. Take her away. Lock her up. (*WGWB*, pp. 37–8)

So that's the situation. Elaine's father is dead. Her mother is ineffectual. Society, as personified by Mr McNamara, the chorus of townspeople and a local doctor, all want her to either conform or be incarcerated. Elaine, dyslexic and half-fey by nature, overwhelmed by grief and caught in what Rosemary Ross Johnston has called her 'troubled "interior infinite"',[3] seems doomed to a life of either madness or crushed conformity. Fortunately, however, she has the imagination of an artist, what Almond himself in an Afterword calls 'a bold creative spirit, brave enough to yell and scream at death, brave enough to outface it, brave enough to keep returning to her wilderness and to discover – or create – the means to transcend her pain. This', Almond says, 'is what the writer does' (*WGWB*, pp. 86–7).

The transcendent imagination

On the most literal level, once again, Elaine specifically cannot write. She may be totally dysgraphic. She is, however, creative, a painter we're told; in fact her pictures of birds and animals decorate her bedroom throughout the play, and she is a storyteller, a creator of poems, incantations, interpretive dances and imaginative fantasies. It is through her art, in fact, that she retains or perhaps recovers her sanity, alleviates her sorrow and eventually transcends the limitations placed on her by society. And she does so by creating Wild Boy.

Since Almond's play begins *in medias res* after her father's death, Elaine remembers him in a series of flashbacks, his death having become the central fact of her existence. The story she is attempting to write, *Wild Girl, Wild Boy*, recalls her life, but is also her first, perhaps unconscious attempt to bring her father back to life. Elaine is the Wild Girl of the title and her dead father is the Wild Boy, as she shows when she cries out in frustration:

> Wild Boy? Wild Boy?
> He's gone.
> He was here, and now he's gone. (*WGWB*, p. 11)

To Elaine, once again, this is the central fact of her existence, the only fact of any importance. Without her father she sees herself as stupid and without value:

> Dooley, dipstick, thicko
> dense, Can't read, can't write, can't see
> straight, can't think straight ...
> ....
> Can't ... anything ... .Can't
> even wake the dead! (17)

But, of course, she can. Through her imagination, her memory, and her art, Elaine can transcend death. Her imaginative re-creation of the finest moments of her life with her father, those moments of rare and transcendent joy spent in the allotment garden, represent, as Latham suggests, 'inner geography as much as outer landscape',[4] what Elaine calls a 'place of dreams and magic' (*WGWB*, pp. 20–1).

Returning to the allotment in reality, Elaine, using her imagination as her father taught her, begins to work magic spells. Catching a 'seed' in mid-air, she spits on it and cries out, 'Grow like mushroom, grow like magic, grow like happiness in the heart (*WGWB*,

p. 32). Noticing that McNamara is watching her with disapproval, she attempts a magic spell intended to kill him, but, of course, it doesn't work. Finally, feeling despair, she begins to draw, all the while shaking a seedhead rattle and rocking back and forth like an autist or a shaman. And then, 'coming out of the wilderness' (*WGWB*, p. 33), his manifestation heralded by the song of the lark, Wild Boy appears.

Paralleling Elaine's dysgraphia, Wild Boy cannot speak; he can only 'sing weirdly', and Elaine spends much of the latter part of the play attempting to teach him a few basic words. She considers the possibility that he may indeed be a fairy and she describes him as having 'No wings. Heavy. Fur on your hands and feet. You're ... ugly. No not ugly' (*WGWB*, p. 35), like some nature spirit, a faun, or perhaps like a brownie from Almond's own Northumberland. Repeatedly, however, through his actions and through Almond's stage directions, Wild Boy is associated not only with nature – and particularly the larks – but also with Elaine's dead father, and it is significantly worth noting that Almond constructed the play so that one actor can perform both roles. Of course neither Elaine's mother nor Mr McNamara can see Wild Boy. At first, the audience is implicitly invited to assume that he is nothing more than a figment of Elaine's seriously disturbed mind, though Almond does give us hints of Wild Boy's reality from very early on.

Her mother, beside herself, shouts to Elaine that 'You'll drive me wild' (*WGWB*, p. 41). 'Wild', however, in this context is clearly associated not just with anger, but also with both the wildness of nature and with madness. It is a charged word, a symbolic word. Perhaps to be driven 'wild' is exactly what Mrs Grew needs. Soon after making this statement, she begins to sense Wild Boy's presence. We are told in a stage direction that, although 'She does not see Wild Boy [who is on stage and standing right in front of her] ... she appears to feel that something is wrong' (*WGWB*, p. 42) and moments later, she notices 'That ... smell or something. No, not a smell' (*WGWB*, p. 42). Drawing back from this moment of potential revelation, she can only scoff when Elaine tells her that she must look for Wild Boy with her 'inside eye' (*WGWB*, p. 43). Then, in the next scene, when a doctor attempts to examine Elaine's eyes (the traditional window to the soul), stating that he needs to 'look inside, deep inside', again according to the stage directions, Wild Boy 'pulls the Doctor's hand away' from Elaine, causing him to be 'alarmed, amazed, uncomprehending' (*WGWB*, p. 46). Not long after that Mr McNamara also notices 'a smell' (*WGWB*, p. 50) in Wild Boy's presence. But none of these hints are enough to convince anyone that Elaine is any more than mad, a victim of poor parenting and too much imagination. Children,

Mr McNamara insists, need to be 'train[ed] ... proper, just like plants. You got to stake them and prune them and shape them' (*WGWB*, p. 51). Like St Paul, that notorious killjoy, he would have Elaine 'Put away the things of childhood [and] .... Come into the real world' (*WGWB*, pp. 51–2), this despite the fact that Wild Boy is staring him in the face. Repeatedly receiving hints that something beyond his ken is going on, McNamara can only react with violence and threats, shouting incoherently:

> What do you get up to, in here, in the
> dark, in the light of the moon? What's
> that ... something? Wild girl. Wild girl.
> We'll have to tame you. (*WGWB*, p. 53)

Elaine names her Wild Boy with the nonsense syllable 'Skoosh', a name she says comes from 'the deep of [her] heart', and wonders 'How to make the noises from inside your heart match up with letters in the world?' (*WGWB*, p. 54), a question which I would suggest every true artist must ask. She promises Wild Boy that the two of them will create a wilderness in her room, re-creating the symbolically unfallen state of her earlier childhood (*WGWB*, p. 55), and notes that her dad said that 'the greatest of all gardens is the mind' (*WGWB*, p. 56). But it soon becomes clear that this isn't enough. Wild Boy and Elaine both become dispirited and ill, retreating further and further into fantasy. After her mother, with difficulty, pulls Elaine back to reality, they go to the garden, a place Mrs Grew has not been since her husband's death.

This sets the stage for the transcendent moment which is the climax of the play. Acting as independent corroborators of what is about to occur, the Greek chorus of townspeople note:

> –The birds?
> –Aye. Did you hear the way they were
> singing?
> ....
> –Never heard them that loud.
> –And never seen that many.
> –Like the sky was filled with larkybirds. (*WGWB*, p. 72)

Elaine's mother is filled with wonder the moment she enters the allotment garden. Merely experiencing the sight and smell of the place makes her relax and, with very little hesitation, she joins in when Elaine demonstrates how to grow a fairy; soon both of them are chanting, 'Grow like mushroom, grow like magic, grow like happiness in the heart' (*WGWB*, p. 74). And then, the stage directions tell us:

The larks sing. Mum and Elaine hug each other. Wild Boy emerges from the wilderness. He watches them. Mum sees him over Elaine's shoulder. (*WGWB*, p. 76)

Wild Boy's vocabulary is still rather limited. At Elaine's request he says her name and his own, or at least the one Elaine has given him, 'Skoosh'. When Elaine's mother, who has never been identified by name throughout the play, asks him what her name is, he calls her what Elaine calls her, 'M-um' (*WGWB*, p. 77). The implications of this monosyllable are interesting. Although Almond has connected Wild Boy to Elaine's dead father both symbolically and through his stage-craft, and although Wild Boy clearly does recognise the older woman, he can do so only within the context of Elaine's viewpoint. She is Elaine's mother, not, it seems, his wife. Wild Boy, although objectively real, is, or so it appears, merely Elaine's re-creation of her father, rather than her actual father re-created.

Waking the dead

This, however, seems to be enough. Elaine shouts, 'Come on, Mum. Come on, Wild Boy. Let's wake the dead!' The word 'wake' in this context may well be a pun, as Elaine and her mother are indeed holding a wake of sorts for the dead father, complete with a highly cathartic bout of dancing and singing. This is immediately followed by Elaine's discovery of a piece of shell from a lark's egg, a symbol of both birth and transcendence. Elaine repeats what her father had previously told her, that 'A little lark grew out of this. From yellow yolk and salty white and flew away. A miracle' (*WGWB*, p. 78).

But Almond, it seems, being after all in charge of the tale, can play it both ways. Wild Boy may only recognise Mrs. Grew as Elaine's mother, but her father can still appear on stage to bless the moment. As the two women stand together, 'absorbed by their memories and by the miracle of the eggshell' (*WGWB*, p. 78), Elaine's father reappears for one magical moment, his presence again heralded by the lark's call. He chants:

Go on. Go on.
Crawl deep into wilderness.
Just call out if you get lost.
Grow like mushroom, grow like magic,
grow like happiness in the heart.
....
Wild girls, wild girls.

And then, again, we are told that the larks sing.

The play, however, has one last, brief scene. Mr. McNamara enters. He too has noticed the larks and, although he can't verbalise it, has perhaps seen some of the miracle that has just occurred. Moved beyond what he has heretofore seemed capable of, exclaiming incoherently about 'The larks so loud. The sun so bright' (*WGWB*, p. 79), he has brought to them raspberries that Elaine's father had planted, but that have, tellingly, grown over the fence into his allotment. Calling them 'sweeter than any I ever grew' (*WGWB*, p. 80), he has evidently brought them as a way of acknowledging the miracle he has witnessed. He then withdraws.

Whether or not McNamara, Mrs Grew and Elaine have a future together is as yet unclear. As the play ends, however, the broken family is, for the moment at least, re-created: Wild Boy returns and, at his behest, he, Elaine, and her mother 'move into the wilderness' of their allotment together.

Conclusion

Natalie Babbitt, another great children's writer, once told me that 'for children, it can never be too late for a happy ending', a statement she worked variations on in a number of essays and speeches, as well as her novels. Though his books are somewhat darker than Babbitt's, Almond ultimately seems to feel much the same way. His child heroes, from Michael in *Skellig* to Elaine in *Wild Girl, Wild Boy*, to Billy in *The True Tale of the Monster Billy Dean telt by hisself*, survive horrible events, some physical, some more existential, from abandonment, bullying and abuse, to the near-loss of a sister or (repeatedly) the actual loss of a parent, to, in *Billy Dean*, the killing of a wicked father in self-defence. They meet people like McNulty in *The Fire-Eaters* whose suffering actually drives him to madness, violent self-abuse and suicide.

And yet, though nothing is ever perfect and the bad times cannot disappear completely, their lives always improve in the end. Michael's sister survives and Skellig, who may be an angel, may have gained salvation. Elaine, though still dysgraphic, has regained some semblance of her father, reconciled with her mother, and drawn back from the edge of insanity. Even Billy Dean gains a muted happiness and a family significantly more functional than any he had previously known. In Almond's novels and plays good characters survive the darkness around them. They are not plaster saints who simply forgive those who have hurt them, but they do come to terms with their pain and move on, drawn back to life by the small miracles of nature – fresh raspberries, the song of the larks, and love – the transcendent things that make life worthwhile.

Notes

1. Don Latham, *David Almond: Memory and Magic* (Lanham, MD, Toronto and Oxford: Scarecrow Press, 2006), p. 3.
2. George Meredith, 'The Lark Ascending', http://allpoetry.com/poem/8475727-The-Lark-Ascending-by-George-Meredith (accessed 5 February 2014).
3. Rosemary Ross Johnston, 'Carnivals, the Carnivalesque, *The Magic Puddin'*, and David Almond's *Wild Girl, Wild Boy*: Towards a Theorizing of Children's Plays', *Children's Literature in Education* 34(2) (2003): 142.
4. Latham, *David Almond*, p. 55.

10

Of Writing: *The True Tale of the Monster Billy Dean telt by hisself*

Rosemary Ross Johnston

The telling of the telling ...

The True Tale of the Monster Billy Dean telt by hisself was published in September 2011, with two different covers, one designed for adults (Viking) and one for the young adult market (Puffin), thus presumably implying an expectation of two different readerships. It was widely noted as David Almond's first book for adults. The tale is told retrospectively through the voice and idiosyncratic written language of its protagonist. The bare bones of the story are revealed in a sort of brief prolegomenon, written from the perspective of the grown-up narrator who is now a father and who in the last two lines of the book puts down his paper, pencil and knife (all of which have been developed throughout the novel into strong and related textual and thematic motifs) and goes 'to play in the water with my son' (*BD*, p. 255). The title of the book is telling (no pun intended); it is explicitly labelled a 'tale', that is, a story that is *told by a teller to an audience*. In this case the actual *telling* of the tale to an audience of reader or readers is integral to both the story and the discourse, and the language, processes and artefacts for recording that telling in written form constitute a fundamental part of its structure, narrative and themes.

This chapter will discuss the multiple and sometimes metafictional layerings of this *telling* of narrative to implied but unknown (and hoped for) *readers* ('Is enybody reedin this?', *BD*, p. 47), and the complex constructions both of that teller and those readers, relating these to the Bakhtinian idea of the superaddressee.[1] And, because the title tells us that this is a 'true tale', the chapter will consider the intricacies and challenges of writing *truth*, especially in *fiction*. Further, noting the idea of the *ethics of hope*[2] implied in Billy's story (and in other books by this author), it will discuss the contribution that *Billy Dean* makes to the literary world of its ultimate teller, David Almond himself.

Almond is an unusual writer with a world-view and understanding of life and language that transcend conventional reality and logic. This book in some ways feels like a culmination of Almond's artistic and philosophical thinking, not so much in its story but in its ideas and themes. In particular, the earlier book *Clay* (2005) – set in the past ('Not so long ago, but it was a different age' *C*, p. 1), whereas *Billy Dean* is set in a future (one we would hope never eventuates) – prefigures some of these: the 'monster' Mouldy, the making of figures (this time out of clay) and trying to give them life, knives and angels, seeing 'with the eyes of the spirit' (*C*, p. 84), the idea of the Master ('What do you want of me, Master?' *C*, p. 207), and even the idea of truth and the telling of the tale:

> So now I've written it down, all of it. I don't care if there's craziness in it. I've learned that crazy things can be the truest things of all. You don't believe me? Tell yourself it's just a story, nothing more. (*C*, p. 296)

At the textual level of *Billy Dean*, the protagonist narrator drifts in his telling from third-person singular into first- and second-person singulars and plurals, and the script reproduces spellings that are phonetic and idiomatic, consciously and perhaps self-consciously reflecting both dialect and childish ignorance. These devices assume a guise of simplicity but simultaneously make available to the reader densities of both innocence and knowingness, and of past and present – and prescient – acuity. As noted above, the process of telling is part of Almond's deeper themes, and its most obvious manifestation – that is, playing around with reproducing language (as it does) – is a surface reproduction of significant intention. *Billy Dean* involves a deep engagement with the idea of truth ('*The true …*'), its sometimes dubious relationship to language ('*tale*'), and its even more dubious relationship to *telling* ('*telt by hisself*'). This book plays with the conundrum of language and the purposes it serves – ways it can be recorded (and the desire to record and publish and make available to others); what it tells and what it doesn't tell; how it can both manipulate and be manipulated; how the veracity of any telling is inflected and infused with personal desires and perspectives; and how it is influenced by time and place (the *then* and *now*): 'Facts and dreams and peopl and gosts get all mixed up' (*BD*, p. 255). Billy Dean, once the 'Aynjel Childe', has, he informs us from the hindsight of the prolegomenon, 'dun the deeds of monsters'. Yet, despite all these limitations, this text iterates and reiterates that there is a capacity in language that somehow detonates, through its very limitations and beyond its words, glimpses and indeed revelations of subtlety and perplexity. Almond the writer uses the sparseness of Billy's telling to create, both as immanence (emerging from deeply within) and transcendence (being tuned to and by something way beyond himself), a delicate and compassionate portrait of the human spirit – its strength as well as its weakness, its capacity for good as well as its capacity for evil, its capacity to love as well as its capacity to hate.

The tools of telling: words as thematic and narrative focus

Almond has created Billy Dean as a narrator/protagonist/*teller*/writer who, locked in his room for most of his childhood, his only human interaction with a mother who cares for him and a father who visits spasmodically and sometimes violently, is fascinated by both the intrinsic and extrinsic qualities of the building blocks of language, words – the *writing* of words, the *sounds* of words, the *reading* of words, and the way that words unravel *stories*. Billy's father, Wilfred, a priest, has told him stories and tried to teach him letters; 'words ar wot make us human', he tells his son. But Wilfred both loves and hates Billy; he sees him on the one hand as a product of his own sin and weakness, a 'bluddy idyot' who should have been killed in the womb or at birth, and on the other as a son whom he 'bluddy love[s]' (*BD*, p. 32). As an imprisoned child Billy knows the outside world only as words that are 'meaning-less'; apart from glimpses through the skylight window of stars and birds, there was no way for him to understand: 'The pitchers had no meanin for me just as the words abowt them had no meanin for me' (*BD*, p. 9). Yet the incomprehensible stories his father tells him so inspire Billy that he desperately wants to use words himself, to write them and 'publish' them in his own book. To obtain the materials for this he dissects and carefully skins mice to make a form of vellum or parchment, and uses feathers and blood from a dead bird as quill and ink – and when that isn't enough, takes blood from his own arm (*BD*, pp. 49, 56–7). He then writes nine pages of 'lyns of tiny meaningless byutiful shayps mixd in with the handful of words I new', telling and illustrating the story of Billy Dean 'who grew in secret at the hart of things' *(BD*, p. 61):

> I drew pitchers of the boy that the story was abowt. I drew pitchers of the boy that rote the tale ...

> I rote it with the fether of a bird on the skin of a beest just lyk in ayn-
> shunt tymes & it wos very byutiful. (*BD*, p. 61)

When Billy shows his 'masterpees' to Wilfred, Billy tells his father
that their names have been written there together in ink and blood,
that his book has beasts, birds, humans, and words and stories in it, and
that when he was writing it, 'I shwd payshens & dedicayshon & I had
my mind on hiyer things' (*BD*, p. 66). This is a *telling of the writing*, and
what Billy does here both is and is not like the writing that forms the
novel, and implies so much about what writing is, what it does, and
how it does it.

In the tag of the title ('*telt by hisself*') and throughout, attention is
drawn to actual *words* – thought, spoken and written – through the
narrative device of representing Billy's awkward – sometimes very
awkward – phonetic spellings. This is hard to read at first, and some
have found it off-putting,[3] noting the inconsistencies, occasionally
even in the same sentence (but Billy tells us at the end that at various
times he has asked his mother or Elizabeth to help with spellings). It
is true that (mis)spellings and devices such as the use of the ampersand
are not consistent but neither of course are 'correct' English spellings
(and having overworked the anxiety of my computer in copying small
extracts from the text, it is quite possible that the publisher's computer
may have won with the correction on a few occasions). This issue does
not concern me. What is important in this book about telling and the
tools of that telling – words – is not consistency but rather the idea of
what the phonetic spellings emphasise, what words look like, the physical marks that pertain to and contain both visible and invisible traces:

> Just let the pensil wark. Let it move like footsteps throu the dust and leev
> its marks behind. Let it leev its marks just like birds and beests leav ther
> misteryous footprints in mud. (*BD*, p. 5)

This book is about writing, and about both what words can say and
most of all, and most deeply of all, about what words cannot say but
somehow nonetheless carry in the telling; about how and what words
mean and the relationship between words and actions; about official
words and private words; about how they reveal and how they cover
up. Words can be used both to fool oneself and to fool others. Wilfred
seduces Billy's mother Veronica not only with the stroking of 'preshus
oil' but with the use of sanctifying words to bewitch and confuse her
(she did not understand their meaning), and to convince himself and
perhaps hopefully God into seeing this as a sacred act. Veronica tells
Billy: 'He mutterd some weard words I cudnt understand. He mingld

my name up with the weard words like I was part of the prare &
part of the spel' (*BD*, p. 149). Even worse is his awful irony and spe-
cious duplicity, when, taking the pregnant Veronica to Mrs Malone
and seeking her help, Wilfred says, pretending Christian concern but
hypocritically covering up his own role in the pregnancy, 'It cud happen to eny of us … it is up to us to show compassion.' Billy writes
that Mrs Malone reports Wilfred as saying, 'This baby has been sent
by God abuv … and it is we who hav bene chosen to receev it and
protect it' (*BD*, pp. 158–9).

My intention is to be literary rather than to engage in formal
linguistic analysis, but Almond's text also provokes consideration of
how speech sounds are conceived, perceived and recorded, and how
spoken language relates to idea and written sign or signifier. In his
Cratylus Dialogue, Plato began the science of semantics by arguing
that words denote concepts that exist in the world of ideas. The first
chapter of *Billy Dean* ('The Start of It') begins with the grammatical
evidentiary declaration, 'I am told I will lern how to rite the tale by
riting it. 1 word then anotha 1 word then anotha (*BD*, p. 5).

As in the prolegomenon, there is a sense of going back to that
beginning of 'Darkness with a boy in it' (*BD*, p. 5). That little boy Billy
did not have the necessary tools that the grown Billy, now writing
retrospectively, has. The boy Billy began learning to write by touching, sniffing, and staring deep into the objects available to him in his
imprisoned world. This is both a semantic and pragmatic exercise; he
uses this context (his only real world references) as stimuli for the idea
of the word, and then for learning the word, and how to write the
word so that he can tell his story. This makes the stories start, with
all their 'memries feelins thorts and horras loves & dremes', churning together 'like tormented water' (*BD*, p. 5). Billy's father tries to
teach him to read letters and write, using Bible stories and fairy tales,
spelling out the letters of his son's name from the text of the story of
Moses. When Billy asks if he is in that story, his father laughs, but then
tells him that 'Billy Dean can be fownd like that in any tale you care
to menshon' (*BD*, p. 29). Wilfred, of course, is referring to the letters
that constitute Billy's name, and Billy is wholly self-centred, but there
is also an implication here of the fabulous; somehow Billy's story has
a greater pertinence.

The idea of words fills Billy's life. So much so that when he is
released from his bedroom prison into the war-ravaged world outside,
he sees words and language – signs *written* to be *read* – in the tracks of
animals and the landscapes of the natural world. But meaning – like
truth – remains elusive, paradoxically somehow beyond words, just

as his father tried to show him in one of his early frustrating lessons: 'Wot do you see beyond the words between the words[?]' (*BD*, p. 33). And even one's own words can't always be trusted, and can become part of trickery and deception. When Billy discovers the 'healin tuch', the often rude nonsense words of his incantations are interpreted by those listening as 'the words of aynjels and spirits': '*Comp yor blip to us! Comp yor blip & chang yor chop & kink yor kop!*' he yells (*BD*, p. 211). Nonetheless they encourage others into experiencing delusions and possibly healings of illnesses and ailments that may or may not be real. And Billy realises he can fool the people who say, 'O lissen how byutiful its is! Lissen how gloryus he is'; he writes: 'How rong they are. It is just sounds and chants and noyses and yels. It is noys with no meening in it but with weard byuty and weard strength' (*BD*, p. 211). In fact, he says, 'nonsense danses off my tongue. Ha! Ha! Bluddy ha!' (p. 212). And whilst he tells them that what comes through him is 'absolutely bluddy nothing and nort' (*BD*, p. 213), they don't believe him; he remains to them the Aynjel Childe.

Almond has crafted, through phonetic representations, the construction of a speaker/writer/teller who is both innocent and knowing, who has been confined to a microcosm that, though a prison, is safe and where his relationship with his mother (but not his father) is secure; then exposed to a desperately unsafe macrocosm, where he will be judged, misinterpreted and manipulated to develop his seemingly special powers.

From the beginning the act of writing has been an act of the senses, a sensuous act, and this sensuousness relates to the physical connection of Billy's early memories of his parents: his father holding him as a baby ('O the feel of his breathin against my body', *BD*, p. 6) and his mother, a hairdresser, cutting his hair ('I feel her fingers & her thums. ... They hold my head and tilt it', *BD*, p. 7). The act of writing for Billy becomes touch, smell, sight, hearing, the intimacy of invading the body of the mouse, the feel of blood and bone and feather. The ultimate sensuousness of lovemaking is of course at the heart of Billy's situation, his mother's helplessness and his father's despair; Wilfred writes to Billy: 'All my actions have been born of lust and the abuse of power and of cowardice' (*BD*, p. 36). Despite this, the priest continues to exert his power and fulfil his lust: 'I heard gasps and cries. ... Wilfred! O Wilfred! Veronica! Veronica!' (*BD*, p. 16). Billy's parents are far from perfect; Wilfred agonises about his weakness in begetting Billy, locks him up not only to conceal his fatherhood but also because he was 'curious' to know how a child would grow in such conditions (*BD*, p. 36), and sways between love and hate, tenderness and frustration at what he perceives as Billy's slowness. His mother is a mixture of weakness and strength – weakness in acceding to Wilfred's injunction to hide Billy away from the world, weakness in retreating and leaving Billy to face Wilfred's rages ('Mam had shuffld acros the flor away from us', *BD*, p. 31); strong in that she perseveres as her own person in her own world; even on the Island she 'has customers for her hairdressing', but now 'goes alone without her sissor carryer' (254) – who of course used to be the young Billy.

This story tells how words not only record life but create life, how they can be gifts (Billy writes his favourite words on scraps of paper and squeezes them into the broken Jesus statue – 'words like star & sky & sun & sea', *BD*, p. 202), how for Billy the footprints and pawprints and clawprints of birds and animals are like a 'weard langwag ritten on the surfas of the world' (*BD*, p. 192), with the birds 'singin the sounds of the words that they have rit' *(BD*, p. 196). It is part of his enchantment ('I am entrancd', *BD*, p. 193) with the beauty of the natural world, with the 'lejons of the lovely living things'. But his own 'possessions' make him very aware of the power of illusion, make him question 'reality': if he can imagine things so intensely, 'what dos that meen for all the things arownd him that seem reel?' *(BD*, p. 197).

But Billy has to continue his telling, and becomes, as he has intermittently before, his own addressee, as he forces himself and the pencil to write the words that will describe the perfidy of the 'disypls' Jack and Joe, and the terrible events of the last chapters. As he hears his mother's screams the narrative shifts from the first person of the preceding chapter to a second-person narration, in which the deixis increases, and then to the opposite, an interpolated narration where the simple definite article 'the' takes on a very precise meaning; there is no other house, no other door at this moment: 'You run to the house. You open the dore. Insyd thers just silence' *(BD*, p. 236). Confronted by Jack and Joe in the next chapter, the narrative reverts to the first person again. At the end of these events – Jack and Joe, his father and Mr McCaufrey all dead (three of them by Billy's hand) – Billy writes that the world goes on, the sun still rises, and the birds all sing songs 'that cum from the furthest reaches of the world & from the depths of time & from the deepest distant casms of ourselves' (*BD*, p. 250).

Telling and generic affiliations

Generically, *Billy Dean* has elements of horror, perhaps most apparent in the obsequious evil of the Angel Child's 'disciples' Jack and Joe, and elements of fairy tale: a locked-up child as in *Rapunzel* (a story

Wilfred has told his son), weak if not evil parents prepared to sacrifice their child for their own ends as in *Hansel and Gretel*, a sort of good witch/bad witch in Mrs Malone, and perhaps most of all a happy ending (which has attracted some negative criticism[4]). The book is set in a dystopic world of war and terrorism; on the day of Billy's birth (5 May), three suicide bombers came into the town of Blinkbonny and set off multiple devices before blowing up themselves and everyone around them. This type of war has become all too familiar in the twentieth-/twenty-first-century world, but what the war actually is (some readers and reviewers have complained they can't work it out) is not relevant; it is sufficient to know that it is recent, it is ongoing and apparently transglobal, and there is a fear that the world is turning 'bak to wilderness' (*BD*, p. 213). The point is that this is a world not at peace, a world of humans – not 'beests' – engaged in dirty killings of other humans, unlike the 'clean' killings of Mr McCaufrey's butcher shop. Wilfred has told his son that 'words ar wot make us human', but words are not saving the world.

However, the book is generically most clearly linked to fable, perhaps fable linked with parable, perhaps as a fable and/or parable of our time. Almond's fictional world, and earlier the real world, almost went to war in *The Fire-Eaters* (in 1962 at the time of the Cuban missile crisis); but in *Billy Dean* war has come, not carried by massive nuclear bombs sent from a faraway place, but carried by nameless individuals into the small world of Blinkbonny. Fables commonly but not always feature animals, not humans, but Billy sees himself – or has seen himself – as a 'monster', and writes that he grows up with 'birds & mise as frends' (although how much these creatures are actually his friends is debatable). He also plays a sort of Creation game with a wooden box of 'beests' given to him by his father and, as his last act in his bedroom cell, tries to make a 'Mowsbird' by splicing wings from a dead bird on to a dead mouse (*BD*, pp. 68–72). There are obvious resonances of Christian symbology in this – 'breath' and 'blood' and a sort of echo of 'And behold it was very good';[5] Billy writes: 'and the blud of the mows trickld down my fingas & the stink of the wings mixd with my breth but I new I had madyd sumthin new & speshul' (*BD*, p. 69). When he is taken from his prison room and enters the outside world, he writes (in an unconscious paraphrase of the hymn 'All Things Bright and Beautiful', sung by his mother): 'Most wundrus and most stranj are the livin creaturs passin by' (*BD*, p. 83). Fables don't usually have human actors but of course parables do, and this book, with its affiliated concerns relating to the power of innocence, the power of illusion, the power of celebrity and the self-delusions of fame, has strong overtones of parable, and Christian parable in particular. That the time of action is hard to pinpoint – suicide bombers, Billy's mother giving perms (later, at least, it seems she uses sugar-and-water paste), he writes with a 'pensil' but he drinks 'lucozayd' (*BD*, p. 8) – adds to the sense of a sort of modern mythic fable or parable; it's a 'Once upon a time … ' or a 'There was once a man … ' sort of story set in the contemporary world. I suspect that Almond wants us to understand that the events of this story could have happened yesterday, or tomorrow. (In passing, it is interesting that 'Glucozade' is part of the Newcastle story: it was first manufactured in 1927 by Newcastle chemist, William Owen, becoming 'Lucozade' in 1929. The Newcastle area, of course, is deep in Almond's mindscape.)

At a fundamental level, both fable and parable are concerned with the expression of some sort of truth and/or moral. The dreadful antithesis that points to the truth of the parable, the moral at the heart of the fable, is that, in the end, words themselves are not enough; there has to be truth – a lived and living truth – between the words, beneath the words, behind the words, *in* the words, if the words are to mean anything at all. That is, there has to be, in what Wilfred called 'beyond the words' *(BD*, p. 33), an intent to honour moral integrity; without this, being able to write and publish such words for readers is just another form of meaninglessness. This is clearly also an expression of what Almond feels about authorial purpose and authorial responsibility. On the last page of the text, almost the last lines, and in what he calls a 'final writing', Billy tells his readers: 'Let the wars be done. Let us continue. Let my child grow' (*BD*, p. 256). This is prayer, plea and moral all in one; humankind is on the one hand immense ('us') and on the other deeply and vulnerably personal ('my child'), the survival of each is dependent on the other, and wars must stop.

The Aynjel Childe and the question of truth and telling

How Billy learns to read and write and 'tell' has far-reaching consequences. The process whereby he eventually (after a time of deliberate pretence) begins to act as a spiritual medium – apparently reaching beyond the seen into the unseen, communicating with those who are dead, soothing the bereaved – is directly analogous to how he has learned to write and read. Then, his father began introducing him to new words and new ideas by telling him stories ('How can I understand the noshon of an aynjel or a saynte? But the mistry dusnt matta. I luv his voys I luv him nere me luv the way the storys move acros his lips & throu the air and into my ere & into my brain', *BD*, p. 13).

Later, Mrs Malone does the same thing to teach him to develop and use what she calls his 'speshal senses'.

When Wilfred shows Billy his wounds from the bombings, Billy, not understanding (or perhaps understanding too deeply?), collapses in a sort of fit; when he recovers his father asks his son to heal him. As his father goes on teaching Billy about the world, sometimes despairing at his son's slowness, Billy learns very quickly to dissemble: answering yes or no as his father hopes, even though, as he says, 'I didn't reely hav a clew what he wos on abowt' (*BD*, p. 21). Whether or not he is eventually possessed by 'poseshun & poseshun' & pose-shun' (*BD*, p. 184), or simply dissembles until he convinces even himself, Billy feels 'completely overtook' and thus becomes 'The Aynjel Childe at last' (*BD*, p. 184). He heals memories just as his father long before had asked him to heal the wounds on his hands. And just as he learnt words from objects then, and used real-world references as signs and signifiers to convey, assign and process meaning, so he now uses objects to find the dead: a shoe, scarf, brooch, seashell, pen, pipe, doll: 'It is a marvel to me how the tales and memrise and spirits & bodys seem to be raysd by such little things. ... It is the same with the things of my own that I tuch & hold' (*BD*, p. 189).

At the end of the book, on the island, writing the final lines of his story, surrounded by praying pilgrims and a peaceful seascape, Billy contemplates the issue of truth, in a sort of personal evaluation of its epistemic modality (the reliability of his own memories) and the justification for his title (*The True Tale* ...):

> Truth? Is it truth? Maybe everything did not happen exactly as I remem-ber it and exactly as I have told it. There is so much confushon. Facts and dreams and people and gosts get all mixed up. The tales of 1 person mingl with the accounts of others and what we dred and what we wish are all mixed up with what we kno. The living & the dead are all mixd up. But that is how this world is. That is how the mind of Billy Dean is. So that is how this tale must be. And yes. Everything is true. (*BD*, pp. 255–6)

Most of Almond's books, but *Billy Dean* in particular, ignite if not actually engage – or perhaps more accurately they engage without resolution? – with the paradoxes and problematic nature of truth. There are no ready answers; Skellig, when asked who he is, merely replies, 'Something ... something like that.'[6] Billy, of course, is claim-ing to write a 'true tale'. The paradox is that in the little book he cre-ated for his father he has told, with the tools and knowledge available to him at that time, the truth about the world as he understands it. He has, in the subsequent telling of the narrative, recorded (but with the

clear perspective of hindsight) the events of his life as best he can: the
cell-like beginning, his release and stint as the Angel Child, and the
terrible events leading up to the killing of his father. That his father,
just before he tries to strangle Billy, produces that little book – Billy's
'aynshent book ritten with the fether of a bird on the skin of a beast'
(*BD*, p. 242) – invites not only contemplation of the effects of that
act of writing and of the power of words to recall the past or bring
the past into the present ('And do you remember how you rote on
me? … And do you remember the words drew blood & how our
blood mingld?' asks his father, *BD*, p. 242), but also contemplation of
the allegorical significance of father/son relationships, of 'blessings'
and 'wounds', of the oft-repeated words 'ancient' and 'masterpiece',
and most of all, of the imperative to tell until the telling is finished:
'Sharpen the pensil. Finish it qwik. Tel what we did' (*BD*, p. 247). The
irony – or is it resolution? – is that at the end of the story, when Billy
finishes the story from the now self-imposed isolation of the island,
he is in a way back where he started, albeit in the role of father rather
than son, this time living in the picture rather than just looking at it on
his wall, and living in the words rather than just writing them. And he
still knows very little about the external world; he does not even know
if the world is still at war. But perhaps that is one of Almond's points –
it is in the interior world, in our rich private worlds, that we flourish.

There are other allegorical resonances: Billy may be seen as a sort of
saviour figure, a Messiah who heals, a little child who leads them,[7] or as
a version of Everyman (but Almond's Everyman, who is far from conventional). It is a human version of a divine story – the breath of life –
that restores his mother. That the giver of that life, Mr McCaufrey, then
dies creating a funeral pyre, evokes a sense of sacrifice. The novel, simple
as it may appear, is rich in imagery (much of it Almond's familiar imagery) and language is clearly used in metaphorical and symbolic ways.

The idea of the superaddressee

An intimate part of any telling is the audience – the person or persons to
whom the story is addressed. Billy explicitly talks to his readers at certain
times. Of course, the 'reader' who is addressed directly by Billy is assumed
to be someone who could have been present; this is, in Wolfgang Iser's
terms, the implied reader – the reader implied by the text.[8] Billy hopes
for a reader – it is his reason for telling: he or she (they) for whom the
words are 'ritten', into whom the words 'enter', to prowl into 'yur blud &
bones & to infect yur dremes' (*BD*, p. 2). My interest is in the readers for
whom Almond is writing. As an author he also hopes for readers – in the

case of this book, pragmatically, perhaps two different sets of readerships. *Billy Dean*'s construction of readers is particularly interesting because, for whatever reason (perhaps the market of adult readers as well?), it is in this book that we can most clearly see what has been part of Almond's writing across all his books: the assumption of readers who will understand not only his style (think about both *Skellig: the Book* and *Skellig: The Play*) but his unique vision of a world at once deeply rooted in a real and easily discernible landscape (the north of England) and yet perilously, sometimes miraculously, sometimes magically, sometimes mystically, on the edge of somewhere else.

Such a story written in such a way could easily become parody, or a more oblique form of magic realism, of which latter there are indeed elements (simply put, 'mundane' mixed with 'magical/mystical'). Indeed, I argue in the first chapter that Almond's mode of writing is better described as 'mystical realism'. The unusual presentation of the text and the melodramatic plot (priest gets simple hairdresser pregnant, keeps son locked away, son has visions, son kills father) could be used to trivialise the story. If we see *Billy Dean* as the protagonist Billy's story, which it is in narrative terms, it could perhaps be interpreted as self-indulgent. However, ultimately Billy Dean's story is written by Almond (just as Jane Eyre's story is ultimately written by Charlotte Brontë, and David Copperfield's is ultimately written by Charles Dickens). I make these obvious points because, as the chapters in this volume make clear, David Almond – like Brontë and Dickens – has a literary world, just as much as he has a literary landscape and a literary mindscape. And in this, his first book for adults, as in his earlier books for young people, Almond trusts his readers. In *Skellig* he trusted readers to accept a cranky old fellow with angel's wings and some sort of special healing powers. He has instinctively written this book for – and implicitly constructed – readers who are prepared to persevere and 'desifer the words' (*BD*, p. 47) and 'the weard langwaj' (*BD*, p. 192), and who most of all commit to engagement with his artistic impulse, not necessarily with his point of view, but with his points of viewing; not necessarily with his world-view, but with the delicate netlike reticulum of ideas that are part of it.

In his discussion of text production and consumption, the Russian theorist Mikhail Bakhtin claims that all utterances (spoken or written) are shaped according to three variables: the object of discourse (the speaker or writer – the first person), the immediate addressee (the second person – in this case, the readers actually addressed by Billy within the narrative), and a 'third person', the superaddressee. This superaddressee (*nadadresat*) is not a higher authority as such but one who is a 'constituitive aspect of the whole utterance', who 'under deeper analysis, may be revealed in it', and whose 'absolutely just responsive understanding' is taken for granted.[9] This, I think, is a metalinguistic, more sophisticated idea not so much of the reader, *but of the writer*, and of the reason writers write: I'm writing this now because I trust that someone will truly understand what I am trying to say. The superaddressee exists as a sort of promise to the writer, and also for the reader, who assumes that the writer has something worthwhile to say, and even if it is difficult, puts up with it. Philosopher Maurice S. Friedman draws a correlation between Bakhtin's concept of the superaddressee and Martin Buber's concept of the 'eternal Thou'.[10] Buber described a relationship which rather than being '*I to It*', in this case, a writer (I = Almond) to a reader (it = he or she), and which Buber saw as a sort of 'user' or functional relationship, is a more personal '*I to thou*' (you) relationship. Thus in this case, it is a writer (I = Almond) and a reader ('you').

The essential point of distinction is the nature of the relationship; it implies not any particular 'cleverness' or authority but rather readers – and writers – who make themselves available and open, which in Buber's view (and whilst he was a theologian he postulated this as the essence of relationship between people as well as between people and God) is powerful, unbounded, sharing, enlarging, enhancing and dialogic. *Billy Dean* models multiple ideas about the what and why of writing, about the feelings of a writer and the implements needed, about ways of writing and about scripts: Wilfred's letter, Billy's pain in remembering and recording the past, his struggles to learn and write, to tell a difficult story, to make a book. It also models multiple ideas about reading and ways of reading, and about readers, inviting them to understand that no matter what he says, he is neither monster nor angel child; inviting them on the first page to participate as characters in the story ('Mebbe you alredy no him' *BD*, p. 1). Billy hopes for a reader who will understand, even when he is unsure whether there is a reader beyond his family: 'Perhaps beyond Elizabeth & my Mam there will be no readers' (*BD*, p. 256). In the healing session he prays to an absence; now he writes to an absence that he hopes to fill by speaking of and to its existence: 'Leen close to my lips. Rede and lissen' (*BD*, p. 47). Transposing this into terms of the grammatical second person, used by Almond at various times throughout the book, this 'thou-ness'–'you-ness' gives a sense of immediacy and synchronicity; Billy whispers to the mouse, 'Its just me, I say. Its just you' (*BD*, p. 8). Almond expects the reader (expects a 'you'?) to understand and accept that, given certain inescapable conventions – print and printing information, page numbers – and using his own capitals, ampersands, inconsistent spellings and misspellings, this book is written by a boy brought up in isolation, at a time of global war, learning to read and write and spell without any reference points from the very beginning.

Readers – and writers – are part of markets, and I began this chapter by referring to the two reader markets targeted by the different editions of this book –adults and young adults.[11] I am not sure which market – that is, which readership – will be or has been most attracted to this book. As Almond's first book designated for adults, it is interesting to explore any differences from his other books written for children. These have been very successful and popular: *Skellig* won the Whitbread Award and the Carnegie Medal, and in 2010 Almond was awarded the prestigious Hans Christian Andersen Award for his contribution to children's literature. Apart from the obvious phonetic rendition of words and language, which young people of the mobile-phone generation may well find easier to read than older people, it seems to me that any major differences between this book and his earlier children's books relate to two areas: first, the organisation of the book into a long list of short episodic chapters which flag both inter-textual biblical associations and the conventions of literature of earlier periods, such as the Victorian era ('The Story of a Girl in Trubbl'); and secondly, and most conspicuously, a greater sophistication not in thought or thematic intent or writing necessarily, but in actual plot and thence the more 'adult' issues it confronts, such as lust and murder.

An ethics of hope

In Gérard Genette's terms, Billy is an autodiegetic narrator,[12] the 'hero' (or antihero) of his own story. Almond's linguistic techniques, his emphasis on words and writing, his use of language motif and dialect, of free indirect discourse, create a narrative which is at once distinctive and intimate, yet, as fables do, as parables do, implying some idea of ethical or moral or practical truth beyond the personal. In *Billy Dean*, this is not a simple idea or concept but a complex one: it is not that good will prevail in any struggle between good and evil – sometimes it doesn't; it is not that innocence or the innocence of a child can prevail – often it doesn't; it is not that this is a world condemned to war because of the evil that humankind does to itself – that doesn't tell the whole story. *Billy Dean* has intimations of all of these: Mr McCaufrey, hugging Billy, wonders aloud: 'ther you were just beyond the warl – a little beat-ing heart of goodness in all this senseless waste' (*BD*, p. 171); Billy prays to God's absence, using the power of words – depending on the power of words – to infill that absence; Billy and Veronica (his mother), praying to the broken statue of Jesus that Billy has found and dragged out of the mud, feel that being together in the kitchen 'with Jesus & with all the reassembld sayntes and aynjels & with the wilderness of Blinkbonny all around' is 'like being inside Hevan' (*BD*, p. 203).

But Almond's themes are not neatly circumscribed nor contained. Rather, *Billy Dean* – and indeed all his stories, the novels such as *Skellig* and *The Fire-Eaters*, the play *Wild Girl, Wild Boy* – are characterised by what I have elsewhere called an *ethics of hope*, a sense of the potential of the future (especially for young people); a sense of the capacity of the human spirit to choose its own interior response no matter what the external circumstance; a sense of the beauty of creation not only as creation but, no matter how perplexingly, as part of a world that has somehow been created, even if by a God who is now leaving it 'to its own devises' (*BD*, p. 220). This hope may be glimpsed as stars through a tiny window (*Billy Dean*), or in an allotment in an untidy city (*Wild Girl, Wild Boy*), or in a sort of danced mystical communion (*Skellig* and *Skellig:The Play*). It is not a nebulous, fuzzy, feel-good hope that everything will turn out all right (it may not and often does not), nor a straightforward religiously-inspired hope. Rather, it is a deep hope that pertains both to creation and the created, and the act of creating (as Billy learns to do with writing words, as he tries to do in making the mousebird, *BD*, pp. 68–9); that recognises absence as well as presence and beauty as well as ugliness: 'I pray to the absens that is filld with things of gorjus wunder & things of deep distress' (*BD*, p. 211). Praying to an absence invokes the idea that prayer will make a difference. Derrida,[13] following Ferdinand de Saussure, postulates the concept of *Différance,* which notes that the production of meaning always depends on that which something is not, to understand that which it is; that is, words have to appeal to additional words from which they differ. Billy says that Mr McCaufrey has told him: 'I am my father's son … but unlike my father I hav hansomness insyd as wel as owt' (*BD*, p. 170).

It is also a compassionate hope that recognises failings, and perhaps most of all the tendency of humans to engage in self-deception – McCaufrey comments of Wilfred: 'He said he cud see to the goodness of the heart. But he did not let us see the wickedness of his own' (*BD*, p. 170). Billy's 'possessions' are ambiguous but they are possibly the ultimate in self-deception – both of Billy and of his audiences. (Nonetheless, if they feel better, for them it is arguably 'real').

This hope is best expressed by Wilfred, despite all the lies he tells and the havoc he wreaks, when he says: 'Sumtyms the world seems filld with evil. But if we look close enuf we wil fynd that ther is goodness at the hart of evrything' (*BD*, p. 22). Billy himself, wondering if anyone will ever hear what he is saying or read what he is so laboriously trying to write about his dissections, asks of 'enybody ther': 'Rede and lissen. ... Yes it looks like monstrousness but it mite be a kind of tenderness. A kind of love' (*BD*, p. 47). People are complex mixtures; self-interest can even influence those who are basically 'good' and who love Billy: Veronica accedes to Wilfred's injunction to keep Billy the baby and small child locked away; both Mr McCaufrey (because of increased custom) and particularly Mrs Malone (who takes money from those who seek out Billy) profit from Billy becoming the 'Anyjel Childe'.

This idea of goodness, tenderness, love and compassion – all despite rather than because of being human and consequently being flawed, imperfect, frail – is at the heart of Almond's ethics of hope. It is a deep 'innerly' idea that the hope of humanity is humanity itself as part of a created world, despite its frailty, self-centredness and propensity for conflict. Billy's knife and Billy's pencil are strong symbols, and are both positive and negative: the knife can be used for killing (and is), can be used for pulling apart and dissecting (but we are asked to understand why), and can be used for sharpening the pencil (and is). Thus the knife is a force both of destruction and creation. The pencil can be used for the creation of words and images, for the re-creation of the beauty of the world ('I rite bits of my tale in 1 or 2 short weard sentenses that mingl with the weard sentences of the beests & birds' like 'weard langwaj ritten on the surfas of the world', *BD*, p. 192); but it can also be used to manipulate and to create illusions, and to make fantasies real.

If we consider the ethics of hope in *Skellig* (Almond's most famous book), it is, as I have written elsewhere, not so much related to the fact that the baby sister of the protagonist Michael, who has been desperately ill, survives, but rather to 'growing knowledge of the possibility of beauty in the apparently unlovely, of love in unexpected places, of hope in the face of the seemingly hopeless'.[14] The image of the birds on the windowsill is similar to the birds that Billy watches and in which he rejoices, and to the moving episode at the end of *The Fire-Eaters*, in which the internal crisis of the sick father plays out against a specific world context of great crisis. The crisis has been averted, and the narrator Bobby and his friend Ailsa are watching a stag and doe come looking for their lost baby, which they have closed (locked up?) in a garden shed for safety; the words are intensely evocative of Katherine Mansfield's short story 'The Birthday Party', but they are also another expression of what Billy also discovers: the capacity of the natural world to restore and inspire hope and faith in what can only be called the *good*:

> '... I watched them coming through the fields,' [Ailsa] said. 'They've been there half an hour now, just watching. They come for their little 'n, Bobby.'
> We went to the garden shed and opened the door.
> 'Howay, little 'n,' said Ailsa.
> It stood up and walked out with us. It sniffed the air and jumped. We led it to the edge of the garden.
> 'Look!' said Ailsa. She pointed to the deer. 'It's your mum and dad. They found you.' She laughed. We looked out on the hugeness of the land around. 'God knows how, but they've found you.' ...
> 'Sometimes,' said Ailsa, 'the world is so amazing.'
> 'I looked into her eyes.
> 'It is,' I said. (*FE*, pp. 248–9)

Conclusion: Billy Dean and Almond's world

Billy Dean is arranged in three sections –'The Hart of Everything', 'Blinkbonny' and 'The Island'. The first two have multiple chapters, with oddly dated titles (as noted earlier) replete with capital letters ('I see Him Fase to Fase', 'Just There She Lys & She is Dead') – but the last ('The Island') consists of only four pages: this is the present from which Billy concludes the book. Billy, his mother and Elizabeth have left the destruction of Blinkbonny, skirting around the city, going through the wilderness and following the river until reaching the seashore. Here they see the island, familiar to Billy from childhood through the pictures on his wall, a place which long ago his mother had told him was 'like a little bit of Heven ... a plase that sumtyms floted on water & sumtyms rested on the land' (*BD*, p. 8). It has been part of the imagery of his thinking from the beginning, a mystical place that is ambivalent and ambiguous – sometimes part of the mainland, sometimes a separate island that seems almost part of the sea. It is an *other* world, a heterocosm – a heaven that sometimes drifts into earth, an earth that sometimes drifts into heaven. Finding it now, he sees it 'as it always had been in pitchers and dremes ... Sea sky sand grass ... A centre for pilgrims because it is a holy plase' (*BD*, p. 254).

The island is clearly identifiable as Lindisfarne, the 'Holy Island' off the coast of Almond's Northumberland, where the Irish monk St Aidan founded a monastery around AD 634, of which Northumberland's patron saint, St Cuthbert (whose life and miracles are recorded by the Venerable Bede), was later to become bishop. It is here, where stars, sea, sand and land are 'astounding', that Billy, letting 'the sunlite and the breeze and the sound of the sea move over me and throu me', and watching his little son at play, reflectively engages with the idea of truth, the impact of any of the words he has written and the tale he has told, and the state of the world: 'let all the destruction be done at last. Let us be gone. Let all the words be dust. Let there be peace' (*BD*, p. 256).

Almond's particular gift as a writer – or one of them – is to depict the chaos and complexities of human weakness starkly but through a tender – perhaps tenderising – lens. Some have seen this as 'saccharine',[15] but to me it is simply an expression of Almond's world-view, at once idealistic and eschatological, the hope mixed with pain at the core of stories 'that for an impossible afternoon hold back the coming dark' (*CS*, p. 157). Perhaps in this book also designed for adults, this is an inheritance of his writing for children. However, Almond's world is not an easy one; in *Billy Dean* it is one of both terrible and beautiful contrasts: the mice are 'nice' to Billy and 'dirty' to his mother (*BD*, p. 28); Billy himself both kills and 'mayks life'; inner worlds reflect outer worlds in Shakespearean microcosms. The outer world is the dystopic turmoil of a continuing perhaps apocalyptic war, and is mirrored in the confusion and passions of the inner worlds of Billy and his father who as a priest feels he has failed, and as a father (and lover) both loves and hates.

Almond is a subtle and distinctive writer. His works imbricate the intensely personal with the national (even international), the social with the landscapes and 'beests' and birds of the natural environment. There are overlays of crisis, often illness – a sick baby sister in *Skellig*, a sick father in *The Fire-Eaters*, a different kind of sickness in *Billy Dean*, a father who has died in *Wild Girl, Wild Boy*. *Counting Stars* is not a children's book but rewards being read as complementary to the novels; its bricolage of stories offers networks of fine dotted lines from the writer's lived life to his writing life. Its very title points to the significance of one of the most recurrent motifs – stars – in Almond's literary consciousness. In its introduction there is also an intimation of the question of truth that is at the heart of *Billy Dean*: these stories about his childhood, Almond writes, are 'like all stories, they merge memory and dream, the real and imagined, truth and lies'.[16]

Indeed, *Counting Stars* makes explicit that throughout his oeuvre Almond explores what Paul Ricoeur calls a 'terrain of the imaginary'[17] that mixes imagination with the problematic of memory, both its 'cerebral imprint' and its 'imprint in the soul'. As Ricoeur writes:

> Are we not dealing with two different readings of the body, of corporeality – the body as object confronting the body as lived – the parallel now shifting from the ontological plane to the linguistic or semantic plane?[18]

This is precisely what we have seen in *Billy Dean*: Billy shifts from an awareness of his being a baby, a child, in a room with a locked door, to learning both implicitly and explicitly to communicate with and by the signs that bring meaning and form together: words and things, grammar and spelling, social variations in language (as with his deliberate outpouring of nonsense babble during the 'possessions'). So, in a very real sense, *Billy Dean* bears a metafictional relationship to the other books; it is simultaneously a book about writing and an example of the product of such writing. Indeed, it could be seen as an exposé of the writer's life: the struggle to find words, to find the in-between of words, to keep on producing (as Billy has to with his visions), to meet expectations, to be responsible and show 'payshens' and 'dedicayshon' and discipline and integrity, by keeping the 'mind on hiyer things'.

This book resonates with the familiar imagery that in this and Almond's other books become such powerful motifs, and that are used often enough in *Billy Dean* to imagine that they have come to carry a freight of associations for Billy as well. 'Stars' and 'dancing' are notable examples (and the sky is the only part of the world that Billy sees for years): 'Im very small. Im wyd awayk. Im staring up into the square of night. Thers dozens of stars even in that smarl space. They glitta and they even seme to dans' (*BD*, p. 6). In this 'littl memry', Billy describes his father's eyes as glittering like stars, and when Wilfred picks the toddler up and sways with him, it is 'almost lyk hes [Billy] dancing with the stars' (*BD*, p. 6). This leitmotif continues for Billy throughout: in the last few pages, on the Island, he writes that at night 'we all dream of floteing upside down across the stars' (*BD*, p. 254), whilst in the daytime: 'I sharpen the pencil for a final time as he [John, his baby son] dances in the sea and as the rainbows flash around him. He splashes and laghs and calls like the bird that dances in the air abov his head' (*BD*, p. 256).

Billy has known three worlds – the first the cell-world with the small square of starlit window; second, when the door is opened, the ruined world of Blinkbonny; and third, the world of nature – the animals, the river, the glade, the endless sky. However, this third world has been intimated to him from the beginning – by the stars, the birds, the mice – and is to remain a source of beauty and mystery to him, a focus of 'unanserable wundering' (*BD*, p. 198). Watching the day turn into night, he sees that 'the end of things can be as gorjus as ther starts' (*BD*, p. 198), and feels in himself the wish 'to be ended as the day is ended' to discover what is 'to be found in the darknes of drownin and death' (*BD*, p. 198). This is not a death wish but a life wish: a wish to understand more about what life is. There are spaces and gaps in knowing about life as there are spaces and gaps in writing. The place that is sometimes land and sometimes sea can be a breath of heaven that illuminates the here-and-now of earth. The magic of writing is that while it can never tell the whole story, through the alchemy of its semantics and pragmatics, symmetries and symbologies, it somehow can express the inexpressible. Indeed, in the context of the *Billy Dean* text, and apparent in other works in the corpus, there is an implication, a shadowing, of incarnation; of the Word (and/or Greek *Logos*) in, or to be found through, words: 'In the beginning was the Word, and the Word was with God, and the Word was God.'[19] Billy, the son of an unmarried mother and a powerful religious patriarch, could be seen as a new kind of prophet, gathering disciples and a following, helping others, suffering, retreating into the 'garden' of the natural world to be alone; the Word at first unable to speak a word and then learning haltingly to do so. As a new kind of saviour he is the son of an absent father, a 'God' who Billy says has given up and abandoned the world, and who has retreated to live in 'wundrous isolayshon in a place of emtiness and peese' (*BD*, p. 220). And this incarnate Word has power: to bring back the holiness of the broken statue of Jesus, Billy cuts tiny openings into the body with his knife, and squeezes in little bits of paper on which he has written his special words ('star & sky & sun & sea'), and even lets his blood trickle into the neck of Jesus: 'Live Jesus. Accept yor holyness agen' (*BD*, p. 202).

There is a sense that Billy glimpses, and glimpses tantalisingly, but what he sees is incomplete and has inexplicable gaps. In this story about writing and the writing life, and across so many of his other books, this seems to be what and how Almond himself glimpses. The miracle is that writing – and life – somehow do, despite the gaps and inconsistencies, manage to convey the inexpressible that lies at the deepest heart of things. Long ago, Wilfred has said this:

> that words wer mebbe not evrythin. Mebbe the sylens had messijes for us messajes deepa than cud be telt by words. He said that mebbe words got in the way of knowin the most important things of all. (*BD*, p. 33)

Billy writes about his little son: 'I watch him. I write him. And Elizabeth draws him. He is in our words and in our pictures but he is also far beyond them' (*BD*, p. 256). A writer, an artist, can only capture so much, but what he or she do capture can direct and profoundly intimate what they cannot capture. Great art – words, paintings, music – always points to something beyond itself. In *Skellig*, Michael's mother says: '[William Blake] said we were surrounded by angels and spirits' (*S*, p. 122), and Dr MacNabola, asked if love can make people get better, also quotes William Blake: 'Love is the child that breathes our breath / Love is the child that scatters death' (*S*, p. 152). Billy's journey has come from darkness into sunlight – certainly another isolation, foregrounded back in that room by the pictures on his wall, but this is one of his own choosing, on the Holy Island, 'surrounded by the birds of the sea' (*BD*, p. 254), and this one is in the light.

There is a lyrical poignancy and a subtle intimacy in Almond's writing that comes from the rich interweaving of autobiography, memory and artistic creation. It is a corpus of works filled with bigness but focusing on smallness; filled with pain and loss and struggle but focusing on wonder and angels and stars. It is a daring corpus – *Billy Dean* is daring in both how it is presented and what it presents; *Skellig* is daring in creating but never explaining an angel figure and angel wings on a cranky old man who likes Chinese takeaways. It was daring to write quality plays for children – not many do; but what plays they are, and I hope Almond writes more theatre for young people. Within a very specific sense of landscape across his works, there are elements of mysticism, magic realism and the mythic, but they are neither laboured nor elite; they tap into everyday universals. The revelations of the human spirit are also revelations of the everyday, not dressed-up-for-going-out depictions. Birth and death, words and stories, love and loss, words that tell and telling that is too big for words, words that can't tell but create gaps that summon those that can – this is the familiar unfamiliar of Almond's world, a world that is at once profoundly terrible and profoundly beautiful.

Notes

1. Mikhail Bakhtin, *Speech Genres and Other Late Essays* (Austin: University of Texas Press, 1986), p. 126.
2. Rosemary Ross Johnston, 'Childhood: A Narrative Chronotope', in R. Sell (ed.), *Children's Literature as Communication* (Amsterdam, PA: Benjamins, 2002), pp. 137–58. Reprinted in Peter Hunt (ed.), *Critical Concepts in Literary and Cultural Studies*, Vol. III (London: Routledge, 2006), pp. 46–68.

3. Examples of three reviews: 'There's a difficulty, too, in the way Billy tells his tale; his self-taught, mainly phonetic spelling, while effectively conveying his childish simplicity, may be a barrier to some readers' (John Harding, 'The True Tale of the Monster Billy Dean', *Daily Mail* (1 September 2011), http://www.dailymail.co.uk/home/books/article-2032172/David-Almond-THE-TRUE-TALE-OF-THE-MONSTER-BILLY-DEAN.html (accessed 8 January 2014).

'You might get a sense of déjà vu when you read the first few idio-syncratically-written pages of this novel, since writing in non-standard or phonetic English to show a character's lack of language ability is no new gimmick: it goes back to Joyce. More recently it was done with some success in books like David Mitchell's *Cloud Atlas* and Peter Carey's *True History of the Kelly Gang*' (William Kennaway, '*The True Tale of the Monster Billy Dean* by David Almond', *The Times*, 21 July 2012, http://www.thetimes.co.uk/tto/arts/books/fiction/article3479588.ece, accessed 9 January 2014).

'It would be wrong to reveal more of the plot here, but David Almond's first book for adult readers is not only dramatically and emo-tionally suspenseful, it is also vividly drawn and wonderfully well-paced, as one might expect from a master storyteller' (John Burnside, '*The True Tale of the Monster Billy Dean* by David Almond', *Guardian* (3 September 2011), http://www.theguardian.com/books/2011/sep/02/true-tale-monster-billy-dean-review (accessed 17 January 2014).

4. 'The ending is disappointingly saccharine. The build-up, the visceral language, drenched through with religion and butchery, leaves one expecting Armageddon at the very least' (Dinah Hall, *The True Tale of the Monster Billy Dean* by David Almond: A tale of violence, tenderness and linguistic bravado', *Telegraph* (31 August 2011), http://www.telegraph.co.uk/culture/8722822/The-True-Tale-of-the-Monster-Billy-Dean-by-David-Almond-review.html (accessed 8 January 2014).

5. Genesis 1:10.

6. '"Something", he said. "Something like you, something like a beast, something like a bird, something like an angel… Something like that"' (*S*, p. 158).

7. '… a little child will lead them' (Isaiah 11:6).

8. Wolfgang Iser, *The Implied Reader: Patterns of Communication in Prose Fiction from Bunyan to Beckett* (Baltimore, MD: Johns Hopkins University Press, 1978).

9. Bakhtin, *Speech Genres*, p. 126; see also Johnston, 'Childhood', p. 146.

10. Martin Buber, *I and Thou*, trans. Ronald Gregor Smith (New York: Scribner, 2000 [1923]).

11. The latter is a classification that I have recently questioned; there are, I think, 'new pulses of reading power', and the young adult brand, partic-ularly in school libraries, now attracts 'a much younger readership, but not that readership for which it was originally designed' (see Rosemary Ross Johnston, 'Breaking the Boundaries: Liberation or Breach of

Trust?', *Neohelicon: Acta Comparationis Litterarum Universarum* 40(1) (2012): 85–98, p. 7).

12. Gérard Genette, *Narrative Discourse* (New York: Cornell University Press, 1980), pp. 244–5.

13. Jacques Derrida, *Différance*, trans. Alan Bass (Chicago: University of Chicago Press, 1978).

14. Rosemary Ross Johnston, 'Literature', in Gordon Winch, Rosemary Ross Johnston, Paul March, Lesley Ljungdahl and Marcelle Holliday (eds), *Literacy: Reading, Writing and Children's Literature* (4th ed., Melbourne: Oxford University Press, 2010), p. 660.

15. See n. 2.

16. Introduction, *Counting Stars*.

17. Paul Ricoeur, *Memory, History, Forgetting*, trans. Kathleen McLaughlin and David Pellauer (Chicago: University of Chicago Press, 2004), p. 53.

18. Ricoeur, *Memory, History, Forgetting*, p. 15.

19. John 1:1.

Appendix: The David Almond Archive at Seven Stories, National Centre for Children's Books

Hannah Izod

Seven Stories was founded with a mission to preserve and promote the enjoyment of modern and contemporary British children's literature, placing it at the heart of Britain's literary heritage and culture. The Seven Stories collection includes original artwork and manuscripts by over ninety authors and illustrators, including Philip Pullman, Robert Westall, Edward Ardizzone and Judith Kerr, and about 30,000 books. In 2008, David Almond, a patron of Seven Stories and a local writer based in the north-east of England, donated draft material for two of his books, *Heaven Eyes* (2000) and *My Dad's a Birdman* (2007), to the collection.

Although the David Almond archive represents only a proportion of his published works, it is possible to glean considerable information about his creative process from this material. Rough notes for both titles appear in the archive on pages torn from a large, thick-papered sketchbook, which suggest this is how Almond begins the process of writing. These pages of notes are extremely rough and ready, with messy jottings and scribbles of ideas, key scenes, characters and motifs which he feels are important for the story. He often creates pro-files for key characters – in his notes for *Heaven Eyes* the following description is scrawled: 'Little girl. White dress spattered with bleach. Bare-footed→Web-feet. Silvery eyes. Grandfather.' All of these are key features of, and associations with, the character of Heaven Eyes. Similarly, in his notes for *My Dad's a Birdman*, Almond has scribbled down the simple description 'Auntie Doreen – waddles & showy'.

These early notes appear to be unplanned and spontaneous, attempting to capture as immediately as possible the essential ideas which have inspired the story. Key places can be traced in the notes – the abandoned printing works of *Heaven Eyes*, where so much of the action takes place, is succinctly captured in his notes: 'Breeze through skylights. Printing presses. Litter of papers – broken glass – bird droppings. Pigeons & sparrows. A huge herring gull perched in the rafters squealing.' One of the key themes of the book is also pinned down in a brief note that reads 'Digging deep in memory. MEMORY.'

The author's notes also contain brief passages of narrative text from key scenes in the stories. One page of notes for *My Dad's a Birdman* includes the following passage: 'People should stick to being people, that's my opinion. Don't you agree, Elizabeth? Yes, Auntie Doreen. They should keep their feet on God's good earth. Don't you agree, Elizabeth? Yes, Auntie Doreen.' This exchange between Auntie Doreen and Elizabeth is reproduced exactly on pages 39–40 of the published book, suggesting that certain passages and pieces of dialogue become clear in David's mind very early on in the creative process.

The notes also show that Almond uses a 'mind-mapping' approach to planning a story's development. In the notes for *Heaven Eyes*, the following numbered points appear – '1. Leaving. 2. Squeak. 3. The raft. 4. The journey. 5. The printing works'. These points map out the key markers in the plot, and they have been further expanded with rough marginal notes as Almond developed his ideas for each stage of the plot.

These rough notes are the only part of the process which this author does by hand. Once he has captured these first ideas and impressions, he moves on to drafting on a computer. The drafts for *Heaven Eyes* in the archive demonstrate an iterative, organic process of drafting the story. Several early, partial drafts of the story survive in the archive, and the fragmentary nature of these drafts reflects process. He does not start with a clear idea of what is going to happen and write a first draft through from start to finish, before going back to revise and redraft. Instead, he starts writing the story, gets a little way into it, then prints out what he has written and annotates the printout with revisions and alterations. He then goes back to the computer and starts the process again from the beginning, so the story develops gradually. Almond does not keep all of the printouts which are created during the writing process, so the drafts which survive in the archive provide only a partial picture of this creative journey.

However, even this partial picture is illuminating. The earliest drafts are written in the first person, as is the published novel, but the voice is that of Heaven Eyes. In these drafts, Heaven Eyes is a child living at Whitegates, not the mysterious child whom the runaways encounter on the Black Middens. Only later in the process does the narrator become Erin Law, and the character of Heaven Eyes appear in her final form.

As well as being annotated with Almond's notes and revisions, one of the early, partial drafts also bears comments from his wife, whose opinions and responses were crucial in shaping the story. A comment on the opening paragraph in her hand reads 'v. fast [getting into the action] more of where they came from'. Almond took this on board, and elaborated on the background of the children in later drafts before they got under way on their adventure. Similarly, the simple comment 'preachy' beside a piece of Erin's dialogue – *'There are doors inside you,' I said. 'Sometimes you'll find wonderful things behind them. Sometimes you'll be very scared. If you want to open doors, I'll try to help you, Squeak.'* – led to the whole passage being cut in later drafts.

The drafts for *My Dad's a Birdman* do not demonstrate the same iterative process of creation. This may be because Almond simply didn't save his early, partial drafts, but it may also be because *My Dad's a Birdman* clearly had a very different process of creation. Although published as an illustrated book in 2007, *My Dad's a Birdman* began as a play, commissioned by the Young Vic when the theatre was putting on *Skelling: The Play* in 2003. The theatre asked for a play aimed at a younger audience that could run alongside *Skellig*. Almond wrote the play *My Dad's a Birdman*, aimed at 3–6-year-olds, consciously drawing on some of the themes of *Skellig* to tie in with the other performance. It was only in coming back to the play a few years later that Almond began to see it as a picture book, and then started work on adapting the play into a book.

Consequently, the earliest draft material, after the manuscript notes, is a play script. In writing the picture book, Almond was moving from a scripted story to a narrative story and the earliest surviving draft of the picture book shows the residual influences of a play. A note in his hand on the title page of this early draft reads 'More narration. More from Lizzie's p. of v. 1st person. Put competition in view – or suggestions in text for illustrations to show this.' As Almond's note for 'more narration' suggests, the text of this early draft is certainly sparse. The dialogue is largely the same as that of the published book, but there are fewer descriptive passages, and far less insight into Lizzie's inner thoughts and feelings. When redrafting the text, Almond added more descriptive detail and also rewrote some exchanges of dialogue as narrative passages, to improve the flow of the story.

This process of adaptation can be traced in reverse in the archive material for *Heaven Eyes*. The novel was adapted for the stage by Almond in 2005, and toured with the Pop-Up Theatre Company. Several drafts of the scripts for this play survive in the archive and they are heavily annotated in his hand. These drafts show Almond struggling to create the right atmosphere in the script – one scribbled note reads 'get lighter feel, less anxious' – and also show him experimenting with different cuts and alterations to the story in order to make it work in play form. Elements which appear in the novel are removed, and then, in some cases, restored as he experimented with what worked best. For example, Heaven Eyes's webbed fingers are not mentioned in the earliest surviving script, but a later note reads 'Put webbed fingers back in'.

Almond was invited to attend the rehearsals for the play of *Heaven Eyes*, and revisions to the rehearsal script show that he was clearly influenced by the actors and director in their interpretation and performance of the script. Some lines of dialogue have been crossed out and cut completely, and in other cases the order of lines or words within lines of dialogue has been altered. This reflects the fact that the adaptation of *Heaven Eyes* involved repeated revision and reworking of the play in a process which included not just the writer, but directors, producers and actors.

The involvement of the editor in the creative process is also evident in some of the correspondence which survives for *Heaven Eyes*. A letter dated 26 May 1999 from Isabel Boissier, Editorial Director (Fiction) at Hodder Children's Books, runs to eight pages of detailed comments and suggestions for revisions to the text for the novel. These comments cover a range of matters, including characterisation: 'Maureen: This is the only character that really worried me. At the outset she's convincing … But Maureen loses credibility at the end of the novel.' They also address writing style, as in the following editorial note: 'Sometimes Heaven Eyes' dialogue sneaks its way into the narration – see last line "we two" – which I think needs to be avoided.' Almond clearly took his editor's comments on board, highlighting the comments which he felt he needed to do something about and then ticking them off once he had addressed them.

Another interesting angle on editorial input is reflected in a set of rough layouts for the US edition of *My Dad's a Birdman*. These layouts and a small amount of related correspondence illustrate the challenges of presenting this book for a US audience. *My Dad's a Birdman* is set in the North-East of England, and the setting and language carry a very strong sense of that regional identity. The US publisher, Candlewick Press, didn't want to destroy that sense of regional identity, but did face the very real problem of making some dialogue comprehensible to American readers.

On the layouts for the US edition, the copy-editor has queried the use of words like 'aye' and 'mebbe', looking to replace them with 'yes' and 'maybe'. At another point, 'cannot whack' is queried, with the suggestion of changing it to 'can't beat'. The UK editor has then amended this to 'cannot beat', with the explanation 'cannot better than can't for northern idiom'. An email dated 8 June 2007 from Lucy Earley at Walker Books, the UK publisher, to her counterpart at Candlewick Press acknowledges the challenges which were presented by idiomatic language – 'Thanks for being so careful about the Geordie-isms – I agree important to keep those for feel, as long as they're not completely incoherent to your readers.'

Although the quantity of material in the David Almond archive at Seven Stories is not extensive, it does provide a wealth of detail and insight into his creative process, and the process of taking a story from first ideas to published book. The value of this sort of archive material for research is significant, and Seven Stories is committed to preserving such material and making it available for future research. Only detailed study can pull out all of the meaning and insight which such material holds, and fully unlock the potential value of literary archives.

Works cited

All of the material held in the Seven Stories Collection is open to research access, by appointment. More information about our holdings, and complete collection catalogues can be found on our website, at www.sevenstories.org.uk/collection, and any enquiries about the collection and research access should be emailed to collections@sevenstories.org.uk.

Bibliography and Further Reading

This selected bibliography includes references that our contributors have found pertinent, as well as general criticism of Almond's work.

A complete bibliography of Almond's work, with publication details

Children's fiction

Skellig (London: Hodder Children's Books, 1998).
Skellig (New York: Delacorte, 1998, 1999).
Kit's Wilderness (London: Hodder Children's Books, 1999).
Kit's Wilderness (New York: Delacorte, 2000).
Heaven Eyes (London: Hodder Children's Books, 2000, 2001).
Heaven Eyes (New York: Delacorte, 2001).
Secret Heart (London: Hodder Children's Books, 2001).
Secret Heart (New York: Delacorte, 2002).
Where Your Wings Were (London: Hodder Children's Books, 2002).
The Fire-Eaters (London: Hodder Children's Books, 2003, 2004).
The Fire-Eaters (New York: Delacorte, 2003, 2004).
Clay (London: Hodder Children's Books, 2005).
Clay (New York: Delacorte, 2005, 2006).
Jackdaw Summer (London: Hodder Children's Books, 2009).
Raven Summer (US edition of *Jackdaw Summer*) (New York: Delacorte, 2009).
The Boy Who Climbed into the Moon (Somerville, MA: Candlewick, 2010).
My Name is Mina (London: Hodder Children's Books, 2010).
My Name is Mina (New York: Delacorte, 2011).
The True Tale of the Monster Billy Dean telt by hisself (London: Penguin, 2011).
The True Tale of the Monster Billy Dean telt by hisself (New York: Penguin Puffin, 2011).
The Boy Who Swam with Piranhas (with Oliver Jeffers) (London: Walker Books, 2012).
The Boy Who Swam with Piranhas (with Oliver Jeffers) (New York: Walker Books, 2013).
The Tightrope Walkers (London: Viking, forthcoming 2014).
The Tightrope Walkers (Somerville, MA: Candlewick, forthcoming 2014).
Half a Creature from the Sea (London: Walker Books, forthcoming 2014).
A Song for Ella Grey (London: Hodder Children's Books, forthcoming 2014).

Memoirs

Counting Stars (London: Hodder Children's Books, 2000).
Counting Stars (New York: Delacorte, 2002).

Picture books/graphic novels

My Dad's a Birdman, illus. Polly Dunbar (London: Walker Books, 2008).
My Dad's a Birdman, illus. Polly Dunbar (Cambridge, MA: Candlewick, 2008).
The Boy Who Climbed Into the Moon (London: Walker Books, 2014).
Kate, the Cat and the Moon, illus. Stephen Lambert (New York: Doubleday, 2005).
Kate, the Cat and the Moon (London: Hodder Children's Books, 2004).
The Savage, illus. Dave McKean (London: Walker Books, 2008).
The Savage, illus. Dave McKean (Cambridge, MA: Candlewick, 2008).
Slog's Dad (London: Walker Books, 2012).
Slog's Dad (Somerville, MA: Candlewick, 2011).
Mouse Bird Snake Wolf, illus. Dave McKean (London: Walker Books, 2013).
Mouse Bird Snake Wolf, illus. Dave McKean (Cambridge, MA: Candlewick, 2013).

Plays

Skellig: The Play (London: Hodder, 2002).
Wild Girl, Wild Boy: A Play (London: Hodder, 2002).
Two Plays (New York: Delacorte, 2005).

First and selected performances of plays by David Almond

Wild Girl, Wild Boy: A Play

Lyric Theatre, Hammersmith, London, 2001. Pop Up Theatre Company, directed by Michael Dalton.

Skellig: The Play

Young Vic Theatre, Waterloo, London, December 2003. Birmingham Stage Company, directed by Trevor Nunn.

Old Rep, Birmingham, October 2008. Birmingham Stage Company, directed by Phil Clark.

Yvonne Arnaud Youth Theatre, Edinburgh Fringe Festival, Augustine's, August 2008. Sheffield Theatres, directed by Charlie Westenra.

Skellig: The Opera

The Sage, Gateshead, directed by Braham Murray. Libretto by David Almond, music by Todd Machover.

Skellig: The Film

Directed by Annabel Jankel, with Tim Roth as Skellig.

Heaven Eyes

Polka Theatre, Wimbledon, London, April 2007, Pop Up Theatre, directed by Mike Dalton.

My Dad's a Birdman

Crucible Theatre, Sheffield, England, 14 November 2009, directed by Charlie Westenra.

YoungVic, London, November 2010. Oliver Mears Productions, directed by Oliver Mears.

Noah and the Fludd

Community Theatre, The Sands, Durham, May 2010. Unfolding Theatre, directed by Annie Rigby.

Teaching resources

Almond, David, '*Skellig* with Online Teacher Resources' (London: Hodder Literature, 2005).

Brennan, Geraldine, 'Talking Points: CILIP Carnegie Medal Shortlist 2012', http://www.carnegiegreenaway.org.uk/shadowingsite/groupleaders/resources/2012/My%20Name%20is%20Mina%20talking%20points%202012.pdf (accessed 12 February 2014).

Carroll, Colleen, 'Raven Summer' Readers' Guide', http://www.randomhouse.com/catalog/teachers_guides/9780385738064.pdf (accessed 10 February 2014).

Carter, James, *Creating Writers: A Creative Writing Manual for Key Stage 2 and Key Stage 3* (Oxford: Routledge, 2000).

Catron, John and Moore, Jean, '*Skellig* Teacher's Resource', Hodder Literature, http://www.hodderliterature.co.uk/teachers/pdf/SKELLIG%20TRB%2001.pdf (accessed 12 February 2014).

Drew, Bernard, *100 More Popular Young Adult Authors: Biographical Sketches and Bibliographies* (Englewood, CO: Greenwood, 2002).

Hughes, Tricia, '*Kit's Wilderness* Teacher's Resource', Hodder Literature, http://www.hodderliterature.co.uk/teachers/pdf/KITS%20WILD%20Introa.pdf (accessed 12 February 2014).

Scottish Book Trust, 'David Almond Resources', http://www.scottishbooktrust.com/node/83685 (accessed 12 February 2014).

Adult short stories

Sleepless Nights (Northumberland: Iron Press, 1985).

A Kind of Heaven (Northumberland: Iron Press, 1985).

Fast Fiction: The Knife Sharpener (ebook: HarperCollins, 2011).

'The Baby', *Critical Quarterly* 38(2) (1996): 71–9.

Media, interviews and speeches

'The 2001 Michael L. Printz Award Acceptance Speech', *Journal of Youth Services in Libraries* 14(4) (2001): 14–15, 23.

'The 2010 Hans Christian Andersen Author Award Winner Speech', International Board of Books for Young People, http://www.ibby.org/index.php?id=1147 (accessed 17 February 2014).

Barnes and Noble, 'David Almond: Meet the Writers', http://media. barnesandnoble.com/index.jsp?fr_chl=4f1e67180775c0199816531cf6d 28855b99bed39 (accessed 17 January 2014).

BBC Radio 4, 'David Almond: Desert Island Discs', http://www.bbc. co.uk/radio4/features/desert-island-discs/castaway/83028b49#b01r50yy (accessed 10 February 2014).

Birmingham Stage Company, 'Skellig: New York Times Review', http:// www.birminghamstage.com/shows/skellig/reviews (accessed 12 February 2014).

Caird, Jo, 'Brief Encounter with ... *Skellig* Author David Almond', *What's On Stage* (28 December 2009), http://www.whatsonstage.com/west-end-theatre/news/12–2009/brief-encounter-with-skellig-author-david-almond_14860.html (accessed 12 February 2014).

Horn, Caroline, 'Cracking Ahead: David Almond talks to Caroline Horn about being a regional writer and the need for constant re-invention', *The Bookseller* 5349 (12 September 2008): 21.

Meet the Author, 'David Almond: Clay', http://www.meettheauthor.co.uk/ bookbites/1194.html (accessed 10 February 2014).

Page, Benedicte, 'Through Almond's Eyes: David Almond's New Book Brings the Frankenstein Myth to the North-East', *The Bookseller* 5198 (30 September 2008): 20.

PEN America, 'David Almond and Sofi Oksanen in Conversation with Rakesh Satyal', http://www.youtube.com/watch?v=81LaJzK3zL4 (accessed 12 February 2014).

Richards, Linda, 'January Interview: David Almond', *January Magazine*, http://www.januarymagazine.com/profiles/almond.html (accessed 10 February 2014).

Ridge, Judith, 'Misrule: David Almond Interview', *Misrule*, http://misrule. com.au/wordpress/?page_id=91 (accessed 10 February 2014).

Smyth, John, 'The Fertility of Imagination', New Zealand Performing Arts Review and Directory, http://www.theatreview.org.nz/reviews/review. php?id=5046 (accessed 12 February 2014).

Teachingbooks.net, 'In Depth Written Interview: Insights Beyond the Slide Shows, http://www.teachingbooks.net/interview.cgi?id=2&a=1 (accessed 10 February 2014).

'The True Tale of the Monster Billy Dean telt by hisself', interview with and book reading by David Almond, http://www.youtube.com/ watch?v=56kmAq4ZmDc (accessed 10 February 2014).

The True Tale of Billy Dean telt by hisself (David Almond reads the first pages), http://www.youtube.com/watch?v=YhqzewH_UFo.

Word Factory Ink, 'In Interview: David Almond', http://www.the-wordfactory.tv/site/in-interview-david-almond/ (accessed 10 February 2014).

Word Factory Ink, 'David Almond Reads "The Knife Sharpener"', http:// vimeo.com/85431905(accessed 10 February 2014).

Archives

Almond, David (1995–2008). *David Almond Collection* (archival material). Seven Stories Collection. DA. Fonds level. Seven Stories Collection National Centre for Children's Books, Newcastle-upon-Tyne.

References and general criticism

This section includes material that has been referenced in the Casebook, as well as other general criticism.

Ackroyd, Peter, *Blake* (London: Sinclair-Stevenson, 1995; Minerva, 1996).

Almond, David, 'Personal Interview with Nolan Dalrymple', in Nolan Dalrymple, 'North-East Childhoods: Regional Identity in Children's Novels of the North East of England' (doctoral thesis, University of Newcastle, 2008), https://theses.ncl.ac.uk/dspace/bitstream/10443/890/1/Dalrymple09.pdf (accessed 13 May 2014).

——, 'The Necessary Wilderness', *The Lion and the Unicorn* 35(2) (April 2011): 107–17.

——, and Amnesty International, *Free? Stories Celebrating Human Rights* (London: Walker Books, 2009).

Aristotle, *Physics*, III, 4, 203b 25–30, in *Aristotle's Physics Books III and IV*, trans. Edward Hussey (Oxford: Oxford University Press, 1993).

Ashley, Benedict M., OP, *Theologies of the Body: Humanist and Christian* (Braintree, MA: Pope John Center, 1985).

Attebery, Brian, *Strategies of Fantasy* (Bloomington: Indiana University Press, 1992).

Bakhtin, Mikhail, *Speech Genres and Other Late Essays* (Austin: University of Texas Press, 1986).

Baltazar, Eulalio R., *The Dark Center: A Process Theology of Blackness* (New York: Paulist Press, 1973).

Barrie, J.M., *Peter and Wendy* (London: Hodder & Stoughton, 1911).

Baudrillard, Jean, *Simulacra and Simulations* – XVL, 'The Spiraling Cadaver', trans. Sheila Faria Glaser (Ann Arbor: University of Michigan Press, 2004 [1994]).

BBC Radio 4, 'Philip Pullman webchat', http://www.bbc.co.uk/radio4/arts/hisdarkmaterials/pullman_webchat.shtml (accessed 7 July 2014).

Blake, William, *Songs of Innocence and Songs of Experience* (London: R. Brimley Johnson, 1901 [1794]).

Borges, Jorge Luis, *Historia Universal de la Infamia* [1935]. Published in English as *A Universal History of Infamy*, trans. Norman Thomas di Giovanni (New York, Dutton, 1972). English edition: *A Universal History of Iniquity*, trans. Andrew Hurley (London: Penguin Classics, 2004).

Bragg, Melvyn, 'At First, Oxford to Me was Unreal, like Camelot', *Daily Telegraph* Weekend (31 May 2003).

Brennan, Geraldine, 'The Game Called Death: Frightening Fictions by David Almond, Philip Gross and Lesley Howarth', in Kimberley Reynolds,

Geraldine Brennan and Kevin McCarron, *Frightening Fiction* (London and New York: Continuum, 2001), pp. 92–127.

Briggs, Raymond, *The Snowman* (London: Hamish Hamilton, 1978).

Brown, Jennifer M., 'David Almond and the Art of Transformation', *Shelf-awareness*, http://www.shelf-awareness.com/issue.html?issue=1185#m9201 (accessed 31 March 2014).

Buber, Martin, *I and Thou*, trans. Ronald Gregor Smith (New York: Scribner, 2000 [1923]).

Bullen, Elizabeth and Parsons, Elizabeth, 'Risk and Resilience, Knowledge and Imagination: The Enlightenment of David Almond's 'Skellig', *Children's Literature* 35(4) (2007): 127–44.

Burke, Edmund, *Philosophical Inquiry into the Origin of our Ideas on the Sublime and the Beautiful* (London: Routledge & Kegan Paul, 1958 [1757).

Burnside, John, '*The True Tale of the Monster Billy Dean* by David Almond', *Guardian* (3 September 2011), http://www.theguardian.com/books/2011/sep/02/true-tale-monster-billy-dean-review (accessed 17 January 2014).

Butler, Robert, 'Philip Pullman's Dark Arts', *Intelligent Life* (December 2007), http://www.moreintelligentlife.com/story/an-interview-with-philip-pullman (accessed 7 July 2014).

Butler, Robyn (Chair of debate), 'Question of Faith. Phillip Pullman debates religion with the Archbishop of Canterbury, Dr Rowan Williams', *Daily Telegraph*, 17 March 2004, http://www.telegraph.co.uk/culture/3613962/The-Dark-Materials-debate-life-God-the-universe....html (accessed 11 January 2014).

Carpenter, Humphrey and Prichard, Mari, *Oxford Companion to Children's Literature* (Oxford and New York: Oxford University Press, 1995).

Carpentier, Alejo, 'The Baroque and the Marvelous Real', in Lois Parkinson Zamora and Wendy B. Faris, *Magical Realism: Theory, History, Community* (Durham, NC: Duke University Press, 1995), pp. 89–108.

Chanady, Amaryll Beatrice, *Magical Realism and the Fantastic: Resolved vs. Unresolved Antinomy* (New York: Garland, 1985).

Crick, Francis, *The Astonishing Hypothesis: The Scientific Search for the Soul* (Westport, CT: Touchstone, 1993).

Crown, Sarah, 'A Life in Writing: David Almond', *Guardian* (21 August 2010), http://www.theguardian.com/culture/2010/aug/21/david-almond-skellig-writing-books (accessed 31 March 2014).

Dalrymple, Nolan, 'Navigating Borderlands of Fiction, Magic, and Childhood: Finding David Almond', *Bookbird – A Journal of International Children's Literature* 48(4) (2010): 1–4.

——, *North-East Childhoods: Regional Identity in Children's Novels of the North East of England* (doctoral thesis, University of Newcastle, 2008), https://theses.ncl.ac.uk/dspace/bitstream/10443/890/1/Dalrymple09.pdf.

D'Ambra, Adrian, 'On Selecting David Almond's "Skellig"', *Idiom* 48(2) (2012): 11–14.

Derrida, Jacques, *Différance*, trans. Alan Bass (Chicago: University of Chicago Press, 1978).

Doherty, Berlie, *How Green You Are* (London: Mammoth, 1996).

Dorsch, T.S., *Classical Literary Criticism* (Harmondsworth: Penguin, 1965).

Eagleton, Terry, *After Theory* (London: Allen Lane, 2003).

Falconer, Rachel, *The Crossover Novel: Contemporary Children's Fiction and Its Adult Readership* (New York and London: Routledge, 2009).

Fish, Stanley, 'One University Under God', *Chronicle of Higher Education* (7 January 2005), http://chronicle.com/article/One-University-Under-God-/45077 (accessed 10 January 2014).

Flores, Angel, 'Magical Realism in Spanish American Fiction', *Hispania* 38(2) (1955): 187–92.

Ford, Lewis S., *The Lure of God: A Biblical Background for Process Theism* (Minneapolis, MN: Fortress Press, 1978), http://www.religion-online.org/showbook.asp?title=2217 (accessed 31 August 2014).

Frye, Northrop, 'The Anatomy of Criticism', http://northropfrye-the-anatomyofcriticism.blogspot.com.au/2009/02/tentative-conclusion.html (accessed 13 January 2014).

García Márquez, Gabriel, *One Hundred Years of Solitude* (London: Penguin, 1972 [1967]).

——, 'A Very Old Man with Enormous Wings', in *Collected Stories*, trans. Gregory Rabassa and J.S. Bernstein (New York: HarperCollins, 1999).

Garner, Alan, *The Stone Book Quartet* (London: Collins, 1983).

Genette, Gérard, *Narrative Discourse* (New York: Cornell University Press, 1980).

Gray, James R., *Modern Process Thought: A Brief Ideological History* (Lanham, MD: University Press of America, 1982).

Greene, Brian, *The Elegant Universe: Superstrings, Hidden Dimensions, and the Quest for the Ultimate Theory* (London: Vintage, 1999).

Griffin, David R., *A Process Christology* (Lanham, MD: University Press of America, 1990).

Grigson, Geoffrey, *Samuel Palmer: The Visionary Years* (London: Kegan Paul, 1947).

Grosz, Elizabeth, *Volatile Bodies: Toward a Corporeal Feminism* (Bloomington: Indiana University Press, 1994).

Hall, Dinah, 'The True Tale of the Monster Billy Dean by David Almond: A tale of violence, tenderness and linguistic bravado', *Telegraph* (31 August 2011), http://www.telegraph.co.uk/culture/8722822/The-True-Tale-of-the-Monster-Billy-Dean-by-David-Almond-review.html (accessed 8 January 2014).

Harding, John, 'The True Tale of the Monster Billy Dean', *Daily Mail* (1 September 2011). http://www.dailymail.co.uk/home/books/article-2032172/David-Almond-THE-TRUE-TALE-OF-THE-MONSTER-BILLY-DEAN.html (accessed 8 January 2014).

Harland, Richard, *Literary Theory from Plato to Barthes* (Basingstoke: Macmillan, 1999).

Harrison, Tony, *Selected Poems* (Harmondsworth: Penguin, 1985).

Hart, F. Elizabeth, 'The Epistemology of Cognitive Literary Studies', *Philosophy and Literature* 25(2) (2001): 314–44.

Hateley, E., '"In the hand of the receivers": The Politics of Literacy in *The Savage* by David Almond and Dave McKean', *Children's Literature in Education* 43(2) (2012): 170–80.

Heaney, Seamus, *North* (London: Faber & Faber, 1976).

——, 'The Tollund Man', Internet Poetry Archive, http://www.ibiblio.org/ipa/poems/heaney/the_tollund_man.php (accessed 27 March 2014).

——, 'The Tollund Man in Springtime', The Saturday Poem, *Guardian*, http://www.guardian.co.uk/books/2005/apr/16/poetry.seamusheaney (accessed 27 March 2014).

Heidegger, Martin, *Letter on 'Humanism'* [1949], http://archive.org/stream/HeideggerLetterOnhumanism1949/Heidegger-LetterOn (accessed 10 January 2014).

Hocking, William, *The Meaning of God in Human Experience* (New Haven, CT: Yale University Press, 1912).

Hofweber, Thomas, 'Logic and Ontology', in *Stanford Encyclopaedia of Philosophy* (30 August 2011), http://plato.stanford.edu/entries/logic-on-tology/ (accessed 17 January 2014).

Hollindale, Peter, 'Autograph No. 142: David Almond', *Books for Keeps* 142, http://booksforkeeps.co.uk/issue/142/childrens-books/articles/authorgraph/authorgraph-no142–david-almond (accessed 1 September 2003).

Hopkins, Gerard Manley, 'There lives the dearest freshness deep down things', 'God's Grandeur' [1877], in *Poems and Prose of Gerard Manley Hopkins* (Hammondsworth: Penguin, 1985).

Hunt, Peter, 'The Loss of the Father and the Loss of God in English-language Children's Literature (1800–2000)', in Jan De Maeyer *et al.* (eds), *Religion, Children's Literature and Modernity in Western Europe 1750–2000* (Leuven: Leuven University Press, 2005), pp. 295–303.

Hurt, J.S., *Elementary Schooling and the Working Classes 1860–1918* (London: Routledge & Kegan Paul, 1979).

Iser, Wolfgang, *The Implied Reader: Patterns of Communication in Prose Fiction from Bunyan to Beckett* (Baltimore, MD: Johns Hopkins University Press, 1978).

Jackson, Brian and Marsden, Dennis, *Education and the Working Class* (Harmondsworth: Pelican, 1961).

Johnson, Christopher, 'Metaphor vs. Conflation in the Acquisition of Polysemy: The Case of See', in Masako K. Hiraga, Chris Sinha and Sherman Wilcos (eds), *Cultural, Psychological, and Typological Issues in Cognitive Linguistics* (Amsterdam, PA: Benjamins, 1999).

Johnson, Mark, *The Body in the Mind: The Bodily Basis of Meaning, Imagination, and Reason* (Chicago: University of Chicago Press, 1990).

Johnston, Rosemary Ross, 'Carnivals, the Carnivalesque, *The Magic Puddin'*, and David Almond's *Wild Girl, Wild Boy*: Toward a Theorizing of Children's Plays', *Children's Literature in Education* 34(2) (2003): 131–46.

——, 'Childhood: A Narrative Chronotope', in R. Sell (ed.), *Children's Literature as Communication* (Amsterdam, PA: Benjamins, 2002), pp. 137–58. Reprinted in Peter Hunt (ed.), *Critical Concepts in Literary and Cultural Studies*, Vol. III (London: Routledge, 2006), pp. 46–68.

——, 'In and Out of Otherness: Being and Not-Being in Children's Theatre', *Neohelicon* 36(1) (2009): 45–54.

——, 'Literature', in Gordon Winch, Rosemary Ross Johnston, Paul March, Lesley Ljungdahl and Marcelle Holliday (eds), *Literacy: Reading, Writing and Children's Literature* (4th ed., Melbourne: Oxford University Press, 2010), pp. 492–686.

——, 'Breaking the Boundaries: Liberation or Breach of Trust?', *Neohelicon: Acta Comparationis Litterarum Universarum* 40(1) (2012): 85–98.

Jones, Nicolette, 'David Almond: Story is a Kind of Redemption', *Daily Telegraph* (25 October 2008), http://www.telegraph.co.uk/culture/books/3562549/David-AlmondStory-is-a-kind-of-redemption.html (accessed 31 March 2014).

Joyce, James, *A Portrait of the Artist as a Young Man* (Melbourne: Penguin, 1960 [1916]).

Kant, Immanuel, *Prologomena to any Future Metaphysics* [1783], trans. and ed. Gary Hatfield (2nd ed., Cambridge: Cambridge University Press, 2004).

Kennaway, William, '*The True Tale of the Monster Billy Dean* by David Almond', *The Times* (21 July 2012), http://www.thetimes.co.uk/tto/arts/books/fiction/article3479588.ece (accessed 9 January 2014).

Kundera, Milan, *The Book of Laughter and Forgetting*, trans. Michael Henry Heim (Harmondsworth: Penguin, 1981).

Lakoff, George and Johnson, Mark, *Philosophy in the Flesh: The Embodied Mind and Its Challenge to Western Thought* (New York: Basic Books, 1999).

——, *Metaphors We Live By* (Chicago: University of Chicago Press, 2003 [1980].

Lane, Richard (ed.), *Global Literary Theory* (London: Routledge, 2013).

Latham, Don, *David Almond: Memory and Magic* (Lanham, MD, Toronto and Oxford: Scarecrow Press, 2006).

——, 'Empowering Adolescent Readers: Intertextuality in Three Novels by David Almond', *Children's Literature in Education* 39(3) (2008): 213–26.

——, 'Magical Realism and the Child Reader: The Case of David Almond's "*Skellig*"', *The Looking Glass: New Perspectives on Children and Literature* 10(1) (2006).

Levy, Michael, 'A Non-Believer Reads Religious Fantasy, First Opinions – Second Reactions', *Purdue e-Pub*, http://docs.lib.purdue.edu/fosr/ 2009 (accessed 2 December 2014).

——, 'Children and Salvation in David Almond's *Skellig*', *Foundation: The International Review of Science Fiction* 88 (Summer 2003): 19–25.

——, 'The Tiger Within: Images of Masculinity in the Recent Young Adult Fiction of David Almond', *Foundation: The International Review of Science Fiction* 102 (Spring 2008): 49–60.

——, '"They Thought We Were Dead, and They Were Wrong": Children and Salvation in *Kit's Wilderness* and *Heaven Eyes* by David Almond',

Foundation: The International Review of Science Fiction 88 (Summer 2003): 26–32.

——, 'Transcendence in David Almond's *Wild Girl, Wild Boy*', *New York Review of Science Fiction* 21(4) (December 2008): 19–21.

——, 'Visions of the Snow Queen in Recent Fantasy by Almond and Billingsley', *New York Review of Science Fiction* 16(6) (February 2004): 15–18.

Lloyd, A.L., *Folk Song in England* (London: Panther, 1969).

Lodge, David, *Consciousness and the Novel* (London: Penguin, 2002).

'Longinus, On the Sublime', http://evans-experientialism.freewebspace. com/longinus01.htm (accessed 17 January 2014).

Lovejoy, Arthur, *The Great Chain of Being* (Cambridge, MA: Harvard University Press, 1936).

Lyotard, Jean-François, *The Postmodern Explained: Correspondence 1982–1985* (Minneapolis and London: University of Minnesota Press, 1992).

Macey, David, *The Penguin Dictionary of Critical Theory* (London: Penguin, 2000).

Marwick, Arthur, *The Sixties* (Oxford: Oxford University Press, 1998).

Mayhew, Henry, *London Labour and the London Poor* (London: Penguin, 1985).

Mendlesohn, Farah, 'Rhetorics of Fantasy', http://www.farahsf.com/extract. htm (accessed 24 January 2014).

Meredith, George, 'The Lark Ascending', http://allpoetry.com/ poem/8475727–The-Lark-Ascending-by-George-Meredith (accessed 5 February 2014).

Merleau-Ponty, Maurice, *Phenomenology of Perception*, trans. Colin Smith (New York: Humanities Press, 1962 [1945]).

Michaels, Anne, *Fugitive Pieces* (New York: Vintage, 1998).

Miller, J. Hillis, *Charles Dickens: The World of His Novels* (Cambridge, MA: Harvard University Press, 1958).

Nesbit, E. [Edith], *Five Children and It* (London: Newnes, 1904).

Newsome, David, *The Victorian World Picture* (London: Fontana, 1998).

Nikolajeva, Maria, *The Magic Code: The Use of Magical Patterns in Fantasy for Children* (Stockholm: Almqvist & Wiksell, 1988).

Nodelman, Perry, *The Hidden Adult: Defining Children's Literature* (Baltimore, MD: Johns Hopkins University Press, 2008).

——, and Reimer, Mavis, The Pleasures of Children's Literature (3rd ed., Boston, MA: Allyn & Bacon, 2003).

O'Sullivan, Keith, 'Binding with Briars', in Valerie Coghlan and Keith O'Sullivan (eds), *Irish Children's Literature and Culture: New Perspectives on Contemporary Writing* (New York and London: Routledge, 2011), pp. 99–113.

Otto, Rudolf, *The Idea of the Holy*, trans. John W. Harvey (Oxford: Oxford University Press, 1958).

Oxford English Reference Dictionary (2nd ed., 20 vols, Oxford: Oxford University Press, 1996).

Purdy, Anthony, 'The Bog Body as Mnemotope: Nationalist Archaeologies in Heaney and Tournier', *Style* 36(1) (Spring 2002): 96.

Ricoeur, Paul, *Memory, History, Forgetting*, trans. Kathleen McLaughlin and David Pellauer (Chicago: University of Chicago Press, 2004).

——, *Time and Narrative*, trans. Kathleen McLaughlin and David Pellauer (Chicago: University of Chicago Press, 1984).

Robson, Geoff, 'Killing God? Secular and Spiritual Elements in Some Recent Literature for Children', *British Journal of Religious Education* 35(1) (2013): 87–97.

Rodia, Becky, 'David Almond, Mining the Past', *Teaching Pre K-8* 32(1) (2001): 76–8.

Roh, Franz, 'Realismo mágico: problemas de la pintura Europea más reciente', trans. Fernando Vela, *Revista de Occidente* 16(47) (abril–junio 1927): 274–301.

——, 'Magical Realism: Post-Expressionism' [1925], in Lois Parkinson Zamora and Wendy B. Faris, *Magical Realism: Theory, History, Community* (Durham, NC: Duke University Press, 1995).

Rushdie, Salman, *Midnight's Children* (London: Jonathan Cape, 1980).

Sahm, Danielle, 'Contrary to Expectations: Exploring Blake's Contraries in David Almond's *Skellig*', *Children's Literature* 38(1) (2010): 115–32.

Sawers, Naarah, '"You molded me like clay": David Almond's Sexualised Monsters', *Papers: Explorations into Children's Literature* 18(1) (2008): 20–9.

Schama, Simon, *Landscape and Memory* (New York: Alfred A. Knopf, 1995; Vintage, 1996).

Schroeder, Mark, 'Value Theory', in *Stanford Encyclopaedia of Philosophy* (29 May 2012), http://plato.stanford.edu/entries/value-theory/ (accessed 21 July 2012).

Shields, Rob, *Places on the Margin: Alternative Geographies of Modernity* (London: Routledge, 1991).

Soja, Edward W., *Thirdspace* (Malden, MA: Blackwell, 1996).

Spring, Kit, 'A Hit From a Myth', *Observer* (23 November 2003), http://www.theguardian.com/books/2003/nov/23/booksforchildrenandteenagers.features (accessed 3 June 2011).

Stephens, John, *Language and Ideology in Children's Fiction: Language in Social Life* (London and New York: Longman, 1992).

Steup, Matthias, 'Epistemology', in *Stanford Encyclopaedia of Philosophy* (14 December 2005), http://plato.stanford.edu/entries/epistemology/ (accessed 21 January 2014).

Stewart, Susan, 'David Almond's *Skellig*: A New Vista of Contemplation?', *Children's Literature in Education* 40(4) (2009): 306–19.

Swedenborg, Emmanuel, *Heaven and Hell* (London: Swedenborg Society, 1937).

Tolkien, J.R.R., 'On Fairy Stories', in *The Tolkien Reader* (New York: Del Rey, 1986 [1966]), pp. 3–84.

Travis, Madelyn, 'Flying Across the Tyne: Madelyn Travis talks to David Almond about the inspiration behind My Dad's a Birdman', http://www.booktrustchildrensbooks.org.uk/show/feature/Features%20Interviews/Interview-with-David-Almond-07 (accessed 3 June 2011).

Trites, Roberta Seelinger, *Disturbing the Universe: Power and Repression in Adolescent Literature* (Iowa City: University of Iowa Press, 2000).

Tucker, Nicholas and Gamble, Nikki (eds), *Family Fictions* (London: Continuum, 2001).

Turner, Mark, *Reading Minds: The Study of English in the Age of Cognitive Science* (Princeton, NJ: Princeton University Press, 1991).

Uslar Pietri, Arturio, *Letras y Hombres de Venezuela* (Mexico City: Fondo de Cultura Económica, 1949).

Warner, Marina, *Fantastic Metamorphoses, Other Worlds: Ways of Telling the Self* (Oxford: Oxford University Press, 2002).

Wertheim, Margaret, *The Pearly Gates of Cyberspace: A History of Space from Dante to the Internet* (Milson's Point, NSW: Doubleday, Transworld, 1999).

Westall, Robert, *Falling into Glory* (London: Methuen, 1993; reissued Mammoth, 2000).

Whitehead, Alfred North, *Process and Reality* (New York: Harper & Row, 1957).

Winterson, Jeanette, 'My Hero: Shelagh Delaney', *Guardian* Review (18 September 2010), http://www.theguardian.com/books/2010/sep/18/jeanette-winterson-my-hero-shelagh-delaney (accessed 20 January 2014).

Wintle, Justin and Fisher, Emma, *The Pied Pipers: Interviews with the Influential Creators of Children's Literature* (New York: Paddington Press, 1974).

Wordsworth, William, 'Lines Composed a Few Miles Above Tintern Abbey', in *Lyrical Ballads* [1798], http://www.poetryfoundation.org/poem/174796 (accessed 31 March 2014).

Zimmerman, Jens, 'Western Identity, the Exhaustion of Secular Reason, and the Return to Religion', in Richard Lane (ed.), *Global Literary Theory* (London: Routledge, 2013), pp. 796–806.

Zipes, Jack, Paul, Lissa, Vallone, Lynne, Hunt, Peter and Avery, Gillian, *Norton Anthology of Children's Literature: The Traditions in English* (New York and London: W.W. Norton, 2005).

Index